DATE DUE

GAYLORD   PRINTED IN U.S.A.

ISLAMIC TERROR ABDUCTIONS IN THE MIDDLE EAST

This book is dedicated to the memory of

Nachshon Wachsman, who was abducted and
murdered by Hamas terrorists,

Captain Nir Poraz, who fell during the attempt to
rescue the abducted soldier,

and all other abduction victims in Israel.

ISLAMIC TERROR ABDUCTIONS IN THE MIDDLE EAST

SHAUL SHAY

sussex
ACADEMIC
PRESS

BRIGHTON • PORTLAND

The right of Shaul Shay to be identified as Author of this work has been asserted in
accordance with the Copyright, Designs and Patents Act 1988.

2 4 6 8 10 9 7 5 3 1

First published 2007 in Great Britain by
SUSSEX ACADEMIC PRESS
PO Box 139
Eastbourne BN24 9BP

and in the United States of America by
SUSSEX ACADEMIC PRESS
920 NE 58th Ave Suite 300
Portland, Oregon 97213–3786

British Library Cataloguing in Publication Data
A CIP catalogue record for this book is available from the British Library.

Library of Congress Cataloging-in-Publication Data
Shai, Shaul.
Islamic terror abductions in the Middle East / Shaul Shay.
p. cm.
Includes bibliographical references and index.
ISBN 978-1-84519-167-2 (alk. paper)
1. Terrorism—Middle East. 2. Kidnapping—Middle East.
I. Title.

HV6433.M5S52 2007
364.15′40956—dc22
2006102347

Typeset and designed by SAP, Brighton & Eastbourne
Printed by The Cromwell Press, Trowbridge, Wilts.
This book is printed on acid-free paper.

Contents

Preface

Abductions constitute a central component in the "attack repertoire" of terror organizations worldwide. Since the 1980s, in the wake of the Islamic Revolution in Iran and the ascent of a terror-supporting regime in that country, the establishment of the Hizballah organization in Lebanon, and the foundation of the Palestinian Hamas Movement, Islamic terror entities have become the standard bearers in the Middle East in all matters connected to terror in general and abductions in particular.

This study addresses abductions in four arenas in the Middle East between 1980 and 2006: Israel (in the framework of the Israeli–Palestinian conflict), Lebanon, Yemen and Iraq. Islamic terror organizations acted and continue to act in these four arenas, using abductions as a means to promote the goals of their organizations and patrons.

The central role of Iran as a state that supports terror, and the use that this country makes of abductions perpetrated by terror organizations operating under its patronage or as its representative in order to promote Iranian interests, stands out throughout the analysis to follow.

The ties and reciprocal links among Islamic terror organizations, as well as the relationship between these organizations and Iran in the context of abductions, will be examined in detail. Islamic abductions in the Middle East can be categorized according to periods and several influential factors:

- **Abductions in Lebanon**: the Hizballah Organization, 1984–1992.
- **Abductions in Israel:** the Hamas Movement, 1989–2005.
- **Abductions in Yemen:** under the influence of the Global Jihad, 1998–2001.
- **Abductions/decapitations in Iraq:** under the influence of the Global Jihad, 2003–2005, in the aftermath of the invasion of Iraq by Coalition forces (2003).
- **Abduction of Israeli soldiers and civilians:** June and July 2006, resulting in Israeli military action in Gaza and Lebanon.

Islamic terror organizations regard the citizens of foreign countries (mainly western countries and Israeli nationals in the context of the

Israeli–Arab conflict in the Lebanese and Palestinian arenas) as prime targets for abductions, although local residents constitute the most frequent target for these attacks.

The theoretical aspects of the terror phenomenon in general, and abductions in particular, will be dealt with extensively in the chapters to follow. Abductions can be categorized according to various criteria, which include:

- **The method of perpetration** – overt/covert.
- **The abduction's purpose** – bargaining, murder, obtaining combat means.
- **The abductors' demands** – ransom money, political demands, the release of prisoners, etc.
- **The attack's target** – an individual or group of individuals in a building or a public place, airplane, boat, bus, etc.

The primary focus in this book concerns **abductions of an individual or several individuals for bargaining purposes.**

The examples raised and analyzed are primarily the "Nachshon Wachsman Affair," the abduction of hostages in Lebanon (William Buckley, William Higgins and the "Irangate Affair"), the abduction of western hostages in Yemen and ultimately, the abduction of hostages in Iraq. The challenge issued by the terror organizations to the countries whose citizens have been abducted, and the way that these countries rose to that challenge, will be the central focus of the analysis.

The abduction and murder of Sergeant Nachshon Wachsman by the Hamas Movement in 1994 demonstrate the painful and dramatic process of an abduction, and serves as a model for the abduction attack, which in this case included four main stages: planning and preparations for the abduction; perpetrating the abduction; contacts to initiate negotiations; and the ultimate failed rescue attempt.

ISLAMIC TERROR ABDUCTIONS IN THE MIDDLE EAST

I
Terror and Abductions

Western Vulnerability and Dilemma

Defining Terror

Since the 1970s, following the increased intensity of international terror and the necessity to understand and contend with this phenomenon, a research discipline has developed, mainly among Western democracies, which examines terror from legal, psychological, sociological and historical points of view as well as other aspects.

The 9/11 2001 attacks in the United States served as a watershed in the world's approach to the international terror phenomenon, which overnight was transformed from a marginal nuisance to a central threat to world peace. The global war against terror declared by President Bush shortly after 9/11 defined the struggle against terrorists, terror organizations and states that support terror as a top priority for the United States and the Coalition of countries that it heads. The 9/11 attacks exposed the vulnerability of the Western world to terror, as well as its lack of preparedness to deal with the challenges posed by a post-modern terror, which is unrestrained and knows no geographical limits.

Modern terror is a complex and problematic issue, particularly as it is a characteristically difficult phenomenon to define. This difficulty stems from the fact that it is impossible to arrive at a definition that is universally acceptable. Various approaches have been adopted to distinguish between definitions. A major differentiation is between normative and analytical definitions.[1] The normative stream bases its definitions on political values from which it derives standards for judging political actions. This school characterizes terrorism in terms of the political context in which it is created. Thus it defines terror as "unjustified violence against a democratic country that permits effective forms of non-violent Resistance."[2] Accordingly a black man who detonated a police station in South Africa during the period of the Apartheid is not to be considered a terrorist, while a member of the Irish Underground (the IRA) who attacked a British base is included in this category. This example high-lights the limitations of normative definitions that examine the phenom-enon from a subjective point of view, according to which an ally or friend is defined in positive terms (a freedom fighter) while an opponent is defined negatively (a terrorist). Thus, on the basis of a normative defin-ition it is difficult to define the term "terror" in an unequivocal and universal manner.

Nevertheless, the importance and benefit of the normative definition lies in the very proposition of the issue of the legitimacy of utilizing polit-ical violence as a standard of judgment. A key aspect related to the state's method of handling terrorism is the defense of its legitimization to use violence and nullify the legitimization of the terrorist challenge.[3] To a great extent, the objective of terror is to win legitimacy from the point of view of the population (or part of it) and to negate the legitimacy of the ruling government. Terrorism poses a challenge to a government's right to monopolize power in society and physically undermines its ability to main-tain law and order.[4]

Other issues that stem from the normative approach address the moral aspects of terror. Martha Crenshaw argues that terrorism can best be judged from a moral examination of the consequences alongside a moral examination of the means. Regarding the consequences of terror activity, the criterion is whether the goal of the activity is to establish a just, liber-ated and democratic government or if it serves the narrow and deplorable goals of establishing an authoritarian regime that will grant special privi-leges to a defined group and cause the discrimination of freedom *vis-à-vis* others.

Discussion of the morality of means leads to an examination of the methods and means which terror uses, and particularly to examining the identity of terror victims. Crenshaw defines two main groups of victims: The first group includes individuals that are vulnerable to terror acts due to the roles that they fulfill, and as a result of the fact that they are identi-fied to a certain extent with the "unjust" policy which the terrorists are fighting; the second group includes citizens of the state who do not play an official role, or citizens of other countries who have no connection to or direct influence upon the government's policy. The "transgression" of these people (according to the terrorists) is that they obey the laws of an "unjust" government, thus becoming accomplices to its deeds.

The issue of terror victims constitutes another example of the prob-lematic aspect deriving from normative definitions. The observer's starting point is the factor that determines that individual's moral approach to the case. It would appear to be impossible to develop objective moral judgment *vis-à-vis* the use of terror in various political circumstances; at the very most one might state that the definition of a deed as an "act of terror" does not in itself constitute a moral or ethical determination regarding its substance.

While the normative school of thought strives to address the term of "terror" by examining it via its ethics, the analytical school of thought attempts to find a formula for defining the phenomenon by constructing a neutral, theoretical definition sufficiently general to cover the range of terror variations.

One of the most comprehensive analytical studies was conducted by Schmidt and Youngman.[5] Their study is based on the assumption that despite the disagreement regarding the definition of terror, there exists a common denominator as to the customary images related to the terror issue, and this consent is clear enough to enable the construction of a model that will provide a common language for researchers investigating terrorism. Schmidt and Youngman compiled 109 different definitions of terror and conducted a "content analysis" of these definitions while striving to indicate the identical components among them. Their findings indicate 25 similar components, the most prominent being: The use of violence/force (appearing in 83.5% of the definitions), a political goal (in 95%), spreading fear (51%), threat and exerting psychological pressure (47%), addressing the difference between the terror victims (37.5%), and methodical and/or planned activity (32%).

The list of parameters or components that Schmidt and Youngman compiled does not suffice to provide an exact definition of the terror phenomenon, but their study enables the indication of the main components connected to terrorism, on the basis of which they attempted to construct a definition of terror.[6] According to Schmidt and Youngman, terrorism is a method of assault in which coincidental or symbolic victims serve as instrumental targets for violence. The victims are divided according to group characteristics that constitute the basis of the terrorists' choice of victims. Previous usage of violence or a proven threat to use it also turns other individuals from the target group into victims due to the state of "chronic fear" in which they subsist. This indirect method of attack is meant to motivate the victims to act according to the wishes of the terrorists or to induce secondary targets to change their approach or behavior according to the terrorists' goals.[7] Schmidt and Youngman's comprehensive study contributed much to understanding the phenomenon and to mapping the joint components in the different definitions, but it was unable to produce a universal definition of the terror phenomenon.

In his book *The Labyrinth of Countering Terror*, Boaz Ganor offers the following definition of terror, which is based on three tiers:[8]

Terror is a type of violent struggle in whose framework intentional use is made of violence towards civilians in order to achieve political (national, social-economic, ideological, religious, and more) goals.

- **The nature of the activity** is a type of violent struggle. According to this definition, any activity that does not involve violence will not be defined as terror (for example, peaceful protest activity – strikes, non-violent demonstrations, tax protests, etc.).
- **The goal at the basis of terror** is always a political one, i.e., a goal designated to gain achievements in the political arena: From replacing a reigning government, through altering a regime or replacing powerful position holders, to revising economic, social or other policy, and more. In the absence of a political goal, the said action will not be defined as terror. Violent activity against civilians, which is not backed by a political agenda, can at most be considered criminal wrongdoing, a felony or simply an act of madness; it is unconnected to terror. The motive behind the political goal is irrelevant to the definition of terror, and it can be ideological, religious, national, social, or economic.
- **The target of terror is civilians**. From this aspect terror is to be differentiated from other types of political violence (guerrilla, a popular uprising, etc.). The proposed definition emphasizes that terror is not the result of a coincidental attack against a civilian or a group of civilians that happened to be in a volatile political area but rather it is primarily targeted against civilians. Terror exploits the relative ease of striking out at the vulnerable civilian "underbelly," and the considerable anxiety and media repercussions that come in its wake.

This proposed definition for terror distinguishes between terror and guerilla warfare based on the perpetrators' target. The most significant distinction between terror and guerilla warfare is that terror necessitates "intentional use of violence against civilians in order to achieve political goals" while guerilla warfare consists of "a violent struggle in the framework of which use is made of violence targeted against military targets in order to achieve political goals."[9]

For the purpose of defining terror, the type of goal that organizations strive to achieve is irrelevant (as long as a political goal is the issue). Both the terrorist and the guerilla fighter may aspire to achieve identical goals, but each of them chooses a different way to realize them.[10] According to the proposed definition of terror, a given organization can simultaneously be a terror organization (if its activities are intended to harm civilians) and a national liberation movement (if its goal is national liberation). The proposed definition of terror is meant to provide a means for the analysis of specific incidents and events, and to assist in determining whether the activity is of a terrorist or guerrilla nature.[11]

The failure to find a universal definition for the phenomenon of terror typifies the study of the "by-products" of terror, such as international terror and state-supported terror.

In the 1970s, two American research institutes attempted to define international terror. The first study was conducted at the RAND Corporation, in the course of which the researchers defined international terror as follows: "A single incident or a series of incidents that contravene prevalent law, diplomatic agreements and the laws of war. The goal of international terror is to draw international attention to the existence of the problem being faced by the terrorists, and to stimulate fear. The aim of terror is to influence or effect a change according to the desires of its perpetrators, and the terror's direct victim is not necessarily identical to the entity that the terrorist factor is attempting to influence."[12]

The various forms of state involvement in terror have been bound together within the concepts of terrorist states or state-sponsored terrorism. However, these terms over-generalize the various levels of state involvement in terror. A more focused distinction is required to classify the involvement of states in terror according to the following categories:

- States *supporting* terrorism. This category includes states that support terror organizations with financial, ideological, military and operational aid.
- States *operating* terrorism. States that initiate terror activities through sponsored organizations, while refraining from direct involvement of government entities in terror.
- States *perpetrating* terrorism. States that perpetrate terror worldwide through the state's security networks (intelligence and security agencies).

Paul Wilkinson indicates three conditions under which political terror becomes international terror:[13] when terror is directed against civilians or foreign targets; when terror is perpetrated by the government or an organization connected to more than one state; when terror is designated to affect the policy of another foreign state.

When state-sponsored terror is instigated against one of the targets specified above, this constitutes a specific case stemming from the definition of international terror. Indeed, Wilksinson defines state-supported terror as "direct or indirect involvement of a government, through formal or informal groups, in the generating of psychological and physical violence against political targets or another state in order to achieve desired tactical and strategic goals."[14]

State-supported terror is characterized by an ambivalent attitude towards international law and order.[15] On the one hand, states that utilize terror are willing to deviate from accepted norms and the international "rules of the game" in order to strike out at their adversary. On the other hand, the state utilizing terror strives to keep its involvement in this activity covert in order to prevent the terror victim from retaliating.

Cooperation between the state and the terror organization is generally based on religious, ideological or political solidarity, or on the basis of shared interests. The extent of the patron's control over the terror organization varies according to the cooperation basis and the degree of the sponsored organization's dependence on its patron. The state's involvement in terror may be direct or indirect, and it may express itself on various levels of aid and (moral, political, economic and operational) cooperation. In the majority of cases the links between the patron state and the terror organizations are essentially clandestine.

Nationals of other countries are recruited in order to make it easier for the state to deny involvement when the activity is exposed, thus preventing censure and international sanctions. Terror may be an additional or alternative tool to activating military force in order to achieve the country's objectives; while the state may support an act of terror against another state with which it is involved in conflict, terror recruitment may also apply to a situation in which the countries are not officially involved in a state of war. Terror may be effective for the achievement of goals when there is doubt whether they are attainable through direct military confrontation, such as undermining the political stability of the target state or incurring damage to that country's diplomatic and economic ties with other countries.

A completely different approach is offered by Edward Luttvack, who maintains that "terror is inevitably self-defeating":

> When trying to understand terror, the logic behind the strategy is completely futile. Unlike guerrilla warfare, a conventional war, a revolution, a coup – or any other use of force aimed at achieving a goal – terror is nothing but a violent form of self-expression or self-definition, a sort of graffiti etched in mutilation and blood, as rational as is propaganda through action. It may possibly provide emotional satisfaction to those bound to hatred; it can perhaps assuage those who seek vengeance or maybe even supply sensual pleasure to sadists, but it cannot achieve a victory of any kind: Not the enemy's surrender, nor his physical conquest or even concessions wrung from him. On the contrary, terror is destined to strike at the target, which terrorists claim to be their goal. The only difference is the extent of the damage, from a severely flawed public image to utter eradication . . .

> When the weak assault those who are strong it is natural for them to avoid complicated targets, particularly military forces and their bases. They attack civilians and civilian targets indiscriminately . . .

> What distinguishes between terror and these aspects – which he condemns to futility and irrelevance – is the source of its violence.

> A handful of extremists can perpetrate terror acts of great magnitude, as was

proven on 9/11 . . . It is impossible to carry out guerilla warfare with a handful of extremists. In the case of war or revolution or a coup – each according to its own configuration – the number of individuals involved must be significant.

Luttvack then provides the ultimate reason why terror is sterile: "There is no political or military victory that can be achieved by a handful of extremists who act in isolation – this can be likened to a similar number of Hitlers, without the backing of the Nazi Party."[16]

Defining Abduction

The abduction of individuals for the purpose of bargaining has been used throughout history as a means to achieve personal and political goals based on criminal, ideological, religious or political motives. According to one dictionary definition 'abduction' is described as "assault and capture, captivity, rapid seizure"; according to another definition, it is "the action of forcibly taking someone away against their will." Both definitions do not engage with the terror of the incident. Consider the following:

Seizing an individual or a group of individuals and keeping them hostage against their will through the threat or actual use of violence with the aim of achieving the abductors' goals in exchange for their release.

Bearing this definition in mind, abduction may be perpetrated by abducting an individual or a group of individuals from an "open area," or by taking over a building, or hijacking a means of (overland, marine or aerial) transportation.

An abduction is considered a relatively complex type of terror attack which requires detailed planning and advanced operational skills, as well as the ability to conduct negotiations under pressure in order to reap the fruits of the action. The majority of the Middle East terror organizations have made use of abductions, targeting both security personnel and civilians. However, there are differences between the modi operandi used by the various organizations.

In the Islamic terror organizations, such as the Hizballah, the abductions triggered a religious and moral discussion regarding the justification of abducting civilians. However, almost without exception these dilemmas were resolved by religious decrees justifying and allowing the perpetration of these kidnappings.

To a great extent, abductions match the theoretical model that describes terror as a sort of theater in which each participant plays a role designated to transmit the terrorists' message. Abductions are generally the most prolonged type of attack. Therefore, they require the "best play" as well as the "actors'" (terrorists') ability to adapt the developing drama to the shifting reality in the course of the negotiations.

In contrast to attacks that consist of a rapid, dramatic incident such as drive-by shootings, throwing grenades, or attacks through the use of explosives, abductions are prolonged incidents with characteristic peaks. In this type of attack a dialogue is opened between the various parties: the abductors, the hostages, the state in charge of the negotiations to release the captives, and additional entities involved in the incident (mediators, representatives of international organizations, the media, pressure groups, etc.).

In the case of shootings or detonations, the government cannot influence the event in "real time" due to the speed of developments. Its main activity comes prior to the attack – taking steps to prevent and thwart attacks, and immediately in their aftermath by evacuating the victims, making arrests or apprehending the assailants.

When it comes to abductions, the government is forced to enter a complex process of crisis management while facing moral, political and military dilemmas under a tight schedule, as well as exposure to public and international censure. Thus, abductions constitute a particularly effective tool in the hands of the terrorists to present their worldviews and demands, and to force these views onto the agenda of the decision-makers as well as local and international public opinion. As abductions arouse dilemma and necessitate decisions, they are particularly effective when the terror organization can generate crises in the adversary's country or society (the victim's home). Indeed, abductions can sometimes trigger crises and dispute between countries regarding the manner of handling the negotiations during the crisis. The terror organization constitutes a constant threat to the adversary based on the traumatic incident of the previous abduction, while declaring that similar attacks will follow.

This study does not address the entire spectrum of variations with respect to the use of abductions throughout history, but instead concentrates on the use that terror organizations in the Middle East have made of abductions to promote their goals in the modern age. It does not deal with the abduction of hijacking transportation means (airplanes, boats or on-land vehicles), which are worthy of a separate in-depth analysis of their own unique characteristics.

The chapters that follow focus on abductions of civilians and security personnel in Israel, Lebanon, Iraq and Yemen.

Abduction attacks can be classified according to three main categories:

- The abduction's goal.
- The identity of the hostage (the abduction's target).
- The modus operandi.

The abduction's goal

As a rule, the goals of abductions are no different than other attacks that serve the interests of the terror organization. But in order to realize certain goals they offer benefits and "added value" *vis-à-vis* other types of attacks.

Common goals are:

- **Altering reality in the confrontation arena** (demanding the adversary's withdrawal from a certain area, cessation of an invasion, interrupting a process or negotiations, etc.).
- **Freeing the organization's prisoners in exchange for the hostage's release.**
- **Receipt of a ransom.**
- **A combination of several demands** (among those mentioned above and others).

The modus operandi

Several main modi operandi used by terror organizations can be identified:

- **Clandestine abduction and bargaining**
  According to this method, the terror organization abducts hostages and holds them in a hideaway. The adversary only learns of the abduction subsequently, after the kidnappers and the hostages have been hidden at a "safe place."

  This method grants the terror organization a clear advantage, because so long as the adversary does not know where the hostages are being held it cannot carry out a direct military raid to release them. This type of attack is usually more prolonged than overt abduction and bargaining attacks.
- **Overt abductions and bargaining**
  In this scenario the terror organization takes over hostages in a building or alternatively seizes a means of transportation (whether on-land, aerial or marine).

  A short time after taking over the hostages or sometimes even during that process, security entities become aware of the terror activity and begin to contend with it. Therefore, in this type of attack, the negotiations between the abductors and the authorities begin shortly after the actual attack.

  In this case, the duration of the negotiations is shorter than in a covert abduction; rapid decision-making is necessary, often under time pressure and maximum media coverage.
- **Capture and negotiation attacks**
  In this case, a terror cell seizes a private or public building and holds the individuals populating that building hostage. Negotiations are

conducted with the authorities in order to achieve its goals in exchange for the hostages' release.

- **The seizure of transportation means**
  One of the most common modi operandi used by terror organizations is the hijacking of transportation means. The hijacking of a means of transportation offers several obvious advantages:
  - Hijacking transportation means that it is possible to capture a relatively large number of hostages.
  - The hostages are held in a relatively small area and under crowded conditions, which makes it difficult to rescue them.
  - A means of transportation provides mobility to the terrorists.
  - As long as the means of transportation is mobile it is almost impossible to conduct a rescue attack.

The drawback of the seizure of transportation from the terrorists' points of view is that news of the abduction is revealed fairly quickly to the authorities, which will locate the abduction site and prevent the movement of the transport. From the moment that the means of transportation is located and stopped, negotiations will begin between the abductors and the authorities and/or an attack will be launched to free the hostages.

Abductions can be classified according to the following:

- **The identity of the hostage/hostages:**
  - **A member of the security forces** (soldiers, police force, intelligence, etc.).
  - **Civilians** – (a distinction must be made between government position-holders who are abducted because of their role, or civilians who are randomly abducted).
- **Hostage/hostages as a chance target or a planned target:**
  - **A chance target** – A civilian or a member of the security forces abducted as a random target.
  - **A planned target** – A civilian or a member of the security forces chosen as a specific target for various reasons. The abduction operation is aimed at the chosen target.

Abductions can be small from the aspect of the number of hostages involved, but they may also be more extensive. This can be depicted according to the following ranking:

- The abduction of a single hostage by a small terror cell (2–3 abductors assisted by several collaborators).
- The overtaking of a public building by a terror cell and holding scores of hostages (for example the September 1972 Munich attack).

- A multi-focused seizure and hijacking such as the hijacking of several passenger planes simultaneously with the aim of abducting hundreds of hostages (such as the attacks of the Popular Front in 1968 in Jordan).
- A mega-attack such as the Chechnya abductions and negotiations: At the theater in Moscow or the school at Beslan in North Austia (at least a thousand hostages and several dozen terrorists).

The abduction's timing

Three main categories are indicated for the choice of the timing of an abduction:

- **Random timing** – A terror organization will perpetrate an abduction randomly when that organization has adopted a policy of abducting hostages in principle as part of the organization's struggle. Therefore, when the operational opportunity arises, the organization will abduct hostages, generally as a random target, and use them for negotiation purposes.
- **Planned timing** – A terror organization may plan an abduction at a specific time in order to promote the organization's goals and intensify the abduction's effect. This kind of timing may be chosen to torpedo a political process (such as the signing of a political agreement), a prime minister's visit, a significant state event (such as hosting the Olympic Games), an attempt to sway election results, and more.
- **Timing based on operational constraints** – A terror organization may plan the abduction of a target that is of special importance to the organization. In these circumstances, the timing will stem primarily from the culmination of the ideal operational conditions that will enable the organization to carry out the abduction.

Types of abductions according to the fate of the hostage include:

- **An abduction for the purpose of bargaining over a live hostage** – (with the intention of freeing the abducted individual if the negotiations succeed).
- **An abduction for the purpose of bargaining over a body** – (murder of the hostage and negotiating over the body – with or without the adversary's knowledge that the hostage is no longer alive).
- **An abduction that begins with negotiations over a live hostage, and subsequently (after murder takes place) over the body** –

this scenario can evolve if the negotiations over the release of a live hostage fail and the terror organization murders the hostage. The negotiation process continues in order to arrange the return of the body.

- **The abduction and murder of the hostage without any negotiations** – this type of abduction is perpetrated mainly for the purpose of seizing the hostage's firearm, or due to botched up abduction plans, etc.

Methods of negotiation can include:

- Negotiating with the abductors themselves.
- Negotiating with the organization behind the abduction.
- Anonymous negotiations ("the organization is unknown").
- Negotiating via the media.
- Negotiating via a direct intermediary.
- Indirect negotiations via a third party.

The duration of negotiations to achieve the abductors' goals and release the hostage can take the form of:

- Negotiations under a deadline and ultimatum.
- Prolonged negotiations to enable the abductors to extract the optimal media and psychological effect (the likelihood of this scenario is greater when it is clear to the abductors that the adversary will have a hard time gaining access to them).
- Where the organization holding the hostage publicly denies the abduction but after a significant delay sends a private message through an intermediary, and not via the media, to indicate that the hostage is in their hands, and thereafter negotiations are conducted.

The abduction arena can include:

- The site of the abduction and the venue where the hostage is being held are under the state's control.
- The abduction is perpetrated in an area under the state's control but the hostage and his abductors leave this area in favor of a secure and "friendly" place.
- The abduction is perpetrated in a "third party" area and the hostage is held by abductors in that state or alternatively is moved to a state that sympathizes with the terrorists.

A Model for the Conduct of Abductions[17]

The following model for the conduct of abductions will serve as a template for case histories to be presented in later chapters.

	The Terror Organization	The State
1	Preparations for the abduction.	The state does not recognize the preparations for the attack.
2	Perpetration of the abduction.	The family or any other entity reports that the "abductee" is missing.
3	The organization that perpetrated the abduction claims responsibility.	Verification that the claiming of responsibility is authentic.
4	The abductors present their demands in exchange for the hostage's release and set a schedule (ultimatum).	A decision is taken regarding the readiness to enter negotiations or to refrain from doing so. Intense searches to find the hostage and the abductors. Pressure is placed on the organization that perpetrated the abduction.
5	Negotiations are conducted.	If such a decision is taken, negotiations are initiated with the organization or the abductors.
6	Thwarting a rescue operation. The abductors will strive to prevent military action by threatening to hurt the hostage. During a rescue attempt, the abductors will try to shoot the rescuers and the hostage. An attempt may be made by the abductors to escape during or following the rescue operation.	If the negotiations fail or alternatively if a decision is taken to refrain from negotiations, then the state will initiate a military operation in an attempt to rescue the hostage.

The stages of an abduction will most likely include the following:

- **The planning stage** – Definition of the abduction's goal, the target, the modus operandi, the area where the abduction will be perpetrated, the hideaway where the hostage and the abductors will stay, escape routes, how to handle the negotiations.
- **The preparation stage** – Recruitment of the terror cell, supply of weapons and the equipment required for the abduction, preparation

of the logistical infrastructure, preparation of the hideaway, renting/purchasing vehicles, patrols to become familiar with the area of the proposed attack as well as learning arrival and escape routes, establishing communication means between the perpetrating cell and the organization's headquarters.

- **Perpetration of the abduction** – Abduction of the target and neutralization of the hostage, taking him/her to the hideaway, reporting successful perpetration of the operation to the organization's headquarters.

- **Conducting negotiations** – Handing over identifying details regarding the hostage to the entity conducting the negotiations, conducting of negotiations by senior members of the organization (sometimes by the abductors themselves), conducting psychological warfare via the media. Setting an ultimatum for meeting the organization's demands. During the negotiations the hostage may be hurt or even murdered.

- **The conclusion of the abduction incident** – There are several possibilities:
  - Attainment of the abduction's goals, the hostage's release in exchange for the former, and the abductors' "disappearance".
  - In the event of military action against the perpetrators, their elimination and the hostage's release, the terror organization will strive to extract maximum media advantage despite the abduction's failure.

- **Drawing conclusions** – Learning the perpetration details, examining points of success and failure, and implementing these lessons in the planning and perpetration of future abductions.

Abductions – An "Act of War" or a "Criminal Act"?

One of the dilemmas faced by terror researchers is the question of whether a terror attack is to be considered a "criminal act", an "act of war" or a "semi-act of war"; in the latter cases handling of the event would stem from the norms and laws of warfare. Abductions are perhaps the most salient instances connected to this dilemma, particularly in cases where the terror organization demands ransom money in exchange for releasing the hostages. In such an event, the distinctions that may be made between a kidnapping for criminal reasons and a "terrorist" abduction become hazy. There is disagreement among researchers who study the area of terror as to whether terror should be considered a criminal act or a derivative of an act of war.

The two approaches have far-reaching implications from the aspect of the ability to contend with the phenomenon of terror, as the "criminal approach" entails routine police and legal procedures including compiling evidence, arresting the offender and arraignment, i.e., local handling of the transgressor. On the other hand, the "act of war" approach attributes less importance to individual guilt and identifies the terrorists according to their group and organizational affiliation, as an enemy with whom one is at a state of war. In this event, it is legitimate for security entities to use any means to protect the security of the state's citizens.

Each of these approaches has prominent advantages and disadvantages:

- The "criminal approach" – Advantage lies in its adherence to stringent norms of equality in the eyes of the law and strict measures established by law enforcement authorities regarding the arrest and indictment of suspects. This approach effectively prevents the authorities from manipulating the law and deters legal authorities from acting on the basis of political motives. The main drawback of this approach is that it impairs the effectiveness of the security agencies when attempting to respond to challenges posed by the terror organizations.

- The "national approach" – This approach distinguishes between terror activity and criminal activity, and attributes a completely different meaning to a terror attack (even if there is no actual difference in the act itself or its consequences). This approach advocates granting considerable leeway to the security agencies and enables taking such steps as the use of force – an unacceptable approach when dealing with criminals.

  This approach's advantage lies in the greater scope of effectiveness that it affords to the security agencies. Its greatest drawback is the danger not only that the authorities may employ draconian measures against the external foe, but also that they might "take advantage" of the situation in order to attain illicit political goals domestically.

Either way, the clearest distinction between a criminal act and a terrorist attack lies in the definition of the goal that the deed is meant to achieve. There is little dispute that in contrast to criminal activity, terror is enacted to impose a political agenda. The motivation behind terror activity is not personal or group benefit that may be derived from the act. Nevertheless, terror poses a threat and challenge to personal and public safety as well as the existing governmental order, thus constituting a substantially different threat to society than criminal offenses.

Thus, even if terror abductions are similar or even identical to criminal kidnappings from the aspect of the modus operandi, their context is different because they intervene on the political level via demands directly or indirectly connected to the overall struggle between the terror organization and the rival state. Thus, each demand is examined not only from the point of view of its nominal significance, but also from the wider contexts of national security, international relations, etc.

In consequence, the decision-makers' approach to a terrorist abduction is inherently different than their reaction to a parallel criminal incident due to the political repercussions from the ultimate resolution of the incident and how this will influence the conflict between the opponents in the future.

State Intervention in Abduction and Bargaining Incidents

Each abduction or bargaining incident begins and ends in a sovereign state. This fact stands true even when the abduction is perpetrated in an international zone (such as when an airplane or a boat is hijacked), due to the fact that the abductors or kidnappers came from a sovereign state and ultimately will find refuge in that state's territory.

State involvement in abduction may be expressed in various ways:

- **The "state as a victim"** – The abduction takes place in the territory of a state against state targets, in order to force the decision-makers to give in to the demands of the terror organization which the abductors represent.
- **The "state as the venue of the incident"** – The abduction occurs in the state's territory but the state is not the terrorists' target. This kind of situation may exist with the state's blessing (for example, when a state is willing to allow a hijacked aircraft to land in its territory) or against its will, when it finds itself facing the fact that the abductors and hostages are located in its sovereign territory.
- **The "state as initiator or supporter of an abduction"** – This scenario relates to a state which "supports terror" and stands directly or indirectly behind the abduction, a scenario which will be discussed extensively in the coming chapters.

A state may be involved in an abduction even without a territorial link to the incident, as when state nationals fall victim to a deliberate or random abduction. Another possibility is that the abductors are citizens of the state and, although they may not be acting on its behalf (and generally break its laws), their nationality involves their country in the incident.

As a rule, one can distinguish between two types of abductions:

- **A local incident** – an abduction in which the abductors and the hostages are nationals of the state where the incident occurs.

- **An international incident** – an abduction in which citizens of various states are involved and/or during its course, the incident moves through the territory of several states.

If an incident is sponsored by a state that supports terror or the act is perpetrated with its consent and knowledge, it can aid the terror organization behind the incident on various levels: being a departure base for the abductors; collecting intelligence about the abduction target; providing financial aid, training and weapons; providing documents that will enable the terrorists freedom of movement; providing assistance in negotiation processes between the abductors and the target state; providing refuge for the terrorists after the incident's conclusion.

States that support terror will generally aspire to conceal and downplay their involvement in terror incidents. Thus, most of the above-mentioned aid options will be performed covertly in order to refrain from leaving incriminating "fingerprints" as to the state's involvement.

In the course of an abduction/bargaining incident, the preferred position of a state that supports terror will be that of "intermediary". In such cases the state that supports terror declares that it is not involved in the terror attack but is offering "humanitarian" aid to help resolve the problem. In the event that its proposal to serve as "broker" is accepted, it can then derive maximum benefit from the attack. On the one hand, the state does not take responsibility for the incident, while on the other hand, it becomes a partner to the negotiations and has the ability to influence the latter's results according to its own interests. Thus it profits from the attack to which it served as an accomplice from the start. The state that has most frequently adopted this tactic is Iran, mainly in connection to the abductions of Western hostages in Lebanon but also during abductions perpetrated by its sponsored organizations against Israel.[18]

2

Abductions in the Palestinian Arena and the Nachson Wachsman Affair

Abductions and Bargaining Incidents in the Israeli–Palestinian Confrontation

The State of Israel has always been a target for abductions and bargaining incidents. The entities perpetrating the attacks, and their modus operandi has shifted over time and the following analysis details the development of abductions over four main periods:

1964 – 1970: From the Foundation of Fatah / PLO to "Black September"

The period between the foundation of the Fatah (the first Palestinian terror organization) and the PLO (1964) up to "Black September" in 1970, when the Palestinian terror organizations were routed in Jordan. These years served as a formative period during which scores of Palestinian organizations and offshoots grew and developed. While some were rivals, they were all united around the violent struggle against Israel. In the aftermath of the Six Day War and the defeat of the Arab armies, the Palestinian organizations adopted the concept that the only way to defeat Israel was through guerilla and terror warfare. The years 1967–1979 were a record period for the activity of terror organizations. One of the modi operandi that developed was bargaining attacks. The hijacking of airplanes, led by George Habash's Popular Front for the Liberation of Palestine (PFLP), was particularly prominent.

1970 – 1987: From "Black September" to the First Intifada

After the banishment of the terror organizations from Jordan their focus of activity was transferred to Lebanon. The Fatah, with its overt and covert branches (the "Black September" movement), became dominant in terror activity on the Lebanese border and worldwide.

The first abduction from the Lebanese arena occurred on January 1, 1970 in Metullah and it was perpetrated by the Fatah. From that time until the Peace for Galilee War (1982) and the establishment of the security zone, the majority of abduction and bargaining incidents in the Palestinian arena were led during the 1970s and 1980s by the Fatah and Ahmed Jibril's Popular Front for the Liberation of Palestine the General Command (PFLP-GC). The bargaining incidents were regarded as strategic attacks meant to promote Israeli and global awareness of the PLO's struggle to establish a Palestinian state and as bargaining chips to release Palestinian prisoners held by Israel. This period is characterized by the perpetration of complex bargaining attacks, including taking over buildings and seizing hostages. Attacks of this kind were perpetrated in Israel and abroad.

Examples include the seizure of the Israeli sportsmen's pavilion in Munich in 1973 by a cell of terrorists from the "Black September" movement; the attack perpetrated by Ahmed Jibril's PFLP-GC at the school in Ma'alot on May 15, 1975; the Fatah's attack at the Savoy Hotel in 1975; hijacking buses (the Fatah's attack on the Coastal Road in 1978 and on the no. 300 bus in 1984); the sea-jacking of the *Achille Lauro* in 1985 by the Palestine Liberation Front (PLF), and the hijacking of airplanes, most of which were perpetrated by the Popular Front for the Liberation of Palestine PFLP), of which the most famous was the hijacking of the Air France aircraft to Entebbe in 1976 by Waddia Haddad's faction.

From 1982, in the aftermath of the Peace for the Galilee War and the IDF presence in Lebanon, a Shiite terror threat developed, mainly through Hizballah, which among its other modi operandi adopted abduction attacks. The Hizballah acted in three arenas:

- The abduction of foreign nationals in Lebanon.
- The hijacking of airplanes throughout the world and their diversion to Middle East destinations for bargaining purposes.
- The abduction of IDF soldiers in Lebanon.

In addition to Shiite terror organizations, Palestinian organizations also continued to act in Lebanon, the most prominent being Ahmed Jibril's PFLP-GC, which focused on abductions (the "Jibril Deal" – on 20 May 1985, 1,150 terrorist prisoners held in Israel were released in exchange for three IDF soldiers).

1987 – 1993: The First Intifada

During this period a new "player" entered the sphere of abductions, the Hamas. This organization's first abduction took place in 1989 when they abducted and murdered IDF soldier Avi Sasportas, and demanded the release of 1150 Palestinian prisoners. This abduction symbolized a new pattern for the abduction threat – no longer a complicated attack aimed at the capture of a large number of hostages but rather a random abduction, perpetrated with relative ease, of an isolated soldier standing at a hitch-hiking station in order to bargain over his life or his body.

Following this attack, the terror organizations realized that there was no need for the grandiose abduction of numerous hostages. It was enough to abduct a single individual, preferably a soldier, in order to shock Israeli society and shake its stability. according to this modus operandi. During this period the Hizballah and the Palestinian organizations continued to perpetrate abductions in the Lebanese arena.

1993 – October 2000: The Oslo Agreements

Following the signing of the Oslo Agreements, the Hamas positioned itself as leader of the Resistance to the peace process with Israel and continued perpetrating attacks in order to undermine the implementation of the agreements. It was the first of the Palestinian organizations to perpetrate suicide attacks and – continued in its efforts to perpetrate abductions against Israelis. The main motives behind the attacks were the release of the organization's founder Sheikh Ahmad Yassin and other prisoners, and to obstruct the peace process between Israel and the Palestinians. The organization succeeded in perpetrating several abductions, the most prominent of which was the abduction of Nachshon Wachsman (October 1994), in the course of which Hamas negotiated for the release of the soldier in exchange for the release of Palestinian and Lebanese prisoners. Nachshon Wachsman's abduction and the shock-waves it generated in Israeli society increased the Hamas' motivation to continue carrying out this type of attack. The last abduction that the Hamas succeeded in perpe-trating during this time period took place in 1996.

October 2000 – 2006: The Al Aqsa Intifada

The abduction threat has been renewed in the current conflict, but this time not only the Hamas stands behind the abductions, but also some Fatah entities as well as local terror cells of Israeli Arabs. On September 21, 2005 Israeli national Sason Nuriel, who resided in the Pisgat Ze'ev neighborhood in Jerusalem, was abducted. Nuriel was murdered by his abductors, members of the Iz-A-Din Al-Qasam Brigades (the military branch of the Hamas), and his body was found on September 26. On the 27th, the Iz-A-Din Al-Qasam Brigades claimed reponsibility for the attack and released a video of the hostage while he was still alive, a short time before his execution. In the Hamas' announcement, the organization claimed that the abductors had intended to carry out a bargaining attack, but the widespread arrests that the IDF launched in the West Bank made it expedient to execute him.

The main motivation behind the abduction attacks against Israeli citizens initiated by terror organizations, particularly after the "Defense Shield" Campaign (2002) where Israel captured/arrested hundreds of terrorists, was for the purpose of bargaining to release Palestinian prisoners incarcerated in Israeli prisons. These attacks were also meant to chip away at the fortitude of Israeli society as part of the armed struggle initiated by the Palestinians. At the present time abductions are generally planned along the relatively simple pattern of abducting a soldier or a civilian and negotiating over his return alive or dead, in exchange for the release of Palestinian prisoners. (A different pattern has recently begun to emerge and this will be discussed in the Epilogue.)

The Hamas Movement – Ideological/ Operational Characteristics

The Hamas or the "Islamic Resistance Movement" (Harkat al Mukawma al Islamiya) was established shortly after the outbreak of the Intifada in the West Bank and Gaza at the end of 1987.[1] It grew out of the "Muslim Brotherhood" movement, which was founded in Egypt by Hassan al Bana in 1929. The Hamas developed a concept that combined a national narrative with an Islamic approach, and is an example of the development of Islamic political movements, a common phenomenon among Islamic communities in the twentieth and twenty-first centuries. Its uniqueness lies in its approach of intertwining the goal of national Palestinian liberation with the establishment of a society whose lifestyle is based on the norms and dictates of Islam.

The Hamas serves as the main opposition to the national movement led by the PLO and the Palestinian Authority, and leads the most violent and resolute trend in the bloody struggle against Israel.[2] Hamas flourished due to the PLO's crisis and weakness following the Peace for Galilee War (1982) and the banishment of the PLO and its leaders from Lebanon. The Hamas took advantage of the crisis in the Palestinian public and offered an alternative to the PLO's form of leadership. The appearance of a national Islamic trend within the Palestinian arena served to express the aspiration of Islamic entities, which had been thrust aside for several decades to the margins of the social and political arena, to influence the national agenda and redefine the strategic goals of Palestinian society as well as the ways to achieve them.

Thus, the Hamas had to contend with two arenas simultaneously – the internal Palestinian one against the PLO and the external arena against Israel, which occupied Muslim territory. According to Islam, this reality necessitated Jihad (a Holy War) to liberate the Islamic land.[3]

The establishment of the Hamas movement at the beginning of the Intifada constituted a substantial shift in the traditional modi operandi of the Muslim Brotherhood, whose activity was focused on the overall Islamic and community aspect within the areas of the *Dawa* (Islamic education as well as improving family and community life).[4]

The Hamas did not cease its *Dawa* activities but in addition took on political and military activity against the Israeli invasion and undertook the role of the "extremist symbol" in its stance, which called for Resistance to any historical compromise with Israel. Instead it proposed an alternative vision of the establishment of an Islamic state in all of Palestine. Thus, the Hamas transformed the nature of the Muslim Brotherhood from a social movement with an overall Islamic identity to a framework with a militant national and Islamic identity that possessed long-term goals but also immediate and local ones. The shifting in the priorities of the Islamic movement in favor of the promotion of national interests through violent means over the focus on the overall Islamic vision stemmed to a great extent from the adversity and rivalry with the PLO as to who would influence and control the Palestinian population in the West Bank and Gaza.

Several fundamental issues stood at the focus of the dispute between the PLO and the Hamas:

The future of the Israeli–Palestinian conflict

The PLO adopted an approach that advocated moving towards a political solution (from November 1988), whereas the Hamas resolutely opposed the political process *vis-à-vis* Israel, as stated in the "Islamic Covenant."

The Hamas regarded itself as the leader of an uncompromising Jihad against Israel and Zionism, while the PLO at the end of the 1980s was inclined to abandon the struggle against Israel in favor of political negotiations.[5] The Hamas offered the Palestinians a clear vision: A Palestinian state from the sea to the river Jordan, whose lifestyle would be based on Islam and its principles. This stood in contrast to the PLO concept of establishing a secular state whose borders would be defined through compromise with the State of Israel.

The Hamas expresses a fundamental hatred not only towards the State of Israel but towards Judaism as well, as expressed in the "Islamic Covenant," which uses fanatical wording with a distinct anti-Semitic undertone to describe the Jews as an evil force in the spirit of the Protocols of the Elders of Zion. The Hamas maintains that World War I, "in which they succeeded in destroying the Islamic calipha state" (the Ottoman Empire), stemmed from a Zionist conspiracy, and it is the Jews who caused the outbreak of World War II.[6] The "Islamic Covenant" describes Judaism as a worldwide demonic force which aspires to "topple societies, demolish values, undermine alliances, deteriorate morals and eradicate Islam."[7] The Hamas also aspires to negate the Jewish claim to the Land of Israel. It states: "From an objective historical point of view, the Jews who stole Palestine have no connection with the Jews of the Land of Israel who lived in Palestine."[8]

During the first months of the First Intifada (1987–1988), the Hamas refrained from calling for mass protest activities such as demonstrations and sit-down strikes, possibly due to its fear of a direct and violent confrontation with Israeli forces, which the movement's leaders felt might bring disaster upon the organization before it had the opportunity strike roots in the Palestinian public.[9] The Hamas feared that such initiatives might clash with the national stream or reveal its public weakness and lack of support in comparison to the national leadership. The activities that the Hamas called for its supporters to perform during this period were mainly connected to religious regimen such as fasting, prayer and citing religious slogans, alongside taking advantage of religious events and holidays, in order to call for the escalation of popular activity under its leadership.

During the initial years of the movement's activities the Israeli government treated it with tolerance. In 1984, when it became clear that the Hamas activists had arms arsenals in their possession, its leaders stood trial for security offenses and were sentenced, but the Israeli authorities still allowed its members to continue with their activities.[10] In the course of 1986 clear messages were transmitted to the Islamic leadership in Gaza, demanding that it restrain its involvement in politically subversive activities. But even this request did not yet indicate a substantial change in the approach to the Hamas leaders. Israeli decision-makers continued to regard them as a moderate entity competing with more extremist factors such as members of the Islamic Jihad. Its very existence and activity contributed to a split and dispute within the Palestinian society, a fact that was conceived to serve Israeli interests at the time. Nevertheless, subsequently, when the movement was officially established and its involvement in subversive and violent activity escalated, Israeli security forces began taking more decisive action to restrain and curb Hamas activities.

In July, September and October of 1988 a wave of arrests were carried out among the movement's activists. Among those arrested was Dr.

Ibrahim Yazuri, one of the movement's leaders and Ahmad Yassin's deputy. The movement's members were indicted at the end of 1988. At about the same time, following the arrest of the Hamas leaders in Gaza, Sheikh Yassin (who had not been arrested), reorganized the movement on a geographical basis while introducing strict compartmentalization. Yassin appointed Ismail Abu Shnab the Hamas commander in Gaza, and Nizar Awadallah was placed at the head of the military branch. Gaza was divided into five sectors, headed by commanders appointed personally by Yassin.

The abduction and murder of Israeli soldier Ilan Sa'adon generated another spate of arrests among the Hamas activists, including Yassin himself in May 1989, as well as prominent activists from the military branch, some of whom were responsible for the abduction. In May 1989, the Hamas sustained another blow when about 250 members of the organization (including Sheikh Yassin) and other senior leaders were arrested. In the aftermath of the arrests, large arsenals of the movement's weapons were discovered.[11]

Only in June 1989 did the Israeli government declare the Hamas a terror organization, together with the Palestinian Islamic Jihad and the Lebanese Hizballah. This declaration was backed up by close supervision of the movement and its institutions, as well as organizations and associations that were linked to them. In September 1989 the Hamas movement was outlawed.[12] The Hamas was based on a relatively large group of supporters that were not directly involved in violent activity or organizational–political activity, but constituted a reserve from which activists were recruited to lead political and violent activities. To a great extent this widespread public support explains the movement's ability to recover time and time again despite the arrests and deportations that it has undergone since 1988.[13]

Against the background of the Israeli steps taken against the movement, which included the arrests and deportation of its leaders, the Hamas increased the compartmentalization between its local infrastructures and its headquarters abroad. Consequently, a growing division was created in the organizational authority which blurred the hierarchical ties between the political spiritual leadership and the armed activists (the military branch). The Hamas' choice to take the violent course stemmed not only from its worldview but also from the necessity to compete with the Palestinian organizations that led the armed struggle against Israel. During the first year of its inception, the scope of Hamas violence against Israel was relatively limited – ten attacks that included shooting at military patrols and Israeli nationals in Gaza, as well as detonating roadside explosive charges. The limited scope of activity stemmed mainly from lack of an organizational operative infrastructure, and from concentrating efforts on the purchase of weapons, recruitment, and training in explosives and weaponry. There was an escalation in Hamas' violent activities during the second year of the Intifada, both in the number of attacks (32) as well as their daring and sophistication.

The most outstanding Hamas attacks included the abduction and murder of IDF soldiers Avi Sasportas (January 1989) and Ilan Sa'adon (May 1989). In the aftermath of the abduction and murder of Sasportas, Sheikh Yassin refused to approve negotiations with the Israeli authorities due to his fear that acceptance of responsibility for the deed would trigger a tough crackdown on the movement's leaders. As it was, the Hamas was still recovering from the above-mentioned arrests carried out by the Israeli authorities in September 1988 in Gaza. During 1989, Hamas members perpetrated terror attacks in the West Bank as well, mainly in Hebron. These activities included shooting attacks and lobbing Molotov cocktails at Israeli vehicles. In 1990, activities were extended within the boundaries of Israel and they included torching fields, stabbings and the murder of Israeli citizens in West Bank and Gaza cities, as well as drive-by shootings and roadside explosive charges. The peak of the wave of attacks came in December 1990 in a stabbing attack at a factory in Jaffa. Three Israelis were murdered in this incident.[14]

Thus, the waves of arrests carried out against Hamas activists since its inception had only limited impact from the point of view of the time needed for the Hamas to recover and reorganize itself operationally. In November 1989, a half a year after a wide spate of arrests among Hamas leaders and members, it was clear that a new generation of leaders had arisen in the movement. Rehabilitation stemmed not only from the movement's ability to reorganize itself, but also from the release of activists who had been arrested in the past and served their time. Their return to Gaza pumped new blood into the movement's veins. At that time, changes in the Hamas' deployment in the areas became evident, including an organizational division into areas of activity, and increased compartmentalization between the factors in the field. Another consequence of the pressure exerted by the Israeli security forces on the movement and its activities was the increased dependence of the organization's activists in Israel on the movement's leaders and infrastructure outside of its boundaries, namely its "external" leadership.

Despite the increase in the scope of Hamas' activities and its geographical dispersion in the years 1989–1990, it was still smaller than the other organizations and created less of an impact on the public despite the sophistication and daring of its attacks. However, the power of the religious message of the Holy War (Jihad) within Palestinian society, which the Hamas hoisted as its banner, was prominently expressed in the circumstances that granted the Jihad immediate and defined significance, such as the killing of seventeen Palestinians in violent clashes with Israeli police at the Temple Mount in Jerusalem on October 8, 1990. After the incident, the Hamas called for Jihad against "the Zionist enemy everywhere, on all fronts and using any means." The bloodshed at the Temple Mount triggered a sharp escalation in the scope of attacks perpetrated by lone Palestinian stabbers, who attacked and murdered civilians, policemen and soldiers spontaneously. These perpetrators did not usually have any link with the Hamas, but many were influenced by its religious message, and following their attacks were adopted by the Hamas, which declared their actions expressions of devotion.

In August 1992, many activists in the military branch (the Iz-A-Din Al-Qasam Brigades) were arrested. Nevertheless, towards the end of that year, Hamas activists perpetrated additional attacks, which aside from their growing frequency were also notable due to the perpetrators' willingness to clash directly with Israeli security forces. Among these attacks were the shooting at an IDF patrol, resulting in the death of three soldiers, and a similar ambush against an Israeli patrol which ended in the death of one of the patrol members.

The deportation of Hamas activists to Lebanon in December 1992

Following the abduction and murder of a Border Policeman in December 1992, some 1500 activists of the Hamas and the Islamic Jihad were arrested, including 22 members of the Iz-A-Din Al-Qasam Brigades.[15] With the aim of intensifying damage to the organization's infrastructures and supporters, it was decided to take the unprecedented step of deporting 415 activists, mostly Hamas members, from Israel to Lebanon.

The Israeli government hoped to achieve the following goals:

- Inflict damage on Hamas leadership and weaken its popular support.
- Fortify the PLO and the peace process by crippling the strength of the Hamas and the Islamic Jihad, who were its main opponents.
- Transmit a clear message to the Israeli public that the government was willing to take any necessary step to protect its citizens.
- Hamper the movement's recovery by removing its leaders and activists.

The deportation necessitated unprecedented legal preparation in order to enable its rapid and resolute implementation without becoming bogged down in the procedural impediments surrounding deportation from the territories, including the right of the recipients of the deportation injunctions to appeal. The proposed legal formula defined the step as "temporary deportation"; according to the ruling of the High Court, the "deportees" were granted the right to appeal the deportation outside of Israeli territory within sixty days.[16] Most of the deportees were affiliated with the civilian-propaganda infrastructure as well as the political and religious infrastructures of the Hamas.

The attacks perpetrated by activists identified with the Hamas were the practical expression of the movement's survival capabilities. The immediate cause for the spates of arrests and the deportation of hundreds of activists in this arena was clearly evident at the end of 1992. But the arrests among the Hamas members had a relatively minor impact on the operational capabilities of the Iz a-Din Al-Qasam Brigades. The forces that motivated people to join the struggle were as strong as ever. When members were arrested others replaced them and preserved the movement's strength so that it could continue to shock the Israeli public. The Israeli decision regarding the deportation was described in the media and public opinion as a gross violation of human rights and triggered sharp censure in the international arena. In the Palestinian arena, the deportation caused a closing of ranks between adversaries and supporters in the struggle for the deportees. Although the deportation did indeed cause a temporary setback in the Hamas' activity, it also boosted the movement's prestige in the eyes of the Palestinian public, thus contributing to its long-term reinforcement. The deportation increased inter-organizational solidarity among the Palestinians and triggered an escalation of violence in the territories and within the boundaries of the "Green Line." The contributors to these attacks were entities connected to the national stream such as the Fatah "Hawks," the "Red Eagles" and others.

Against the background of the deportation, and in a gesture that was the first of its kind since the beginning of the Intifada, the PLO and the Hamas published a joint statement denouncing the deportation. The Palestinian public demanded the renewal of the dialogue between the PLO and the Hamas, and suspension of the dialogue with Israel. The Hamas, family members of the deportees, and the Palestinian public in general put heavy pressure on the Palestinian representatives to the peace talks and on the PLO leadership to suspend the peace talks in Washington, and forced the PLO to make the return to peace talks, which had been recessed due to the Christmas break, conditional on the return of the deportees.

In the aftermath of the deportation, the movement's "external" leadership undertook the rehabilitation and strengthening of Hamas infrastructures in the territories.

A central activist, Mussa Abu Marzook, was the life and spirit behind the movement's reorganization in Jordan. The Hamas' new structure was based on a strict hierarchy, functional divisions and rigorous compartmentalization. The Gaza Strip and the West Bank were divided into sub-regions, and headquarters were established in each of the latter. A coordinating committee was set up in order to coordinate between the movement's infrastructures in Gaza and the West Bank. The Hamas' senior leadership acted through three central committees: A political committee, a committee for ideological direction and propaganda, and a military committee.

Following the reorganization, the link between the "external" leadership located in the United States (Mussa Abu Marzook's place of residence) and in Amman grew stronger. The Hamas had an overt infrastructure in Amman which served as a rear headquarters *vis-à-vis* the "interior" leadership and coordinated its ongoing activities, including military action. The influence of the "external" leadership, which was heavily dependent on the headquarters, expressed itself in its control of the financial resources that the Hamas raised outside of Israel's borders and in the financial support that it provided to the families of the organization's martyrs and prisoners.

The mass deportation of the Hamas activists came a short time after the movement's "external" leadership had reached a strategic agreement with Iran.[17] Iran agreed to provide the Hamas with political, financial and military support in order to boost its struggle against Israel and the peace process. In October 1992, one year after the Hamas opened its official offices in Teheran, it was announced that a Hamas delegation, headed by its spokesman Ibrahim Roshaa and Mussa Abu Marzook, arrived in Iran and met with its spiritual leader Ali Khameni and with the commander of the Revolutionary Guards, Mukhsein Razai. Both parties signed the draft of an agreement to establish a political and military alliance.[18] Iran agreed to provide the Hamas with financial, military and political aid and to erect a broadcasting station in Southern Lebanon. This agreement had long-term ramifications and it would appear that the intensification of the Hamas' military activity, which was meant to impede the negotiations between Israel and the PLO, was part of the implementation of this agreement by both parties. In light of the growing cooperation between Iran and the Hamas, the Hizballah came to the aid of the Hamas deportees in Lebanon. The Hizballah and Iran became the patrons of the deportees, offering them aid and financial resources, and took advantage of their time in Lebanon for military training and strengthening of the ties between the Hamas, Hizaballah and Iran.

Benjamin Netanyahu addresses this issue in his book:[19]

In 1992 – prior to the Oslo Agreements – the Rabin administration deported almost 400 Sunni terrorists from the Hamas to Southern Lebanon. There they encountered their Shiite colleagues from the Hizballah, who took pleasure in training them in the artistry of terror including how to detonate car bombs, as well as how to produce explosives and suicide missions. Thus a strong link was created between the two organizations, including the appointment of liaison officers.

In December 1993, after the period of their deportation, many of the Hamas deportees returned to Judea, Samaria and the Gaza Strip. Upon their return they were arrested, and underwent a preliminary interrogation. Subsequently, all those against whom no incriminating security evidence had been found were released.[20] In actual fact, the majority of the deportees returned to their homes and quickly reverted to subversive activity and terror. The Hamas senior members who underwent military training in Lebanon became leaders of the Hamas' military branch after their return. Among these leaders were Abdallah Kawasma, Abd al Aziz Rantissi, Salah Darawzeh, Nasser Jawarish, Abdul Rahman Hamed and others. An examination of the modi operandi of the Hamas' military branch after the return of the deportees indicates an improvement in the movement's operational skills; it significantly expanded its activities and adopted terror methods that it had learned from the Hizballah and Iran such as suicide attacks (which it initiated after the signing of the "Oslo Agreement"), attacks using explosive devices, combined attacks (shooting and explosive devices), and abductions.

Despite the opposition of the Hamas leaders to the Oslo Agreements, the organization's members exercised restraint until the IDF forces completed their withdrawal in Gaza. Following the Oslo Agreements some of the senior Hamas members who had fled Gaza returned, including Abd al Rabo Abu Hussa. The terrorist, a veteran member of the Iz a-Din Al-Qasam Brigades, was known to have assisted in the murders of the late IDF soldiers Avi Sassportas and Ilan Sa'adon. After the attacks he fled to Egypt and from there to Libya, but in July 1994 he infiltrated the Gaza border through the security fence at Raffah and brought new instructions from the Hamas headquarters in Syria. He received a hero's welcome in Gaza, basked in media coverage and had his picture taken in the newspaper; he later became the spokesman of the Iz a-Din Al-Qasam Brigades. Israel issued warnings to the Palestinian Authority about him, but the Palestinian police made no effort to arrest him. Abu Hussa's new instructions from Damascus were that the ranks of the Iz a-Din Al-Qasam Brigades should be expanded and the pace of the terror attacks accelerated.[21]

Up to the abduction of Nachshon Wachsman, Arafat and his colleagues denounced Hamas terror but refrained from actually taking preventive steps, despite the fact that the Israeli General Security Services (GSS) had provided the Palestinian Authority with ample and damning reports regarding the activities of the Iz a-Din Al-Qasam Brigades.

It appears that the Palestinian Authority was pleasantly surprised by the restraint of the Hamas, which declared a temporary lull in hostilities after the last IDF soldier withdrew in the Gaza Strip on May 4, 1994. The Hamas leaders openly refrained from friction with the Palestinian forces in order to avoid being stamped with the negative image of civil war Fitna instigators. Indeed, for over two months the Hamas did not perpetrate even one attack in the Gaza Strip but rather focused its main activities on bolstering its political strength.

The supportive attitude of the Palestinian police convinced the Hamas headquarters that Arafat would not disrupt attacks perpetrated by the Iz a-Din Al-Qasam Brigades against Israel. Members of the movement, who in the first weeks of the Palestinian rule acted as if they were fugitives, came out of hiding and some even walked around openly with their weapons. At the beginning of July 1994, a few hours after riots had abated at the Erez Pass, the Hamas headquarters in Gaza received an urgent fax: "Resume the armed struggle," read the message that had been sent from the Hamas headquarters in Syria.[22] Two days later, on the morning of July 12, 1994, a cell of the Iz a-Din Al-Qasam Brigades set out for the road that led to Gush Katif. Gunfire was aimed at a building contractor from Beer Sheva, who was slightly injured. This shooting symbolized the end of the Hamas' restraint. From July 12, 1994 onwards the drive-by shootings perpetrated by members of the Iz a-Din Al-Qasam Brigades became an almost daily event. On July 19, 1994 Lieutenant Guy Ovadia was killed in a skirmish with one of the movement's terror cells near Raffah, and on August 14, 1994, Ron Sobol was shot by the Hamas' members near the Kisufim Pass.

Abductions and Attempted Abductions by the Hamas

The period of the Intifada until the "Oslo Agreements" (1987–1993)

On February 16, 1989, IDF soldier **Avi Sasportas** was abducted and murdered by the Hamas, after he had hitchhiked a ride at the Hodaya intersection east of Ashkelon. Searches began 24 hours after his disappearance. On the third day of the search a bag containing his army boots and sneakers was found. Two weeks after his disappearance the Israel Broadcasting Authority received an anonymous call demanding the release of 1500 terrorists within 24 hours in exchange for his release. If not, he would be executed. Sasportas' buried body was discovered not far from where he was last seen hitchhiking on May 7, 1989 – three months after his disappearance. Sasportas was apparently killed a short time after his abduction by his abductors.

On May 3, 1989, IDF soldier **Ilan Sa'adon** was abducted by the Hamas. He was picked up by a Subaru car and murdered by two Hamas members who were masquerading as religious Jewish seminary students. Searches were initiated the day after his disappearance. In the wake of the abduction, the GSS arrested Sheikh Yassin. Sa'adons body was found on July 30, 1996 and was interred on August 12, 1996. Subsequently, the terror cell behind the abduction was exposed but the murderers themselves had fled to Libya. On November 19, 2001 an IDF force penetrated the outskirts of Gaza and arrested Abd al Rabo Abu Hussa, one of the planners behind the abduction and murder of IDF soldiers Ilan Sa'adon and Avi Sasportas.

On September 17, 1992, IDF soldier **Ilan Karavani** was abducted by terrorists wearing skullcaps. After his weapon had been confiscated, he was thrown out of the vehicle and saved by Arabs who happened to be passing by. The Hamas and the "Fatah Hawks" claimed responsibility for the abduction attempt.

On December 13, 1992, Border Guard policeman **Nissim Toledano** was abducted and murdered. Toledano was abducted in the city of Lod in the early morning hours while he was walking from his home to the base where he served. On the same day at 10:00 a.m., two masked men appeared at the Red Cross representative office in Elbireh and left a document along with a photocopy of the policeman's identity card. The document, signed by the Hamas' military branch, demanded that the movement's leader, Sheikh Ahmed Yassin, be released by 21:00 that evening. Two days later, Toledano's body was found, bound and stabbed, near the village of Kfar Adomim on the road between Jerusalem and Jericho. Pathological findings indicated that he had been strangled and stabbed to death two to six hours after the ultimatum had expired. The murder had not been committed at the site where the body was found.

On March 7, 1993, IDF soldier **Yehoshua Friedberg** disappeared on his way from Jerusalem to Tel Hashomer. His body was found after an extensive search near Neveh Ilan: his firearm was missing. Indications from the crime site indicated that the soldier had been abducted and murdered by terrorists. On November 16, 1993 the cell that had perpetrated the murder was apprehended. The cells' members, Hamas activists from East Jerusalem, confessed to their involvement in three additional murders (those of Lior Tubul, Ronen Karmani and Rafi Abraamov – cases that did not involve abductions). During interrogation one of the murderers, Ala Jowaad, confessed that on the morning of the abduction he was alone in his car when he picked up the soldier who was waiting at a hitchhiking station at the exit from Jerusalem. When he approached Abu Gosh, he pulled out his gun and shot the soldier four times while driving. He then dumped the body at the village of Neveh Ilan. He took the soldier's firearm and ID card and threw away the rest of his belongings.

On August 5, 1993, IDF soldier **Yaron Chen** was abducted and murdered. He was hitchhiking at the Rama intersection near Ramallah. The soldier, shot to death in Bitunya after struggling with his abductors, was found in a burnt-out car. The Hamas' military branch claimed responsibility for the abduction and murder, its spokesman stating that the soldier had been executed to avenge the death of the two terrorists who had perpetrated the attack on bus no. 25 at the French Hill in Jerusalem on July 1, 1993.

The period of the "Oslo Agreements"

On October 24, 1993, two reserve soldiers, **Ehud Roth and Ilan Levi,** were abducted and murdered in Khan Yunis. The two accepted a ride in a stolen car bearing Israeli license plates. Three terrorists masquerading as Jews occupied the car. One soldier was shot and the other was stabbed. Their bodies were found about one kilometer away from the hitchhiking station. The terrorists confiscated the soldiers' firearms. The Hamas' military branch claimed responsibility for the attack.

On April 20, 1994, IDF soldier **Shahar Simani**, an officers' course cadet, was abducted and murdered. He was abducted on his way from the army base to his girlfriend's house in moshav Masuot Yitzchak near Ashkelon. After his murder, the body was dumped near Beit Hanina. He bore signs of stabbings, shooting and strangling, as well as having cuts on one of his hands, which testified to the struggle he put up against his assailants. His firearm and two magazines had been taken by the abductors. Hamas' military branch claimed responsibility for the attack. A document found several days later featured a photocopy of the soldier's papers. The document also claimed that a secret Hamas cell had infiltrated Israel's southern border, abducted the soldier and dumped his body in Jerusalem. The document stated that the abduction had taken place several days after the Hamas' warning and demand that the Israeli government release Hamas prisoners, including Sheikh Yassin, were ignored.

On July 6, 1994, IDF soldier **Aryeh Zvi Frankental** was abducted and murdered. The soldier had set out from his base in the southern part of the country for his home in moshav Gimzu. He was abducted near the town of Kiryat Malachi by a terrorist cell traveling by car. The terrorists shot him in the head four times and dumped his body in a deserted house in the village of Akab near Ramallah. His body bore signs of scratches and stabbings. His personal papers were not taken but his firearm and cartridge chamber were stolen.

The Hamas military branch claimed responsibility for the murder in a manifest published on July 8, 1994, which included a photocopy of the soldier's ID. It stated that the soldier had been abducted by "members of secret unit no. 6." The communique also warned that the Hamas would perpetrate additional abductions if Israel failed to release all Palestinian prisoners, with Sheikh Yassin, Sheikh Obeid and Mustafa Dirani at the head of the list. The characteristics of the attack were similar to those of Shahar Simani and the same terror cell claimed responsibility for both murders.

On August 12, 1994, the cell that killed the two soldiers and stole their weapons was exposed. Interrogation of the cell's leader indicated that Frankental's abduction was meant to serve for bargaining purposes but the plan went awry when the soldier struggled with his captors. After the murder they had planned to negotiate over the return of the body but its discovery in an abandoned house thwarted that plan.

On May 12, 1996, a Hamas cell led by the wanted leader of the movement in Judea and Samaria, Muhi Aldin Sharif, attempted to abduct **Lior Avital**, a cadet at the Mishor Adumim military academy. Lior accepted a ride at the French Hill intersection. There were two bearded young men wearing skullcaps in the car. During the drive, Lior was hit on the head with a club by a third passenger who had been hiding in the back seat. At the same time, the passenger seated next to the driver took out a gun and pointed it at the soldier. Lior fought his abductors, succeeded in escaping through the car window and was lightly injured.

On May 17, 1996, Hassan Salameh, a senior member of the Hamas' military branch in Gaza, was arrested. In the course of his interrogation he revealed the existence of an Eastern Jerusalem Hamas cell which included three members led by Muhi Aldin Sharif. These were the members of the cell that had made the failed attempt to abduct Avital. It seemed that the abduction had been attempted following instructions issued by the Hamas leadership to suspend suicide attacks until after the elections, which were scheduled for May 29, 1996. The orders were to abduct soldiers, transfer them to Gaza, and negotiate for the release of Sheikh Yassin and other Palestinian prisoners.

On September 9, 1996, IDF soldier **Sharon Edri** was abducted by a Hamas cell from the village Tsurif. The cell that perpetrated the attack was uncovered on March 21, 1997, following the suicide attack at the Apropo restaurant in Tel Aviv. Sharon Edri's body was found on April 19, 1997.

The Abduction and Killing of Nachshon Wachsman

On October 9, 1994, IDF soldier Nachshon Wachsman was abducted at the Bnei Atarot intersection near Lod when he accepted a ride. He was held captive by his Hamas abductors in a house in Bir Naballah (northern Jerusalem). The Hamas demanded the release of Hamas leader Sheikh Yassin, Sheikh Karim Obeid (Hizballah) and Mustafa Dirani (The Faithful Resistance), as well as Palestinian and Lebanese prisoners in exchange for the soldier's release. The movement threatened that if by 21:00 on October 14, 1994 Israel did not meet its demands, Nachshon Wacshman would be executed.

Israeli intelligence located the safe house in Bir Naballah several hours before the expiration deadline and a military operation was launched in an attempt to rescue him. Nachshon Wachsman was murdered before the IDF force could extricate him. Captain Nir Poraz was killed in the rescue attempt and eight other soldiers were wounded.

Nachshon Wachsman's abductors were killed in the raid and the cell's collaborators were arrested and brought to trial in Israel. A description of the abduction's planning stages, the perpetration and the abductors' actions until their extermination by the IDF force, were revealed in the subsequent interrogation of the collaborators. Their testimonies shed light upon the Hamas' modus operandi, its motivation and the dangers inherent within this murderous organization.

The Hamas was one of the main opponents to the peace process between the State of Israel and the Palestinian Authority. When Israel and the Palestinian Authority began implementing the Oslo and Cairo Agreements, the Hamas instigated a wave of terror attacks aimed at torpedoing the "Oslo process". It was the first organization to perpetrate suicide attacks and rapidly became a significant security threat to Israel. It was granted military, economic and propaganda aid from opponents of the peace process, led by Iran and its sponsored organization, the Hizballah.

Thus, during the years 1993–1994 the Hamas was embroiled in its conflict with Israel but also in adversity with the Palestinian Authority, which attempted to clip the organization's wings and curb its influence but avoided a face-to-face confrontation with the challenges posed by the organization.

The Hamas leadership, including its military and political arms, acted from several focal points: Hamas' leader, Sheikh Yassin, was incarcerated in an Israeli prison; the main political and military branches both acted out of Gaza, and another area of activity was Judea and Samaria. At the same time, the movement had headquarters in Jordan, Syria and Lebanon (the "external" leadership). Despite the leadership's decentralization and dispersion, the Hamas acted as a hierarchical organization with reciprocal links and coordination between the "internal" and "external" leadership.

The movement's leadership formulated the strategy while the "military infrastructures" translated the policy into its terrorist attack policy.

Due to the delicate relationship between the Hamas and the Palestinian Authority, decisions regarding "strategic attacks", such as Nachshon Wachsman's abduction, necessitated decision-making by the organization's most senior echelon and were not the initiative of the "field levels". Thus, it is reasonable to assume that the Hamas' most senior echelons in Gaza and Judea and Samaria, and outside of these territories, were involved in the abduction of Nachshon Wachsman. Moreover, it would appear that Iran and the Hizballah were partners to the abduction even if they were not aware of the actual details of the attack. (For an in-depth discussion of Iran's involvement, see chapter 3.)

The interrogation of some of the members of Hamas' terror infrastructure who were involved in the abduction indicates that two of his abductors participated in previous abductions of soldiers and members of the Israeli security forces.[23] The two, Hassan Taysir Natsche and Abd Al Karim Bader, were also involved in a shooting incident with policemen near the Rockefeller Museum. Hassan Natsche was injured in the skirmish and the two fled to Jericho where they hid for a month.[24]

From Jordan, the two moved to Nablus, a stronghold of the Hamas' military arm. The plan to abduct a soldier for bargaining purposes was formulated during their stay in Nablus.[25] It seems that the instructions to carry out the abduction were issued by Muhammad Def al Masri, one of the senior commanders of the Hamas' military branch in Gaza, apparently in coordination with and/or under the direction of the movement's leadership abroad. The members of the terror cell in Nablus were given the mission to perpetrate the abduction and update the headquarters in Gaza, which was to handle the negotiations *vis-à-vis* Israel.

The main terrorists involved in the abduction were:

- **Muhammad Def al Masri** – dubbed "Abu Khaled", one of the leaders of the Hamas' military branch in Gaza. He activated the terror infrastructure. A resident of Gaza.
- **Abd al Rabo Abu Hussa** – a senior member of the Hamas' military branch in Gaza. He was involved in the murder of IDF soldiers Avi Sasportas and Ilan Sa'adon.
- **Salah a-Din Nur a-Din Rada Drawza** – dubbed "Abu Nur", a senior member of the Hamas' military branch. He planned and perpetrated the abduction.
- **Salah a-Din Hassan Salem Jadallah** – dubbed "Abu Muhammad", commander of the abductors' cell. He took part in abductions of three soldiers and Israeli security members. A resident of Gaza. Salah Jadallah served as the aide of Imad Akel, one of the commanders of the Iz a-Din Al-Qasam Brigades in Gaza.
- **Hassan Taysir Natsche** – took part in three abductions of IDF soldiers and members of the Israeli security forces as well as the shooting incident near the Rockefeller Museum in which he was injured. A resident of the Ras al Amud quarter of Jerusalem.
- **Abd al Karim Yassin Bader** participated in the shooting attack near the Rockefeller Museum as well as the abduction of Nachshon Wachsman. A resident of Beit Hanina.
- **Jihad Yamur** – collaborator to the cell that abducted Nachshon Wachsman. He participated in the abduction and served as liaison

with the movement's activists in Gaza. A resident of Beit Hanina.

- **"Abu Ali"** – collaborator to Muhammad Def "Abu Khaled". He maintained contact with Jihad Yamur, and through him with the abductors' cell. A resident of Gaza.
- **Zachariya Lutfi Najib** – dubbed "Abu Abdallah" – he was collaborator to the cell that abducted Nachshon Wachsman. He helped to organize the hiding place for the abductors and provided them with food twice during the abduction.
- **Ahmad Jadallah**[26] – Salah Jadallah's ("Abu Muhammad") younger brother. He worked as a Reuter's photographer in Gaza.
- **Hisham Shams**[27] – photographer for Reuters in Gaza. He filmed the Iz a-Din Al-Qasam Brigades members on a cassette prepared in Gaza.

Organization and preparations prior to the abduction

Information regarding the preparations was revealed during the interrogations and testimonies given to the Israeli police and at the trial of some of the terrorists involved in the abduction.[28] Central testimony, which shed light on the preparations and perpetration, was that of Jihad Yamur, who as mentioned earlier was a collaborator. He participated and served as liaison between the abductors and the attack commanders in Gaza. A description of the events, divided according to various categories, is presented below:

On Tuesday, October 5, 1994 or a date close to it, Jihad Yamur went to the branch of Bank Hapoalim on al Zahara Street in Jerusalem in order to make a deposit. Two other men arrived at Bank Hapoalim in a red Volvo. One of the two, who introduced himself as "Sami," approached Jihad Yamur while the other (who later turned out to be Zachariya Najib "Abu Abdallah") remained near the car. "Sami" explained that he had been sent to Yamur at the request of Hassan Taysir Natsche. In order to verify his mission, Sami stated a fact related to Yamur himself, which was known only to Natsche. In light of this fact, Yamur was persuaded that Sami had indeed been dispatched by Natsche. Yamur asked Sami why Natsche had sent him and Sami explained that Natsche wished to meet with him. Yamur agreed to go with Sami and Zachariya and traveled with them to Nablus to the Refediya Mosque, where the defendant prayed the midday prayer with the two men.

At that point Zachariya left his car at the mosque and accompanied Yamur to meet with another person – Salah a-Din Nur a-Din Rada Drawza ("Abu Nur").

Drawza took the two to another mosque in Jabel Alshimali where they met with Hassan Taysir Natsche and Salah Salem Jadallah known as "Abu

Muhammad." Yamur learned from "Abu Muhammad" and Hassan Natsche that the two had been declared wanted by the Israeli security forces. The latter told him that during a shooting skirmish with Israeli policemen near the Rockefeller Museum, Natsche had been injured in his leg and head. They also told him that after the attack, the two had fled to Jericho with the help of Areb Abadin (another wanted terrorist who was killed following the attack at the Museum). They stayed in Jericho for a month and then traveled to Nablus where they met with "Abu Muhammad" who had arrived from Gaza.

Yamur was informed that they were acting on behalf of the Iz a-Din Al-Qasam Brigades of the Hamas. During the meeting Yamur noticed that Natsche was armed with a black handgun and magazine. Natsche and "Abu Muhammad" also told Yamur and Zachariya that they were planning to abduct an Israeli soldier in a bargaining attack and for this purpose they needed a hiding place in the Jerusalem area and a car. Yamur and Zachariya agreed to help the two to bring their plans to realization.

The cell members asked Yamur to help with the following: To rent a large van that would serve for the abduction; to rent a safe house where the captive would be held; to rent a video camera in order to tape the abductee; and to serve as a liaison between the cell and the organization's headquarters in Gaza.

Preparations for the attack

At the end of the meeting with Natsche and "Abu Muhammad," Yamur and Zachariya returned to Jerusalem in the latter's car. During the ride, Zachariya suggested to Yamur that they use the house of his nephew, Ziyad Najib (also called "Abu Allah"), which was located in the village of Bir Naballah. The two drove by the house on their way to Jerusalem to check it out.

Yamur liked the idea and the two agreed that Zachariya would give Yamur the keys to the house three days later after the prayer service at the Al Aqsa Mosque, on Friday, a date which had been set earlier. Zachariya asked his nephew to rent him the house and told him that it was for Hassan Natsche, a fugitive hiding from the Israeli security forces who wanted to meet his mother, whom he hadn't seen in a long time. Ziyad Najib agreed to the proposition and gave the keys to Zachariya. On the agreed date Zachariya handed the keys over to Yamur.

Immediately afterwards Yamur drove his brother's car to Nablus where he met with Natsche and Abd al Karim Bader, according to the plan previously agreed. Yamur informed them that he had found a house in Bir Naballah. The members of the terror cell agreed that Yamur would drive ahead in his brother's car and the three cell members would follow him in the white Transporter van with license plates bearing the letter "S" (license plates issued in the city of Nablus). The vehicle was driven by Drawza who had met Yamur earlier.

Yamur noted that each of the cell members carried a blue knapsack and a black plastic bag in which they concealed their firearms. The cell members traveled in the two vehicles to the A-Ram intersection where Yamur switched with the driver of the white van and asked him to wait there in the car owned by Yamur's brother.

From there, Yamur drove the three cell members to the house in Bir Naballah and they arrived there at about 18:30. Zachariya's nephew was waiting for them and showed them their rooms. Yamur drove back to the intersection where he and the other driver switched cars. Yamur returned to the house in Bir Naballah in his brother's car and talked to the three other cell members. Zachariya's nephew was angry when he realized that Natsche would not be there alone but in fact would be accompanied by two other fugitives, and he berated his uncle for misleading him. Later, after it became clear that the abducted soldier had been held at the house, "Abu Allah" fled with his family to Jordan.

The plan to abduct the soldier

During the planning stages the cell members agreed that during the abduction they would masquerade as religious Jews so that the Israeli soldier would be easily enticed into the car. They asked Yamur to purchase skull-caps and black hats usually worn by ultra-Orthodox Jews. On Saturday October 8, 1994 (after leaving the members of the cell in the house), Yamur drove to the Old City of Jerusalem where he bought four small knitted skullcaps and two black hats in a shop for $25. He also purchased iron chains to shackle the soldier. That night he returned to the hiding place and gave the items he had bought to the cell members.

Renting the vehicle for the abduction   After the cell members had settled down in the house they asked Yamur to rent a van with Israeli license plates, as they had agreed earlier. Yamur explained to his colleagues that as the next day was Saturday, all of the car rental agencies would be closed, but he promised to take care of the rental first thing on Sunday morning. In the meantime, on Saturday October 8, 1994, Yamur dealt with other arrangements connected to the abduction. On Sunday October 9, Yamur tried to rent a van from several car rental agencies in West Jerusalem but he was unsuccessful because he did not have a credit card. Ultimately he found one agency that agreed to a cash deposit instead of a credit card. Yamur successfully rented a maroon coloured van (license no. 2491358) at 14:00 from the "Shako Land" agency after leaving a $1,000 cash deposit.

After renting the van, he drove to the hiding place in order to inform the cell members that he had succeeded in his mission. The rented van was used in the abduction and subsequently served Yamur when he handed over the cassette and the soldier's ID to the Hamas commanders in Gaza. The rented van was parked far away from Bir Naballah and was not used for Yamur's visits at the hideaway. During these visits Yamur used other cars or taxis. Three days after the abduction Yamur returned the van and was even offered a refund for the days that he had not used the vehicle.

Weapons at the terror cell's disposal   The members of the cell had various weapons at their disposal. For the purposes of perpetrating the abduction the members were equipped with weapons, which were concealed in their bags: An Uzi sub-machine gun (stolen from a security company in 1991); handguns; and a Galil rifle (stolen from an IDF base).

When they got into the vehicle, Yamur noted that Natsche was carrying a Galil rifle and a handgun, Bader toted an Uzi submachine gun, and "Abu Muhammad" brought a gun, handcuffs, iron chains and black bags. Yamur was carrying the black handgun which Hassan Natsche had given him prior. Before Natsche gave him the weapon, Yamur told him that he didn't know how to shoot it and the former instructed him.

The abduction

The cell members set out from Bir Naballah to perpetrate the abduction in the van rented by Yamur. Jihad Yamur drove the van with a skullcap on his head. Karim Bader was seated next to him, wearing a black hat. Seated behind Yamir was "Abu Muhammad" in a black hat. Natsche sat behind Karim Bader with a skullcap on his head.

The cell members drove from Bir Naballah to the Jerusalem–Tel Aviv highway. From there they continued to the Ben-Gurion intersection and turned towards Petach Tikva. As they encountered a gridlock, Yamur turned around and headed for Tel Aviv. Shortly afterwards, he turned back and drove towards the airport. On the Yahud–Ben-Gurion road, the cell members saw a soldier disembarking from a gray Subaru car, which then continued on its way towards the Yahud industrial zone. Yamur watched the soldier and saw that he had stopped at the bus station and was hitch-hiking. The soldier they saw was Nachshon Wachsman, who was on his way to visit a friend at an army base in Ramle. Nachshon was wearing a crocheted skullcap and an army uniform with a beret of the Golani Brigade under his shoulder strap. He was also armed with an M-16 rifle and a magazine.

He was carrying some civilian clothing to change into as he had slept at a friend's house the night before.

The terrorists stopped the car near Nachshon and Yamur asked in Hebrew, "Where are you headed?" Nachshon replied that he was interested in reaching Ramle. Yamur said, "Get in" and Nachshon sat down on Natsche's right, between the side door and Natsche. A few minutes later Nachshon asked Natsche where he was from but he didn't reply. Then, when they arrived at the airport near the Tel Aviv–Jerusalem highway, Natsche wrapped his arm around Nachshon's neck and forced him into a sitting position on the car's floor. Nachshon attempted to struggle and tried to load the magazine into the rifle but at this stage Bader grabbed the weapon away from him. In order to stop Nachshon's struggles Bader bashed him on the head several times with the rifle's butt.

Natsche and "Abu Muhammad" snapped on handcuffs and shackled his feet with locked iron chains. They covered his eyes with a black blindfold and placed a black bag over his head. Nachshon was thrown on the car's floor. Natsche and "Abu Muhammad" continued hitting him while Yamur drove towards Bir Naballah.

The terrorists arrived at the hiding place where Yamur dropped off his three comrades and helped them carry Nachshon, who was still tied up, chained and blindfolded, into one of the bedrooms. Food, a radio and a television set had been brought in earlier. Yamur drove away in the rented van and parked it in a parking lot in Jerusalem so that his family would not know about the rental vehicle.

After Yamur had parked the van at a parking lot on Salah a-Din Street in East Jerusalem, he approached a camera shop owned by Ramzi Selhab and rented a video camera for 24 hours, paying IS 150. He explained that he needed the camera to film the wedding of his friend's sister. He also purchased two video cassettes, each 180 minutes long. Yamur returned to Bir Naballah with the equipment.

Yamur spoke to the soldier in Hebrew. He learned that his name was Nachshon Wachsman and that he lived in the Ramot Quarter of Jerusalem. Nachshon told Yamur that he was doing his army service in the Golani Brigade and that he had been stationed in Southern Lebanon for three months. He explained that he had been on his way to Ramle to visit a friend who was stationed in an army base nearby. Yamur explained in Hebrew that the objective of his abduction was to force Israel to bargain and swap him for Palestinian prisoners. He also instructed him about what he should say on the tape.

"Abu Muhammad" was filmed making the demands in Arabic with his face covered. In his announcement he stated that the Israeli soldier had been abducted by the Iz a-Din Al-Qasam Brigades and they were demanding the release of many prisoners from Hamas and other terror organizations who were serving long prison sentences in Israel. He clarified that the Israeli soldier would be released only if their demands were met. "Abu Muhammad" also posed several questions in Hebrew which Nachshon was forced to answer. Yamur was seated opposite Nachshon, helping "Abu Muhammad" to formulate some of the questions and translate them into Hebrew.

Immediately after filming the cassette, "Abu Muhammad" wrote a letter in which he described the abduction process. He gave the tape, the letter and Nachshon's ID to Yamur and asked him to hand them over to someone named "Abu Ali" who lived in the Yarmuk neighborhood in Gaza, near the block factory. "Abu Muhammad" also gave him "Abu Ali"'s phone number and explained that the latter would hand the tape and letter over to "Abu Khaled," one of the commanders of Iz a-Din Al-Qasam Brigades, who was to negotiate for the release of Palestinian prisoners.

The next day, on October 10, 1994, Yamur drove the rental car to Gaza and handed over the items to "Abu Ali". Yamur and "Abu Ali" agreed that the latter would contact him again at 21:00 to verify that "Abu Khaled" had indeed received the goods. A second cassette was filmed at "Abu Ali"'s house. The photographer who filmed the cassette in Gaza was Hisham Shams, a former Reuters employee.

Claiming responsibility for the abduction

On October 10 several items of information were received regarding the abduction:

- An anonymous tip was received at the offices of the Red Cross in Gaza that the Iz a-Din Al-Qasam Brigades had abducted a 20-year-old religious IDF soldier. His hair was light, he was dressed in an army uniform and he had a skullcap on his head. The soldier was in the Jericho area. The anonymous caller demanded the release of security prisoners including Sheikh Yassin by 11:00 on October 10. If not, the soldier would be executed.
- The Reuters news agency received a demand from the Hamas with the following message:

The Iz a-Din Al-Qasam Brigades claim responsibility for the abduction of Nachshon Mordechai, ID no. 03228629. He is alive and being treated as a prisoner, according to the laws of Islam. We demand:[29]

1 The immediate release of the leader of Islamic Liberation Ahmad Yassin, Sheikh Salah Shehada, Sheikh Abdel Karim Obeid and Sheikh Dirani.
2 The release of all of the Iz a-Din Al-Qasam Brigades prisoners.
  (a) The liberation of 50 Hamas prisoners serving prolonged prison sentences.
  (b) 25 members of the Islamic Jihad.
  (c) 50 Fatah members.

(d)   20 members of the Habash faction.
(e)   10 members of the Democratic Front.
(f)   20 members of the Hizballah.
(g)   15 members of the Jibril faction.
(h)   Liberation of all the female Palestinian prisoners.

The abduction was a gift to the souls of Hassan Abas, Osama Mahana and Ismail Jahri.[30] If the Israeli government refuses to meet our demands, it will bear responsibility for the soldier's execution, and then we will negotiate for his body. The deadline is at 21:00 on Friday October 14, 1994.

Subsequently, a slightly different demand from that which originated in Gaza was broadcast from Damascus on Al-Qud's Radio:[31]

Here follows an announcement that we received from the Iz a-Din Al-Qasam Brigades:
In the name of merciful Allah:

"Fight them and God will remove them from your hands and abase them and strengthen you against them and reward the wrath of a faithful people" (from the Koran).

A military announcement from the Iz a-Din Al-Qasam Brigades:

The Iz a-Din Al-Qasam Brigades announce that they are responsible for the abduction of the Zionist soldier called Nachshon Mordechai, ID no. 03228629. He is alive and being treated as a prisoner, according to the laws of Islam. Therefore, we demand the following from the government of the Zionist authority:

1   The immediate release of Sheikh Ahmad Yassin, Sheikh Salah Shehada, Sheikh Abdel Karim Obeid and Sheikh Mustafa al-Dirani.
2   The release of all prisoners from the Brigades of the martyr Iz a-Din Al-Qasam.
3   The release of 40 Hamas members, 25 Islamic Jihad members, and 50 Fatah members – all serving long prison sentences. In addition – 20 members of the Popular Front for the Liberation of Palestine, 10 members of the Democratic Front for the Liberation of Palestine, 20 Hizballah fighters, 5 members of the Popular Front for the Liberation of Palestine – the General Command, and all female Palestinian prisoners.

The announcement also stated:

"We promise you to continue along this path until the last prisoner has been liberated from Zionist prisons, no many how many martyrs we may sacrifice. We dedicate this attack to the memory of our brave martyrs Hassan Abas and Ismail Jahri.

If the Zionist government refuses to meet our demands, we will place upon it the full responsibility for the soldier's death and it will pay a high price for his body against its will.

The final date for the liberation is Friday, October 14, 1994 at 21:00."

Some time after the Damascus message, the deputy head of the Red Cross delegation in Gaza informed the IDF that at 13:05 on October 10, 1994, an anonymous caller contacted the organization's offices and asked that the following message be conveyed to the delegation head:

"Iz a-Din Al-Qasam Brigades, the group of IKHEIL fugitives, announces that it is responsible for the abduction of the religious soldier aged 20 and three months (no name was mentioned). His hair is light, and he was wearing a uniform and a skullcap. The 'dog' Rabin must be updated as quickly as possible before midnight that he must release all of the prisoners of the Fatah Eagles, the Red Eagle, our wanted brothers, heroes and leaders, such as: Muhammad Abu Atiya, and Sheikh Ahmad Yassin. In the event that this does not happen at the specified time, the soldier will join those executed Sasportas and Sa'adon. At this time the soldier is located in the area of Jericho in the Palestinian Authority."

Signed by Iz a-Din Al-Qasam Brigades, the Hamas' military branch, in the name of the leader Abu Hussa."

The deputy head of the delegation in Gaza noted that the anonymous caller had spoken with the organization's receptionist who wrote down the message word for word. The Red Cross representative office in Beirut then received the following message on the afternoon of October 10 from a member of the Iz a-Din Al-Qasam Brigades:

"Iz a-Din Al-Qasam Brigades are willing to extend the deadline set for Friday night on the condition that the Israeli government expresses its willingness to enter negotiations regarding the condition stated and set by the group (Iz a-Din Al-Qasam Brigades) earlier."

The caller was informed that the Red Cross was not fulfilling the role of neutral intermediary at that time because it had not been asked to do so by the parties involved, but it would nevertheless convey the message to the Israeli government and was willing to convey other messages.

In addition to the announcements broadcast over the radio, the video cassette filmed in Gaza was distributed and aired by most Middle East television stations as well as international broadcasting networks worldwide. The picture from the cassette showing Nachshon Wachsman with a masked and armed terrorist standing behind him reading out the organization's announcement and list of demands was published in all of the Israeli newspapers, as well as the Arab and international press.[32]

On **October 13, 1994**, at 13:00 the following message was conveyed through an anonymous call that was received at the Red Cross offices in Gaza:

"We inform the Israeli government and verify that it will be completely responsible if the soldier Nachshon Wachsman is killed. We promise that the abducted soldier will not be found in the area of the autonomy but rather within the Green Line. This is the policy of the "Kassam Muhbarat" (intelligence) and there is nothing new about it. We assure you that the execution of Nissim Toledano was the result of the Israeli government's obstinacy. We do not want this obstinacy to repeat itself. We are holding him as a captive of Islam. We are treating him as you saw on television. We warn Rabin not to persevere with his stubborn policy because he knows who the Kassam Brigades are. We verify once again that the soldier is safe within the Green Line boundaries and ask that you meet our demands. The Red Cross is being asked to inform Monte Carlo and London because the warning is vital."

On **October 14, 1994,** the International Red Cross passed on a proposal to Israel to extend the ultimatum that Nachshon Wachsman's abductors had set in exchange for Israeli consent to launch negotiations for the exchange of the Israeli soldier and Palestinian prisoners. This message was faxed on Friday at 10:04 a.m. from the Red Cross offices in Tel Aviv to the IDF's liaison officer to the Red Cross.

The abductors' ultimatum was to have ended eleven hours later. The announcement that a man who had arrived at the Red Cross offices in Beirut and identified himself as a representative of the Hamas' military branch alerted that "the Iz a-Din Al-Qasam Brigades are willing to postpone the ultimatum on the condition that the Israeli government enters into negotiations *vis-à-vis* the previously stipulated conditions" (this was apparently in reference to the ultimatum to release Sheikh Yassin and some 200 other prisoners).

The head of the Red Cross offices in Israel, Jean Jacque Gassond, informed the liaison officer that his organization told the man who had brought the message that the Red Cross was not an intermediary but it was willing to relay messages between the parties involved. Gassond stated that the Red Cross offices in Gaza had received similar messages in telephone calls received on Tuesday and Thursday from people who identified themselves as representatives of Iz a-Din Al-Qasam.

The decision-making process

Following the publication of the Hamas announcements regarding the abduction of Wachsman, a status evaluation was conducted on the evening of Tuesday, October 10, 1994 at the Prime Minister's office in the presence of Prime Minster Yitzhak Rabin, the Chief of Staff Ehud Barak, the Minister of Police Moshe Shahal, the Deputy Chief of Staff Brigadier General Amnon Lipkin Shahak, the substitute for the director of the GSS, Brigadier General Danny Yatom, and director of the Intelligence Department Uri Sagie. Discussion revealed that the intelligence branch had no information about the abduction. The parties involved therefore decided to focus attention on Gaza, based on the assumption that the terrorists would prefer to take cover in that area, which was under Palestinian control. At that meeting, the Prime Minister decided to place all of the responsibility for the soldier's welfare on Yasser Arafat.[33] "If we controlled Gaza," Rabin stated, "we would upend the Gaza Strip. As we are not there, we must place all of the responsibility on Arafat."[34]

Rabin assumed that heavy pressure placed on Arafat would lead to the soldier's release. Rabin and his advisors were aware that Arafat was not pleased with the unrestrained activities of the Hamas and Islamic Jihad in Gaza and their premise was that the key to Wachsman's welfare was in Arafat's hands. At the same time, it was decided to focus efforts on the operational and intelligence areas in order to bring about his release. IDF elite units were instructed to be on standby for a military operation to extricate the soldier.

During the discussion, Prime Minister Rabin said that he was willing to use considerable force to rescue the soldier without the Palestinian Authority's permission, despite the fact that according to the Oslo Agreements he could use military power within the boundaries of the Palestinian Autonomy only after prior coordination with Palestinian entities. In addition, the Prime Minister decided to seal the "territories" (Gaza, Judea and Samaria). This decision had two goals – to prevent the relocation of Nachshon Wachsman or his body from Gaza, and to escalate the pressure on Arafat.[35]

Rabin himself conducted several conversations with Arafat in which he was vehemently adamant that the responsibility for Wachsman's welfare was in the latter's hands. He instructed Arafat to inform the media that the discussion between them had taken place.[36] Following the meeting headed by the Prime Minister, efforts focused on three channels: In the diplomatic channel, all of the efforts focused upon the PLO and Arafat. Egyptian President Mubarak, the American Secretary of State Christopher and Dennis Ross were recruited to reprimand Arafat. The second, the intelligence channel, focused on Gaza. While the third, the military channel, had the elite units competing among themselves to carry out the rescue mission.[37]

On the night between Tuesday and Wednesday the Palestinian intelligence service arrested 60 suspects, but Israel remained unimpressed, claiming that Arafat was careful to limit himself to the "small fry". On Wednesday morning Rabin convened the cabinet. The conclusion at the end of the meeting was that at that time activities would be based on the assumption that the soldier was being held in Gaza. Cabinet ministers who were interviewed by the media placed responsibility for his welfare on Arafat. The focus on Gaza increased during Wednesday morning due to a rumor that Nachshon Wachsman's abductors had moved him the previous night from one hiding place to another with the knowledge of the PLO. This rumor was subsequently proved to be false. On Wednesday a house was found in Gaza where according to information sources the soldier was purportedly being held. Intensive intelligence efforts were introduced near the house. During the evening suspicious activity was noted. Hamas activity was indeed identified in the house but it had no connection to the abducted soldier. The second cassette featuring Nachshon Wachsman's message was released at noon on Wednesday. This was the cassette that was filmed in Bir Naballah on Sunday, and handed over by Yamur to Gaza on the second day of the abduction. On Wednesday, Rabin spoke at length with Nachshon Wachsman's father, Yehuda.

Nachshon's father suggested ransoming his son for money and asked Rabin why he would not release Sheikh Yassin in exchange for his son's liberation. In the afternoon hours Rabin called Arafat and reprimanded him severely. Towards evening, Rabin convened another meeting at his offices in Jerusalem to be updated regarding any progress made in the activities to save the soldier. On Wednesday night, it became increasingly apparent that the terrorists may have set a trap and that Wachsman was being held at a completely different location than was originally thought. The next day, on Thursday, Rabin sent his new advisor on matters related to terror, Yossi Ginosar, to Gaza. Ginosar met with Arafat, and reiterated that in Israel's view he was responsible for the soldier's well-being. Arafat replied that he was making every effort to locate the missing soldier.

During the meeting with Arafat the possibility of a compromise was raised – Wachsman in exchange for Sheikh Yassin.[38] Ginosar refused to commit himself and told Rabin that he did not believe that the proposal could be taken seriously due to the fact that Arafat had no control over the events and he could not negotiate in the name of the Hamas. From the beginning Rabin preferred a swift rescue operation to giving in to Hamas' extortion, but due to the lack of information regarding the soldier's location, Rabin agreed to enter negotiations to explore the possibility of his release. In this matter Prime Minister Rabin decided that if Arafat could get the Hamas' consent to release Wachsman in exchange for Sheikh Yassin's release, Israel might consider the proposal.

In the security establishment many entities claimed that it would be best to release Yassin because his incarceration in Israel merely provided an excuse for the Hamas to plan additional attacks in order to release him. But Rabin feared that the Sheikh's release would be interpreted as a sign of Israeli weakness. At the same time that intelligence efforts were being invested in Gaza, Israeli intelligence tried to uncover information in Jerusalem as well as in Judea and Samaria, and finally there was a lead. On

Thursday, the GSS learned of Jihad Yamur. Yamur was arrested at his home. During his interrogation he revealed his part in the abduction as well as information about the house in Bir Naballah where the hostage was being held. At 6:30 a.m. the GSS briefed the Chief of Staff about the development and immediately afterwards the Prime Minister was informed.

Under the circumstances, Rabin preferred a military operation to extricate Wachsman. But in order to gain time to locate him and make preparations, Rabin decided to keep his plans a secret and therefore refrained from sharing them with the cabinet. He even created the impression among the government ministers that Israel preferred to release Sheikh Yassin in exchange for the captive soldier, thus ensuring that the desired information was leaked to the media and to the Hamas.[39]

Rabin also refrained from convening the security cabinet because he feared that such a meeting might expose the military plans to rescue the soldier. On Friday morning the GSS gave the IDF operational intelligence about the house in Bir Naballah. Jihad Yamur disclosed everything he knew from his visits to the house. He claimed that the last time he had seen Nachshon Wachsman – on Wednesday – he had been lying on the couch shackled in chains. While the IDF forces were preparing for the military operation to liberate the soldier, Dr. Ahmed Tibi and MK Taleb A-Sana'a, two leading Israeli Arabs, attempted to mediate between Israel, the Hamas' political leadership and the Palestinian Authority.[40] Rabin did not cooperate with them as he regarded their activities as a way to rake in political support. His assumption was that even if Mahmoud a Zahar, the Hamas spokesman in Gaza, was willing to negotiate, he would have little influence on the abductors. And if he did have some influence, the price they demanded would be far higher than Israel was willing to pay; in any case, a transaction would undoubtedly encourage additional abductions (see Appendix B).

The prime minister's office insisted that up to the moment that the military began its operation no concrete proposition had been received from the abductors, neither to extend the ultimatum nor to conduct a barter deal. From Prime Minister Rabin's point of view, the operation started at the last minute, one hour and a quarter before the abductors planned to murder the soldier, and therefore there was no other option other than to prepare a rescue plan.

The Palestinian Authority

Entities in Gaza reported that after Arafat had been updated about the kidnapping and talked on the phone with Rabin, he became very angry. Due to the abduction Israel announced that it was suspending the peace process. Arafat ranted in his office for several hours, and instructed his men to leave no stone unturned in Gaza and to arrest Hamas activists.[41]

Based on Arab sources in Gaza, on the morning of Wednesday, October 11, 1994 the Israeli media reported that the cell members who had abducted Wachsman had transferred him to a different hiding place with the full knowledge of the Palestinian Authority. That same day, the house where Nachshon Wachsman was supposedly being held captive was found, and Palestinian policemen began surveillance. However, within several hours it became evident that the soldier was not there.

On Wednesday night, Arafat convened his security committee and instructed them to take a harsher stand against the Hamas. Following Arafat's instructions, some 200 Hamas members were arrested the same night. Nasser Yousouf, commander of the Palestinian police, was the power behind the full-fledged attack against the Hamas, and he was quoted as saying, "If we don't destroy them, they'll destroy us."[42]

The Israeli defense community, which had been unimpressed by the Palestinian Authority's initial anti-Hamas steps, began to sit up and take notice.

On Thursday and Friday, the Palestinian Authority stepped up its activities against the Hamas. On Friday, large Palestinian Authority forces were active in the village of Abasan near Khan Yunis. This was where the terrorists were allegedly holding Nachshon Wachsman. This operation ended without the desired outcome, but Israel started to believe that Arafat was actually taking serious action to rescue the abducted soldier.

The Nachshon Wachsman rescue operation[43]

By Friday morning, the GSS had accurate information about the house where the abducted soldier was being held as well as other details. Shortly thereafter, Prime Minister Rabin gave the green light to begin planning the rescue mission. Two elite units – the IDF's general headquarters' reconnaissance unit and the Israel police's special counter-terror unit – presented plans. For various reasons, it was decided to give the mission to the IDF general headquarters' reconnaissance unit. The plan was ready in principle, but the GSS requested a few hours' delay in order to "tie up as many loose ends as possible" and gather more information. The Central Command was instructed not to deviate from routine activity at Bir Naballah or on the road passing through it. Apparently the abductors did not notice the reconnaissance teams or GSS activity. Every piece of intelligence information was gathered, such as entrances to the house, the roads leading to it, the house's internal design, each and every room, including the kitchen and bathrooms.

At 14:00, the Chief of Staff Ehud Barak, his deputy Brigadier General Amnon Lipkin Shahak, and senior officers convened at an army camp near the Givat Ze'ev neighborhood in northern Jerusalem. The operational plan had been prepared down to the tiniest detail (see Appendix A). Several Israeli Air Force (IAF) helicopters were on alert as well as emergency and rescue teams. The IDF posted scouts who observed the house from afar. The house was large and set at a distance from the other houses in the village. It had several entrances but all of them were blocked with iron gates. The windows were covered with railing protruding outwards, which made penetration difficult. All of the windows were covered with blankets. There was no movement inside or outside the house and there was no telephone connected. No electricity was turned on during the day. For a moment the fear arose that Nachshon Wachsman had been transferred elsewhere.

Despite this possibility, preparations for the mission continued. The prime minister's green light was not cancelled. But it was vital to verify that Wachsman was still being held there. As darkness fell, activity began at the entrance to Gaza. The Ashkelon–Gaza road was blocked. Convoys of ambulances headed for the south. The media were quick to ask questions: Was it true that the IDF had initiated a military attack in Gaza? This step was meant to mislead the Hamas and the abductors in order to ensure the element of surprise for the rescue mission in Bir Naballah.

Several options were raised during the mission's preparation. One idea was to bring Sheikh Yassin or other Hamas prisoners to the site and show them to the abductors. There was a television in the house and it could be used to transmit messages on the seven o'clock news in Arabic, which they would presumably watch. These ideas were disqualified for various reasons. It was feared that if the terrorists knew they had been exposed they would kill the soldier immediately. The authorities believed that these were not "one time" abductors as was the case in past Palestinian attacks, but rather veteran killers (three-time murderers). The assumption was that they would not surrender as a result of negotiations.

The briefing of the mission force began at 16:30, in the presence of the Chief of Staff. The soldiers made final preparations, learned the details and rehearsed the plans. GSS commanders met with the soldiers and briefed them about the house and the cell members entrenched there. Everything was ready. The prime minister insisted that the mission be conducted prior to the expiration of the ultimatum at 21:00 in order to increase the chances of saving the soldier's life. The force started moving at 18:00. At about 18:30 a Mercedes was seen making its way to the house. A man got out of the car and entered the house. The forces stopped. Several questions arose: Was the arrival of the car a sign that it had been decided to move the soldier to another location? Perhaps it would be easier to rescue him that way? Or was he here to warn the abductors of the rescue mission? Maybe he was bringing instructions to execute the prisoner? Twenty minutes later the man emerged alone, got into the Mercedes and drove away. He was apprehended outside of the house's field of vision.

The man was 37-year-old Zachariya Najib. Najib has been imprisoned during the 1970s for security offences. In his interrogation, Najib said that he had handled the rental deal and had returned to bring them food prior to his arrest. Is the soldier alive? he was asked. He replied that he was. He had seen him lying on the couch eating "knafa". This reply convinced the commanders in the field to continue the mission. After receiving this information, the final decision was taken to act. The frontal command room was situated at an army camp near Jerusalem. Those present were the Chief of Staff, his deputy, the director of Intelligence, Major General Uri Sagie, Commander of the Central Command Ilan Biran, the Commander of IDF Forces in Judea and Samaria Brigadier General Shaul Mofaz, Manpower Director Major General Yoram Yair, the acting director of the GSS, and Director of the Police Department's autonomy district Alik Ron (see Appendix A).

At 19:15, after the sun had gone down and it was fully dark, the fighters, who were already near the destination, began moving towards the house, after splitting up into two forces. One force approached from the village's southern point, and the other from the north. Each force included sappers carrying explosives to be used for detonating the doors. The force moved forward slowly under the cover of darkness. The sounds of a wedding could be heard from the village. Reports were transmitted to the frontal command room. The force approached a mosque and it became clear that several of the worshippers had lingered after the evening prayer. The force was told to wait. Several minutes later the fighters approached the house and hid behind the wall that surrounded it. One force climbed on to the roof in order to find a way to penetrate the house without being noticed. Only when the commanders understood that they had no choice, did they decide to burst in.

The commander instructed the sappers to do their job. They crept covertly to the three entrances designated for blasting, two doors on the ground floor at the house's northern side, one of which served as the main entrance, and the other as a secondary entrance; and the door to the kitchen terrace on the house's first floor facing west. The original plan was to blast the door on the roof too, from which it would be possible to descend a stairway directly to the floor where Nachshon Wachsman was being held. However, it was ultimately decided only to block the door in order to prevent the abductors from escaping. The three explosive charges were detonated at 19:47. Only one went off. Additional explosive charges were set off. Dozens of fighters, who were standing near the doors, started to storm inside.

The details regarding the operation in the building and the attempt to save Nachshon Wachsman became known due to the testimonies given by the elite soldiers at Jihad Yamur's trial.

The force split up into sub-units, each with its own mission. During the force's approach, prior to the noisy breakthrough which was accompanied by gunfire, and also while the forces were still outside the building, no gunfire was heard inside the house and no shots were fired by the force in the direction of the house. At that time, Nachshon Wachsman and his three fully armed abductors – Abd al Karim Bader, Hassan Natsche and Salah Jadallah ("Abu Muhammad") – were in the house. Bader had an Uzi sub-machine gun, Natsche was armed with a handgun, and Jadallah was carrying a Galil rifle. Nachshon Wachsman was lying on the couch, wearing jeans and a white tricot shirt, with chains on his hands and feet.

The force led by Captain L. burst through two doors; the first, the external front door, was made of metal, and the second the internal (inner) entrance door to the section of the house where the soldier was being held. While Captain L.'s force was busy detonating the inner door, other soldiers from the force led by Nir Poraz were already inside the house and from outside the door, L. heard the sound of automatic gunfire. These sounds were the exchange of gunfire between the terrorists and the soldiers from Nir Poraz's force; the terrorists were shooting at the soldiers when Abd al Karim Bader ran into the room next to Nachshon Wachsman's. As a result of the exchange of gunfire, soldiers in Nir Poraz's force were injured and he himself was mortally wounded in the chest.

In the meantime, Natsche and Jadallah barricaded themselves in the room where the soldier was being held. They closed the door and placed a heavy piece of furniture behind it to prevent entry. Jadallah had apparently been gravely wounded as a result of the gunfire and therefore did not participate in the dialogue between Natsche and the IDF soldiers.

At this stage, prior to Bader's escape to the adjacent room, the terrorists shot Nachshon Wachsman with the aim of killing him. To achieve their goal, they shot him in many areas of his body, including in his stomach (after removing his shirt), in the neck, in his chest and in the area of the collarbone. After blasting through the inner door, Captain L. and his men entered the house. On the right side of the inner door there was a closed wooden door which gave way when L. kicked it. After ensuring that the room was empty he continued on to the room where Nachshon Wachsman was being held. L. tried to open the door to the room where Nachshon Wachsman was located, but the door was barricaded.

In the meantime additional forces had arrived, one of which was under Captain N.'s command. When Captain N. and his soldiers entered the inner door they registered gunfire being shot in their direction. Captain N. and two soldiers went into the room on the left and after identifying Bader (who was armed with an Uzi) shot him and headed for the room where

Nachshon Wachsman was situated. As noted earlier, Captain L. had attempted to gain access to the room by pushing and kicking the door.

This time, there were shots being fired from the room's interior outwards. Captain L. decided to try opening the door (which was made of two plywood boards coated with tin and a hollow area in between) by shooting directly at the lock.

Captain L. shot repeatedly at the lock from its left side, aiming from left to right and up and down. Thus the shots were aimed at the lock and/or the floor; Captain L. used a micro-Uzi (while the soldiers were carrying M-16s), carrying weakened bullets. During these stages no gunfire was shot towards the room's interior by any one of the soldiers, aside from Captain L.'s shots. The terrorists continued shooting from the room's interior outwards. The shots aimed at the lock did not open the door and triggered additional shooting on the part of the terrorists barricaded in the room. Captain L. was wounded a second time.

In the course of the terrorists' gunfire, the soldiers heard Hebrew coming out of the room – "Go away!", "Get out!" The spokesman, who conducted the entire dialogue, was Natsche.

Y. and T., two of the force members, began a dialogue with Natsche. They told him that they only wanted the soldier and that Natsche could emerge with his hands up and he would not be harmed. They also called out Nachshon's name several time but received no answer. The spokesman continued yelling in Hebrew, "The soldier is dead," "I killed the soldier," "I'm not afraid to die," and again, "Go away!" Throughout the dialogue, which was conducted mainly in Hebrew and partially in Arabic, Y. and T. heard only one person. No sound came from Nachshon. At that point, Captain L. attempted to open the door with more aggressive means by using a shotgun. These means were applied solely with the aim of opening the door and could not have harmed the room's inhabitants. More shots were fired from inside the room. Finally, as the result of these means, the door opened to a narrow slit, but it would not open further due to the heavy item of furniture on the other side. At this point, in order to ensure a sequence of action and prevent the terrorists from regrouping inside the room, L. decided to use an IDF fragmentation grenade (no. 26); the grenade was placed very close to the slit on the door's right side (the door opened towards the left), thus ensuring that the door itself would absorb most of the grenade's impact.

In the aftermath of the grenade's explosion a wide aperture was created. L. entered the room first and immediately took several steps to the left in order to enable two soldiers to enter the room after him and take positions along the wall facing the room.

To his left, L. noticed Jadallah lying on the floor; a small fire was burning in the farthest corner. The wounded Natsche was lying at L.'s feet.

He picked up his handgun and fired four shots in L.'s direction; the soldiers with L. returned gunfire, killing Natsche. Upon entry, L. saw that in the middle of the 4 × 4 meter room there was a bed (with a broken leg) upon which Nachshon Wachsman was lying on his back. Y. and N. entered the room immediately after and noticed it as well. Due to the position of the body and his extreme pallor, L. understood that Nachshon was no longer alive. L., Y. and N. noticed that there was a kafiyah wrapped around the soldier's neck, his shirt was rolled back and he was handcuffed. The combat time outside of the door was estimated at 4 to 8 minutes, and the time that passed between the explosion of the grenade and the removal of the soldier's body was 25 seconds.

The rescue mission to extricate Nachshon Wachsman had failed. He had been murdered by his abductors. In the course of the mission, Captain Nir Poraz was killed and eight soldiers were wounded. The three terrorist abductors were killed during the rescue operation; some of the cell's collaborators had been arrested earlier by the security forces.

The response of Hamas to the rescue operation[44]

From Damascus, the Hamas movement lauded the abduction and murder of the soldier and declared its intention to continue the struggle against Israel. The movement published two statements in which it accused Prime Minister Yitzhak Rabin of "reneging on a promise he had given to release some Palestinian prisoners in exchange for extending the deadline for Wachsman's execution. The end of the operation, in which our heroes took the Zionist soldier captive, was full of bravery just like its beginnings. It went against what the Zionist war general wanted," bragged the announcement.

The Hamas accused PLO leader Yasser Arafat of disclosing information about Wachsman's location, and claimed that the Palestinian Authority had arrested over 450 people suspected of affiliation with the Hamas in Gaza. The Hamas warned the Palestinian Authority that it would "set Gaza on fire," if the police continued to arrest its members and if it failed to release the detained Hamas activists and supporters immediately. The resistance movement, the Islamic Jihad and the members of the Iz a-Din Al-Qasam Brigades declared three days of mourning to mark the death of the three triangle members who were killed on Friday night by IDF soldiers.

From the early hours of the morning thousands flocked towards the mosques in Gaza and the Imams began chanting verses from the Koran calling to avenge "those who chose blood rather than to release captives." Members of Iz a-Din Al-Qasam patrolled the streets of Gaza condemning the Israeli actions over loudspeakers:

"The Jews violated the agreement despite the fact that the Hamas openly declared before the whole world that it would delay the ultimatum by twenty-four hours. When the Jewish force heard that the Hamas postponed the ultimatum it attacked the house where our heroes were staying and they killed their own soldier Nachshon Wachsman when they detonated the house. It was not our people who killed him – The Jews have proved once again that they are not trustworthy and only desire the death of as many Palestinians as possible."

The Main Characteristics of Hamas Abductions

An analysis of Hamas abductions indicates that they share several prominent characteristics:

- All of the abduction targets were random soldiers (including a Border Guard policeman).
- Most of the abductions were perpetrated within the "Green Line."
- The abductions ended in the hostage's execution (either immediately after the abduction or at a later date).
- In most of the abductions similar modi operandi were employed.
- The State of Israel never gave in to the movement's demands nor did it release prisoners.

Hamas' modi operandi

The goals of the abductions   One can classify the abductions perpetrated by the Hamas in Israel as follows:

1   Abductions for the purpose of murder.
2   The abduction of an armed soldier/civilian in order to confiscate his combat means and ammunition.
3   An abduction for bargaining purposes with the aim of liberating terrorists incarcerated in Israeli prisons.
4   A combination of several goals.

The abduction's location   Most of the abductions were perpetrated when the soldiers were hitchhiking, at out-of-the-way hitchhiking stations or intersections. In the majority of the incidents, the preferred area for the abduction was within the 1967 borders because the perpetrators believed that the soldiers would be less alert there. The abduction cells also acted along other routes such as roads that lead from the pre-1967 borders to Judea and Samaria, or between the former and the Jerusalem area, as well as roads leading from Judea and Samaria to the Jerusalem area.

The abductors' identity and their behavior   In most instances there were three abductors in the vehicle, two in front and one in the back. The abductors were disguised as religious Jews with beards and skullcaps. In several cases, one of the abductors spoke fluent Hebrew and he was the individual who conversed with the soldier. The other abductors were silent and refrained from speaking to each other or to the hostage. In some cases, Israeli music was playing in the car. In several of the abductions at least some of the cell members, who were residents of East Jerusalem, carried authentic Israeli ID while the others carried false Israeli ID. This made it easier to pass through roadblocks and collect intelligence prior to the attack.

In the course of abductions for bargaining purposes, a short time after the hostage got into the car, one of the abductors (not the driver) threatened him with a gun and demanded that he hand over his weapon. If the hostage attempted to resist and a struggle developed, in most cases the soldier was killed. Nevertheless, it is noteworthy that in some instances resistance and struggle saved the lives of the hostages as in the cases of **Ilan Karavani** and **Lior Avital**.

The type of vehicle   In many of the abductions, the act was carried out in stolen cars or in Arab vehicles whose license plates (blue) had been replaced with Israeli plates (yellow). Sometimes the abduction was perpetrated in an Israeli rental car (as was the case with Nachshon Wachsman).

Combat means and equipment   The main weapon used in the majority of abductions was at least one handgun, and in several incidents weapons like a knife or a spike were used too. In the case of Nachshon Wachsman several types of weapons were used. In abductions for bargaining purposes handcuffs and ropes were used to bind the soldier.

3

The Hizballah and Abductions in the Lebanese Arena

Iran and its Use of Terror[1]

In the course of the twenty-six year reign of the Islamic regime (1979–2005), Iran has projected the image of a state with a radical foreign policy where all is fair, including terror, in order to export the Islamic revolution and promote its political goals. The use of terror as a tool to realize political interests is not exclusive or unique to Iran, but there is no doubt that during the period under discussion Iran was among the most prominent nations to encourage terror and to utilize it to realize Iranian goals on the international level.[2] In a speech that US President Bush delivered in February 2002, he defined Iran as one of the "Axis of Evil" states that supports terror and strives to create weapons of mass destruction. Since the early 1980s Iran has appeared on the US State Department's list of states that support terror. Indeed, since the Islamic Revolution in 1979, Iran has stood out among countries that use terror to promote their goals in the international arena.

The Iranian terror activity is operated cunningly. Iran endeavors never to leave "fingerprints" that might serve to implicate the country as the entity behind the terror. Moreover, in its public statements the Iranian leadership expresses its reservations about terrorism and even condemns it. This stands true even in regard to its own sponsored organizations such as the Hizballah, which operates in Lebanon and latterly prefers to define terror activity as legitimate resistance. The concealment of Iran's connection to the terror activity in which it is indeed involved enables it to draw optimal benefit: On the one hand, the terror victim's desire to avenge itself against Iran is neutralized, while on the other had, Iran presents itself as an intermediary that is ostensibly striving to mediate between the victim and the terror organization, and through its active participation in the bargaining and negotiation process achieves its goals.

Most of the information exposing Iran's involvement in terror activity has come to light when terror perpetrators have been caught, questioned and brought to trial, and also in the aftermath of terror attacks when the organizations claiming responsibility included declarations and/or demands that clearly reflected Iranian interests.[3] There is a close connection between terror activities and Iranian foreign policy, which clearly reflects the consistent and methodical use of terror in order to impose Iranian will on other countries after this goal failed to be achieved through accepted diplomatic channels. Salient examples are Kuwait and France, which served as central targets for Iranian/Shiite terrorism during the 1980s mainly due to the stances they adopted regarding the Iran–Iraq war and the aid they offered to Iraq.

In many instances the weapon of terror was activated in order to achieve a wide range of Iranian goals *vis-à-vis* the victim. For example, Iranian demands of France in the 1980s included withdrawing its forces from Lebanon, cessation of military aid to Iraq, rethinking its policy *vis-à-vis* the Israeli–Arab conflict, the return of Iranian funds frozen in France, the banishment of exiled Iranians and Iranian Resistance organizations from French soil, and the release of Shiite terrorists arrested in France. These goals were achieved one after the other through a "series" of different types of terror attacks (car bombs, hostage-taking, sabotage and more), which ultimately led to repeated French capitulation to most of the Iranian demands.

The timing of most of the terror attacks was usually chosen carefully and was meant to serve political processes during negotiations with the victim or sometimes to promote the launching of these negotiations. Although one might ostensibly state that Iranian terror policy is both rational and realistic with the aim of achieving Iran's goals, several additional phenomena are important factors in the formation of Iranian policy:

- The use of terror in the international arena is a central bone of contention within the leadership of the Iranian regime, between the circles that are called "moderate" and the "radical" circles that advocate an inexorable struggle against the regime's enemies. Thus, to a great extent, the scope of the use of terror and its targets also reflect internal Iranian power struggles.
- Iran often adopts an ambivalent policy, with the "moderates" pulling towards negotiations and compromise, and radical elements simultaneously continuing to perpetrate terror (sometimes with the aim of undermining the "moderates'" moves).
- Iran's ambivalent policy grants it flexibility in its political maneuvers. This policy has made it difficult for the country's adversaries to advocate stringent policies, which might provide a suitable

response to Iranian terror, due to the assumption that it is important to encourage the moderate entities facing the extremists within the Iranian regime, as it must be considered "the lesser of two evils".

Iranian involvement in terror can be divided into two main periods:

- The "revolutionary" period – the period of Khomeini's reign, 1979–1989
- The period of "Khomeini's successors," which can be further divided into:
  - Rafsanjani's reign – 1989–1997
  - Khatami's reign – 1997–2005
  - Ahmadinejad's reign – 2005–

There is a significant difference in the scope of Iranian terror activity over the full term, which was most intensive during Khomeini's reign and diminished considerably during the terms of office of his successors. During Khatami's reign, Iranian involvement in terror decreased drastically with the exception of the Israeli–Arab conflict in the Lebanese and Palestinian arenas.

Several examples reflecting Iranian willingness to sacrifice political interests at the expense of ideological considerations can be noted. The most salient example is the Salman Rushdie affair. When sentencing the British writer to death, Khomeini also decreed conflict with the Western democracies, as the issue of Islamic values and principles was held up in contrast to the democratic values advocated by Western culture.

The Rushdie affair enlightens the nature of the Iranian leadership: First, there is across-the-board consent (among both extremists and moderates) that Rushdie had to die. Secondly, even after Khomeini's demise, and under the leadership of Rafsanjani and Khatami, it was made unequivocally clear that the decree was still valid, although Iran would not act on the death sentence. Thus, when it comes to several basic religious and ideological values there exists a consensus within the Iranian regime: in issues that are less paramount, Iranian policy is pragmatic and motivated primarily by considerations of cost/benefit.

The dilemma regarding the nature of the Iranian leadership (moderates versus radicals) stems mainly from an angle of observation and judgment based on Western norms and values. A closer examination of the actions and statements of the Iranian leaders, both moderate and radical, leads to the conclusion that in actual reality the more accurate distinction must be made between *radical* and *more radical* leadership. As long as Khomeini's doctrine serves as the source of legitimacy and as a guide for the Iranian leadership, the differences between the moderates and radicals will find expression in different approaches to achieving objectives, but not in their essence.

With regard to Iranian power over the Palestinian and Shiite-sponsored organizations, during the entire period under study, Iran demonstrated both control and influence *vis-à-vis* the latter. However, this statement must also be qualified because control and influence over these sponsored organizations are sometimes to be found in the hands of entities that are not necessarily those standing at the head of official Iranian leadership. Thus, it would be more correct to say that the internal power struggles in Iran have a significant impact on the sponsored organizations operating under the authority of various factions in the Iranian regime.

One must also keep in mind that the sponsored organizations have their own goals and needs which are not always fully compatible with the needs of the "patron". In this context, in most of their terrorist attacks, the Shiite and Palestinian organizations raised demands that included the release of terrorists incarcerated in various countries as well as a monetary ransom (demands that first and foremost serve the organizations themselves). The arrests of Shiite terrorists in various countries worldwide sometimes turned countries that were not originally earmarked as targets of terrorist attacks into terror attack victims (such as Switzerland and West Germany). Attacks against these countries did not usually serve Iranian interests at all; the sole aim was to liberate terrorist prisoners. Iran and its ally Syria are deeply involved in terror, and they finance and operate many of the Palestinian terror organizations.

Khomeini's doctrine, which called for "Shiite activism" and "revolutionary violence," provides religious and ideological legitimacy for the use of terror. Thus, Iranian terror is inspired by a combination of religious and ideological motives as well as political needs.

Iran was the first to introduce the phenomenon of suicide terror into the attack arsenal of the Middle Eastern arena. The suicide terror approach has not changed from the 1980s till today. It encourages the Palestinians to use the weapon of terror and suicide attacks as a strategic means in their struggle against the State of Israel.

Many years of contending with Iranian terror demonstrate that the decision to use the instrument of terror is generally taken on the basis of an evaluation of cost versus benefit, or profit versus risk. From the Iranian viewpoint, a rational decision-making process is usually involved, bearing in mind two qualifications: First, when there is a conflict between political interest and a fundamental religious edict, such as the "fatwa" in the Salman Rushdie affair, Iran usually favours the religious decree. Second, sometimes international terror stems from internal power struggles inside Iran's supreme leadership, between the "moderate circles" and the radical ones. Through these activities, the latter group strives to undermine the moderates' "conciliatory" policy towards entities they perceive as enemies of Islam.

Exporting the Iranian Revolution[4]

The aspiration to export the Iranian revolution to all of Muslim society (as well as all of humanity) is an integral part of the philosophy of the Islamic revolution. At its base is the aim to promote the Islamization of Muslim society, forge Muslim unity and return Islamic society to its proper status in human society.[5]

Khomeini and his disciples strived to ignore the religious differences between the Sunnis and the Shiites, as well as national divisions, and aspired to create a unified revolutionary Islamic power that "would include a billion Muslims."[6] In Khomeini's view, this concept constituted justification for interference in the "internal" business of other Muslim countries and societies, in the form of rhetoric calling for Muslim populations to rebel against their governments (which he regarded as lacking religious legitimization and as lackeys of Imperialism). Even during his exile in Iraq (1963–1977), Khomeini had stated that the leaders of Muslim countries "live as infidels and animals . . . and they do not pay heed to the poor populace that suffers from poverty and need."[7] Khomeini ignored the political boundaries separating Muslim populations in various states, and declared that Iran "views all of the Muslim countries as part of us and ourselves as part of the Muslim countries."[8]

Although the revolutionary message was meant for all of human society, the Muslim states were the first target, and the Shiite community in these countries was naturally designated to serve as the standard bearers of the revolutionary concept. An examination of the movements in the Muslim world that adopted Khomeini's outlook indicates that most of them were Shiite organizations, some of which had been established prior to Khomeini's ascension to power (such as the al-Dawa movement and the Islamic action organization in Iraq) and had undergone radicalization;[9] others arose after the revolution and were inspired by it, such as the Jundullah and the Hizballah in Lebanon. In the eyes of the leaders of these movements, such as Sheikh Fadallah in Lebanon or al-Hakim in Iraq, the Iranian revolution constitutes the epitome of "Husseinism" – the concept of self-sacrifice for Islam as Hussein demonstrated in the battle of Karbala. The Hizballah leaders lauded the achievements of the Iranian revolution, and its lessons are studied in the publications of radical Lebanese and Iraqi circles.[10]

The Iranian model grants legitimacy to an armed struggle, and bases its political policy on Shiite *Khadits* (religious interpretation) that explain when and why it is permissible to use violence, and what regime should be established after ousting a heathen and sinful government. These movements recognize Khomeini as the representative of the "vanished Imam" and also as the leader of the Islamic nation, whose authority is valid throughout the Muslim world.[11]

Among the religious scholars in Iran there were those who viewed the revolution as a gateway towards the modification of all of human society and as an opportunity to turn Muslim society into a leading power in human civilization. Ayatollah Mashkini, one of the extreme advocates in favor of "exporting the revolution," went so far as to state that "the objective of the revolution is to force the Koran on the entire world."[12] However, for the most part even the more radical religious leaders viewed the revolution as no more than the presentation of a message and a model for emulation for oppressed nations. Ali Khamenei expressed the stance of the regime by stating that "the revolution knows no boundaries and cannot be imprisoned by walls, but rather it must be exported."[13] Khamenei compared the effect of the revolution in the Muslim world to that of "whispering coals that will naturally ignite the black reality that encompasses them."[14] Thus, according to his view, the Islamic revolution is only the first stage in the "world revolution". The Iranian Foreign Minister in 1981, Mussawi, declared that the goal of his ministry was to "convey the messages of the revolution to the world." He added that if Iran persuades the world that it possesses a "message, solution, a model for emulation, then there will be a chance to create a large revolutionary movement throughout the world."[15]

During the years of Khomeini's regime, Iran continued to espouse the principle of exporting the revolution and aiding the "freedom movements" in the Muslim world. However, gradually and over time realism and moderation crept into the Iranian declarations, due to pragmatic considerations related to Iranian foreign policy needs; these declarations mainly carried a message regarding the dissemination of the principles of the Iranian revolution for simulation "in peaceful ways". In 1983, Khomeini passed a ruling according to which although the course of history turns the export of the revolution into an unstoppable process, Iran is not interested in "crawling like a worm [into the other countries], but rather prefers to enter through the front door like an invited guest." Until this takes place, it must act to disseminate the revolutionary values and create an awareness of Iran's achievements as a means "to encourage these invitations."[16]

Iran took myriad steps to export the revolution: Starting from its presentation as a model for emulation; through its use of terror, encouraging radical movements and its assistance in establishing revolutionary Islamic movements (Hizballah in Lebanon and Islamic movements in the Gulf and the Magreb); and finally, dispatching forces of the Revolutionary Guards to Lebanon. The means and methods changed in accordance to the character of the society of destination ("third world" countries, Muslim countries or Shiite societies) and of course Iran's internal situation.

A central means for the export of the revolution is propaganda activity aimed at disseminating its values, which is carried out by Iranian embassies, special information delegations, and "culture centers" established in various countries, including Western Europe. Students who undergo ideological training and religious clerics are sent to various countries throughout the world in order to convert people and promote the concept of the Iranian revolution. Another method for the dissemination of the Iranian revolution is based on Iran's presence in international organizations, which it uses as a stage to present its worldview. At the same time an effort is made to draw religious clerics from other Muslim countries to the revolution, mainly be inviting them to attend conferences or by visiting Iran, as well as by hosting various Islamic conventions. For example, in May 1983 some five hundred clerics convened at the "world conference for Imams" and ruled that they regard Khomeini as a man "who has the required qualifications for Muslim Imams"; they undertook "to call on Muslims to follow the path of their appeal."[17]

In the framework of its attempts to export the revolution and to make its ideas attractive for Sunni Islamic circles, the Khomeini regime made use of two separate layers of propaganda: Shiite propaganda for internal consumption, and an ecumenical approach (an approach that strives to play down and lessen the controversy between the two schools) for external consumption. In order to address the challenge of exporting the revolution, Iranian propaganda in Arabic[18] emphasizes the messages shared by all of the Islamic movements, underscores the activities of the Iranian revolution to realize the message in the economic sphere (redistribution of income and property) and the moral area (woman's status, imbibing wine, etc.), and plays down the conflict between the Shiites and the Sunnis. An example of this ecumenical effort can be viewed in the approach to the Shiites' fundamental myth – the myth of Hussein and the battle of Karbala. The ecumenical approach grants this myth an all-Islamic and universal significance in the form of the struggle against injustice and suppression, a struggle that is not to be postponed to the "end of days", but rather it is the duty of every Muslim to participate in it even today.[19]

The dispatch of the Revolutionary Guards to Lebanon in 1982 constitutes an example of an aggressive operational method – the export of the revolution also via military power, and not only through influence and persuasion. Although the Revolutionary Guards were not directly involved in the combat against Israel, they established the Hizballah organization that spearheaded the armed struggle against the Western and Israeli presence in Lebanon.

Iran regards the solidification of the Hizballah in Lebanon as its greatest success (and only one to date) in exporting the Islamic revolution. Even after the IDF withdrawal from Lebanon (in 2001), Iran continues to view Lebanon as its forefront against Israel, and the Hizballah as a key factor in leading the struggle.[20]

Over time, Khomeini's movement became the Muslim world's symbol for the power of Islam in its struggle against the oppressor, whether from within or via external imperialism, but its practical influence did not usually exceed organizations formed by minority militant groups. Several factors combined to limit its influence and prevent it from becoming a leading trend in Islam:[21]

- The Iranian revolutionary regime failed to provide satisfactory solutions for Iran's social and economic problems; therefore, in practical terms it was not perceived as a suitable model for emulation.
- The regimes in Muslim countries were aware of the danger posed by radical religious groups, and therefore took ruthless action against them.
- The promotion of Khomeini's ideas came up against an objective obstacle because they were accepted by a Shiite minority in a Muslim world which was mostly Sunni and was hostile to the Shiites.

The Iranian revolutionary regime made significant efforts to expand its influence and connections to radical Sunni Islamic circles. In this framework, close cooperation was established with the various Islamic Jihad groups (Palestinian, Egyptian), and with radical Islamic movements in the Magreb.

Due to the obstacles that made it difficult to export the Islamic revolution (as specified above), subversive activity to disseminate Khomeinism and the use of terror gradually turned into the main tools to achieve the objectives of the Iranian regime. Subversive pro-Iranian factors instigated riots and agitation in many Muslim countries, and translations of Khomeini's philosophy to local languages became an integral part of the arsenal of Fundamentalist propaganda in these countries.

The assassins of Anwar Sadat in Egypt brought up Khomeini's name during their trial as a source of inspiration for their acts. During a television interview, King Hassan of Morocco accused Khomeini of being behind the wave of riots that struck Morocco in 1983. A series of suicide attacks in Lebanon against French, American and Israeli targets was perpetrated under Iranian inspiration and direction, with the aim of banishing the foreign presence in Lebanon as the first step towards an "Islamic Republic" in that country according to the Iranian model.[22]

The period of the regime of Khomeini's successors in Iran is characterized by the fortification and stabilization of the Islamic rule, the implementation of the revolutionary theory, resolution of the Iranian people's problems and distress, the setting of the revolutionary path, and the continued export of the revolution.[23]

External observers distinguish between radical and moderate entities in the Iranian leadership. Power struggles between radical and moderate elements already took place during the presidency of Rafsanjani, but the struggles became more intensive during the term of his successor to the presidency – Khatami. Khatami appeared to be a reformer who aspires to carry out internal reforms in Iran and improve its ties with countries worldwide, but his ability to realize his vision was restricted due to the power wielded by the traditional circles headed by the spiritual leader Ali Khamenei.

The pragmatism of the Iranian governmental system stems from its internal social and economic problems, and from the knowledge that in order for the regime to survive, it is necessary to cooperate with international bodies such as the UN, and to adopt internationally accepted modes of diplomatic behavior. Although Iran's foreign relations improved accordingly, this pragmatic approach was curtailed with the election of Mahmoud Ahmadinejad as President of Iran in 2005.

The main events that took place in the international arena during the 1990s, which had an impact upon Iran, were as follows: the collapse of the Soviet Union, the US coalition's war against Iraq in the Gulf War, the Middle East peace process, and the Islamic Fundamentalist awakening. The influence of these events was reflected in the intensification of Iranian aspirations to cement its status as a regional leader, while viewing the situation as an opportunity to fortify Iranian hegemony in the Gulf, as a chance to hoist the banner of the Islamic struggle against Israel, and as a means to disseminate Islam through linkage with movements that were not trained or supported by Iran when they were first founded (the Hamas, for example).

It is clear to Iranian leaders that the degree of Iran's stability and success will ultimately stem not from the extent that Islam is implemented, but rather from its success in solving social–economic problems in the countries they aspire to change. This is why they incorporate pragmatism and realism, and as a rule, when revolutionary interests conflict with the country's interests, preference will be given to the latter.

The examples detailed below do indeed reflect the duality of Iran's approach. On the one hand, in regions and at focal points where Iran believes it can act intensively and uncompromisingly to promote the concepts of the Islamic revolution, it aids radical Islamic organizations in terror acts and subversion aimed at ousting secular regimes and striking out at Western interests. This category includes Iranian involvement and cooperation with Sudan in disseminating radical Islam in North Africa (mainly Egypt and Algeria) and in the Horn of Africa (Somalia, Eritrea, Mozambique, etc.), as well as Iranian support of the Hizballah in Lebanon and Palestinian terrorist organizations in their battle against Israel.

On the other hand, where there is a fear that Iranian subversion may be exposed, thus resulting in damage to Iranian interests, Iran adopts a more pragmatic policy. A prominent example in this category is the moderate stand adopted by Iran towards the neighboring Islamic republics, with the aim of maintaining sound relations with Russia and Turkey, and for the time being to prevent the creation of a threatening reality which might cause conflicts with these countries.

To summarize, Iranian policy is inspired even today by a revolutionary and radical ideology, but its implementation is examined opposite prag-matic considerations that ultimately dictate Iran's actions. The American campaign against terror in the aftermath of the 9/11 attacks in 2001, and the American war in Afghanistan and subsequently in Iraq, have generated the creation of a new strategic reality within Iran's boundaries, which forces Iran to reexamine its goals in connection to exporting the revolution and terror in these new geo-political circumstances.

At the end of 2006, Iran under the leadership of Mahmoud Ahmadinejad advocates a foreign policy that perpetuates their nuclear project despite international protest, and continues to support terror orga-nizations such as Hizballah, the Hamas, and the Palestinian Islamic Jihad.

Iranian Intelligence and Terror Agencies[24]

Khomeini's revolutionary regime was forced to provide a response to several central challenges that threatened its very existence:

- Coping with Resistance to the revolutionary regime from among the followers of the previous regime (that of the Shah), as well as with some of its revolutionary partners which later turned into its enemies, such as the (communist) Tudeh party, the Mujahidin Khalq and the Fedayeen Khalq.
- Coping with the Iraqi invasion of Iran (in 1980).
- Coping with the threat posed by foreign powers that supported the Shah's reign and were unwilling to recognize the revolutionary regime in Iran (the United States, Britain, and others).

Aside from coping with these weighty challenges, the revolutionary regime was committed to its revolutionary ideology and to the principle of "exporting the Khomeini Revolution" to the entire Muslim nation. Thus, the regime had to set up intelligence, operational and propaganda agen-cies within a short period of time in order to meet the demands.

The Islamic regime initially used the apparatus that served it during the period of the struggle against the Shah's reign and in the course of the revolution, like the Hizballah militias and the Revolutionary Guards, which had carried the burden of the struggle against the Shah's government. Their most important mission, after the success of the revolution, was to wipe out the military and security power points that supported the Shah's reign.[25] After these entities were eradicated, jailed or fled the country, the regime's main effort was directed against the Resistance organizations (Khomeini's allies during the period of the revolution), while at the same time the regime was forced to deal with the Iraqi invasion in a head-on military confrontation, as well as with Iraqi and Western aid offered to the Resistance circles that were active against the revolutionary regime.[26]

As the army and the Iranian intelligence agencies in Iran had identified with the Shah's regime, the Khomeini regime was forced to establish new intelligence forces and agencies that would be based on loyalists to the revolutionary regime. The Khomeini revolution in 1979 brought about the eradication of the Iranian intelligence service dating from the Shah's reign – the SAVAK – which had served as a central tool for securing the Shah's government, as well as pursuing and eliminating his opponents. During the revolution and in its aftermath, the leaders of the SAVAK became central targets of the revolutionary regime, and many of them were imprisoned and executed.[27]

According to the Iranian constitution, the spiritual leader is the chief commander of the Iranian armed forces. In practice, there are several "armies" and semi-military forces acting under the command of the various political powerbrokers in the Iranian establishment.

Already in 1979 Khomeini's regime had founded its own intelligence service called the SAVAMA, its main role was in the area of internal security (persecuting and eliminating the regime's opponents), and gathering intelligence about Iraq.[28] The first director of the SAVAMA was General Faradost (who was arrested in 1985 and charged with espionage for the USSR). The SAVAMA acted simultaneously with the Hizballah's branches and the Revolutionary Guards, which handles missions that were identical to those of the intelligence service. In 1984 the SAVAMA underwent reorganization: Muhammad Rishari was appointed its director and its name was changed to VEVAK (the Ministry of Intelligence and Security). Rishari's deputy was Ali Falahian, who subsequently replaced him as head of the organization.

The Ministry of Intelligence and Security[29]

The VEVAK inherited the SAVAMA's roles while expanding its intelligence activities *vis-à-vis* Iraq and other foreign targets, and incorporating these activities in "revolutionary export" missions. In order to boost its operational capabilities, military intelligence experts (from the Shah's time) and junior SAVAK agents who specialized in Iranian leftists and in the Iraqi and Arab arena were called back to service.

It appears that during these years VEVAK renewed the intelligence infrastructure established in Iraq and in Arab countries during the reign of the Shah, and utilized the intelligence capabilities for the promotion of Iran's goals despite the difference in ideological approaches between the revolutionary intelligence service and its predecessor.

Due to the allocation of generous funding and extensive personnel, within a short period of time the Ministry of Intelligence and Security became one of the most powerful and influential agencies in the Iranian regime. In 1988, Ali Falahian was appointed Minister of Intelligence. Thanks to his qualifications, connections and status in the regime, he succeeded in establishing work procedures and coordination mechanisms between the various security and intelligence entities, as well as founding and heading the supreme council for intelligence matters, which supervised and coordinated all of Iran's intelligence and subversive activities.

The Ministry of Intelligence and Security is officially subordinate to the president, but in practice the heads of the ministry are appointed from among the close associates of the supreme leader and acted according to his instructions. The ministry is composed of twelve departments that activate over twenty thousand agents inside and outside of Iran. The first department is responsible for internal security, and enjoys a substantial part of the budget allocated for covert activity within Iran to secure the regime. The second department – the popular intelligence – is responsible for the bazaars, markets and mosques, and in practice strives to supervise public places and focuses on group associations. The third department – external security – is responsible for gathering intelligence information, underground activity and terror activities abroad. The department operates the Al-Quds organization spread out at various points worldwide, including Turkey, Pakistan, Germany, Switzerland, and more. The technical service provides communication equipment to agents and supports terrorist organizations; the finance department and administrative center deal with the budget and payroll; while the training bureau deals with the agents' training and instruction. The department for external security and the bureau of revolutionary movements are involved in links and operational activity *vis-à-vis* Islamic and other organizations that cooperate with Iran and are recipients of Iranian funding.

The Ministry of the Revolutionary Guards (Pasdaran) [30]

The aim of the activities of the Revolutionary Guards was mainly to defend the Iranian revolutionary regime against internal resistance. After the Iraqi invasion of Iran (in 1980) the Revolutionary Guards became a central nucleus of the Popular Military Forces, which bore the brunt of the combat against Iraq, due to the weakness of the Iranian army that underwent purges as a result of the revolution. The Revolutionary Guard numbers about 120,000 members, including independent land, sea and air forces. The land forces are divided into thirteen regional commands and twenty divisions (a division of the Revolutionary Guards is parallel to a military division). The Revolutionary Guards are deployed along the borders with Iraq and Afghanistan with the aim of defending the country, and in Iran's large cities for internal security missions. In addition, they are responsible for Iran's non-conventional combat means. Parallel to their missions related to safeguarding the regime and protecting the Iranian homeland, the Revolutionary Guards also undertake tasks related to the "export of the revolution," mainly through the use of terror and aid to Islamic terror organizations worldwide.

The Revolutionary Guards Ministry, which was established in 1983, handles all areas of activity inside and outside of Iran. In all matters relating to activities outside of Iran, the Revolutionary Guards are based on two central entities: (a) the committee for intelligence abroad; (b) the committee for operations abroad. The activity of Revolutionary Guard members abroad is generally conducted under a diplomatic, cultural or commercial guise. The Revolutionary Guards support the training, instruction and indoctrination of activists in Islamic terror organizations worldwide. These activists underwent training in Iran, Sudan, Lebanon or Afghanistan from 1983 onwards. Revolutionary Guard members also assist in the establishment of Islamic terror organizations, such as the Hizballah in Lebanon, and support Islamic entities at conflict arenas worldwide such as Bosnia or Chechnya.

The "Al-Quds Force" ("Jerusalem Force") of the Revolutionary Guards, which has been deployed in Lebanon since 1983, is an Iranian entity that leads Iranian activity in the region and its support of the Hizballah. This force deals with the direction and provision of military aid in terror activity against Israel, particularly that of the Hizballah, and Islamic and secular Palestinian organizations. The entity includes several militia forces that operate under the auspices of or in connection with the Revolutionary Guards:

- The Bassij – This militia constitutes a national guard and is charged with maintaining law and order in the country, and handling disorderly conduct and threats against the regime. The militia constitutes civilians who can be recruited as needed. The Bassij is subordinate to the Revolutionary Guards.

68

- Law enforcement forces – These forces are subordinate to the Ministry of Interior, but in practical terms are operated by leaders of the religious establishment and serve as a kind of "religious police".

The Ministry of Direction and Propaganda [31]

The ministry is responsible for religious and cultural activity, and for the dissemination of the Islamic revolution abroad. In this framework it is responsible for the establishment of mosques, cultural centers, associations, student unions, and religious services worldwide. The ministry is allocated considerable resources, which serve for the financing of propaganda activities, communication and education. The ministry's activity centers abroad often serve as a guise for Intelligence Ministry members, and enable the identification and recruitment of Islamic activists abroad among Muslim communities where ministry members are active.

The Foreign Ministry [32]

The Foreign Ministry is in charge of Iran's foreign policy and its diplomatic ties with states and organizations all over the world. It also assists in the dissemination of the Islamic revolution, and the diplomatic representations abroad serve as central focal points for entities affiliated with the Revolutionary Guards and the Ministry of Intelligence.[33] The Foreign Ministry provides diplomatic camouflage for the activity of intelligence members and terror activists, and aids in the provision of documentation (passports, visas, etc.) and in the transfer of combat means and equipment via diplomatic pouch (which according to international law is not supervised by the host country).[34] Iranian diplomats also deal in the gathering of intelligence and surveillance of potential targets against which Iran intends to perpetrate attacks.

The Supreme National Security Council

The Council was established in order to supervise the implementation of the Islamic revolution and protect the national interests of the Islamic republic as well as the sovereignty and territorial integrity of the state. In accordance to clause 177 of the Iranian constitution, the Council is responsible for the following issues.

- To establish policy regarding national security issues according to the general policy framework formulated by the spiritual leader.
- To coordinate the political, intelligence, social, cultural and economic activities in keeping with the general security policy.

- To develop the country's strategic, economic and security infrastructures in order to provide an adequate response to internal and
external threats.

Various committees function within the Council, such as the defense
committee and the national security committee. The President or a
member of the Council appointed by the President heads the committees.
Council members comprise: The leaders of the legislative, judiciary and
executive branches; the chief commander of the armed forces' supreme
council; the head of the planning and budgetary institution (PBO); the
Council's secretariat appointed by the supreme leader; an additional representative appointed by the supreme leader; the Foreign Minister; the
Minister of the Interior; the Intelligence and Security Minister; and a representative of the Revolutionary Guards.

The Iranian Terror System [35]

Terror activity, subversion and the elimination of the regime's opponents
abroad are subject to the approval of the top decision-makers in the Iranian
regime, including the spiritual leader (Valiat Fakia).[36] Ideas and initiatives
in these areas are first raised for discussion and approval in principle within
a small forum composed of the president and four ministers. Following
their authorization, these proposals are transferred to the Supreme
National Security Council, which processes the recommendations and
prepares them for the approval of the spiritual leader. After gaining the
approval of the spiritual leader, they are then transferred to the Supreme
Council for Intelligence, which ensures implementation via the relevant
ministries and the executive branches.

The trial of Iranian agents in Germany, tried and convicted of murdering four Kurd émigrés in the "Mikonos" restaurant in Berlin, constitutes a
prominent example of the Iranian decision-making chain. Indeed, the
German court unequivocally indicated the responsibility of the Iranian
government's top leaders for this terror activity. In his verdict, the German
judge pointed to the personal and direct involvement of the Iranian
Intelligence Minister Falahian in the planning and implementation of the
terror activity and issued an arrest warrant against him (in absentia).[37]

Since the early 1990s, the Supreme Council for Intelligence Matters and
the Ministry of Intelligence and Security have played a central role in ini-
tiating and conducting terror activity abroad. The Supreme Council for
Intelligence Matters and its head are responsible for coordination between
the relevant ministries in all matters related to the planning and perpetration of operational activity.[38] As stated earlier, the various agencies that deal

in the export of the revolution and international terror recruit and activate terrorists all over the world, who undergo underground training in Iran or Lebanon.[39] For example, terror activity against foreign targets was perpetrated by the Hizballah's "special security agency" in Lebanon[40] and by various cells of Hizballah members abroad, based on Iranian diplomatic infrastructure. Imad Muraniya heads the "Special Security Agency" and receives his instructions directly from Iran.[41] The "Special Security Agency" was responsible for the hijacking of airplanes, the kidnapping of Western hostages in Lebanon and terror attacks worldwide.

The Hizballah Organization

The Hizballah organization was established in 1982 with Iranian help and inspiration, as part of the Khomeini regime's efforts to export the "Islamic Revolution" beyond Iran's boundaries. Lebanon constituted a preferred target due to the large Shiite population residing there and also because of the political reality which made penetration of the Iranian influence into this country fairly easy. The Hizballah is a roof organization that consolidates Shiite organizations, groups and religious clerics that adopted the Khomeinist worldview and recognized Khomeini as the supreme religious adjudicator (Valiat Fakia), and as their undisputed religious and political leader. The organization was founded by members of the Revolutionary Guards who arrived in Lebanon in the summer of 1982. Its founders include Abas Musawi, Sheikh Tsubhi Tufeili and Sheikh Muhammad Yizbak. During 1982 Hussein Musawi joined the organization. Musawi was the leader of the Islamic Amal movement (an organization that had split from Amal, advocated a radical line on the ideological level and perpetrated scores of terror attacks against IDF forces in Lebanon), as well as other religious Shiite organizations such as the Muslim Students' Union, the Lebanese Muslim Ulama Union and the al-Dawa Organization.[42]

Most of the founders of the Hizballah were alumni of Shiite seminaries in the holy cities of Najef (Iraq) and Qum (Iran), who returned to Lebanon in the late 1970s and established religious Shiite colleges that disseminated a radical school of thought among the Shiite population of Lebanon.

The Hizballah ideology is based on the principles of Iran's "Islamic Revolution", in the center of which is the demand for activism via a violent struggle (Jihad), with the aim of ousting the "tyrannical ruler" (a term coined by Iran and Hizballah). In this connection the Jihad is perceived as a legitimate defensive war. At the head of the struggle stands the learned scholar who will also lead the Islamic state based on religious law, when it is established. This is not a local message but rather a universal one, and its goal is the establishment of a global Islamic regime.[43]

The goals of the Hizballah organization are:[44]

1   The establishment of a revolutionary Islamic republic in Lebanon based on the Iranian model (as a strategic goal and as a stage in the establishment of a global Islamic republic).
2   Fighting "Western Imperialism" in Lebanon, reducing its influence and forcing Western entities (mainly French and American) to leave the region.
3   Fighting the Israeli presence in a way that will not be restricted to its banishment from Lebanon, but also concentrating efforts on its annihilation in order to impose Islam upon Jerusalem.
4   Establishing and consolidating the organization's status as the "leading" Islamic organization in Lebanon.

Hizballah's radical Shiite religious ideology played a major role in its formation and in drawing young Shiites to its ranks, by offering an attractive and active alternative to the community's political and religious establishment. The Hizballah perceives the struggle against the West and Israel as part of an overall struggle between Islam and the forces of evil, which are described as dynamic forces: The United States is the "Great Satan", while France and Israel are the "Small Satan". The United States, together with France and Israel, are perceived as the root of evil and the focus of heresy in our world; therefore, it is the duty of the Hizballah to eradicate their control.[45] The focus of the struggle is in Lebanon, particularly after the invasion by Israel, which according to the Hizballah's view plans to enslave the Lebanese people and turn their land into an imperialist base in cooperation with France and the United States. Therefore, their expulsion and the eradication of their influence in Lebanon are among the supreme objectives of the Hizballah.

The struggle against Israel does not end with the banishment of its presence from Lebanon, but with the triumph of Islam over Judaism. The Hizballah views the current struggle as a continuation of the historical struggle between the prophet Muhammad and the Jews.[46] Moreover, the State of Israel was allegedly based on the theft of Arab land, a fact that according to Islamic religious ruling obligates every Muslim to act for the return of the stolen land to its owners. In addition, every Muslim has the basic obligation to liberate all Islamic areas (Dar-al-Islam) from the presence of foreign occupiers. Thus, the Hizballah negates the very existence of the State of Israel, and the struggle against Israel in Lebanon constitutes only the first step in the overall battle.[47]

However, in the array of considerations that guides the leaders of the Hizballah it is possible to discern more pragmatic thinking alongside the radical line, particularly when addressing issues controversial among the religious scholars. There are several prominent examples:

- In the matter of founding an Islamic republic in Lebanon, the organization recognized its inability to impose this type of regime upon Lebanon in the near future, and therefore this principle remains in the framework of a long-term strategic objective which will be realized when the time is right.
- Regarding the question of the struggle against Israel, the organization "compromised" at the initial stage and was satisfied with limiting itself to a struggle against Israeli presence in Lebanon (the security zone – a part of Southern Lebanon previously occupied by Israel in order to protect Israel's northern settlements).
- After the withdrawal of the IDF from Lebanon (in May 2000), the organization redefined its objectives and placed the liberation of the "Shab'a Farm" and support for the Palestinian struggle at the head of its priorities. (Israel captured the "Shab'a Farm" from Syria in 1967, but the Hizballah claims that this territory actually belongs to Lebanon and the Israeli occupation of Lebanese soil is thus perpetuated.)

The various organizations that joined forces with the Hizballah maintain their separate status within the organization to a certain extent, although not in a manner that impairs the organization's unity and activities. This apparently stems from the undisputed personal authority of the organization's leaders – religious clerics – in the eyes of their followers at the Shiite centers, colleges and villages, where they are active and where their powerbase lies. It is important to note that in this traditional environment, particularly in South Lebanon, considerable importance is attributed to family connections; for instance, several members of families hold key positions in the organization – Muramiya, Musawi, and others.[48]

Hizballah is structured upon a hierarchy of councils ("Shura") headed by a Main Council, which numbers anywhere between seven to seventeen members during different periods. The Main Council members include (in 2003) Sheikh Hassan Nasrallah, Sheikh Naim Kassem, Hashem Tseifi Aldin, Sheikh Ibrahim Amin Alsid, Sheikh Muhammad Yizbak, Haj Imad Muraniya and two Iranian representatives. The inherent integration of Iranian entities in the organization's leadership unequivocally reflects the organization's identification and link with Iran.[49]

The Main Council is headed by the secretary-general – Sayyed Hassan Nasrallah. This council controls the secondary councils – including the political council, the military council and the judiciary council – as well as other entities. Therefore, unified leadership controls the organization's various branches, including the military terrorist activities. The activity of all of the secondary councils, particularly the political and military councils, is determined by the organization's secretary-general and the Main

Council, and is translated into an established policy stemming from the organization's ideology and strategy, alongside a series of considerations and constraints rooted in the interests of Iran and Syria, which support the organization.

Sheikh Muhammad Hussein Fadallah, a native of Najef and a pupil of Abu-al-Qassam al-Hawi (the supreme Shiite religious authority during his time), was granted the status of the organization's spiritual leader. Fadallah returned to Lebanon in 1966, established many educational and charitable institutions, and founded a radical ideological school of thought that opposed Mousa al-Sader's doctrine and negated his efforts to achieve legitimization within the existing regime. Even so, Fadallah's approach is currently considered pragmatic and moderate in comparison to the attitudes of the other Hizballah leaders. Fadallah espouses the implementation of the goals of an Islamic state in a peaceful manner and through educating the public, while reconciling themselves to a certain degree of pluralism in Lebanon, at least at the initial stage.[50] Fadallah also opposed suicide attacks at the time, and refused to provide them with the support of a religious ruling (*fatwa*), although he gave them his blessing after the fact. In the matter of taking hostages, he also regarded this issue as damaging to Islam's moral image and as detrimental to the belief pertaining to the more just character of the Islamic state when it is founded.[51]

It is important to keep in mind that these disputes had no effect on Hizballah's adherence to the extreme line that it adopted against its enemies inside and outside of Lebanon, nor did it limit the use of terror to achieve its goals. The organization has a military branch that relies on the infrastructure of the Shiite population. The number of militia members is estimated at several thousand, although the majority is made up of activists who are only partially recruited. The organization possesses an infrastructure that includes bases, commands, hideaways and ammunition depots. The activities are conducted in small groups. Also, the familial ties between many of the members and the joint origins – ethnic or geographical (from the same village in South Lebanon) – make it easier to maintain organizational loyalty and confidentiality.

The senior military command was mostly in the hands of the religious leaders Abas Musawi (until his termination) and Hussein Musawi, who were known as the masterminds of the Hizballah's attack policy in South Lebanon. This policy was executed by religious clerics such as Sheikhs Abd al-Karim Obeid and Afif a-Nabulsi. In addition to the military training provided by the Revolutionary Guards to the Hizballah members, the organization also enjoys financial support and the provision of a wide range of combat means.[52]

In 1989, in the framework of the "Ta'if Agreement", Syria forced the Lebanese government to grant the Hizballah the status of the sole militia organization in Lebanon, while the other ethnic militias were disarmed. The special status of the Hizballah and the weakness of the Lebanese government have enabled the organization, from then to now, to exploit its strength for military and civil conquest of South Lebanon (and several areas in the Lebanon Valley) while usurping the Lebanese administration's place. This process has continued since the withdrawal of the IDF from Lebanon (May 2000). The area of South Lebanon has basically turned into a "state within a state" ("Hizballahstan"), much as it was when the Palestinians controlled it up to 1982 ("Fatahland"). The Hizballah has become the decisive factor in this area, while the control of the Lebanese government is shaky and is expressed mainly in the development of economic projects (subject to the organization's approval).

The Hizballah established an extensive operational military infrastructure in South Lebanon numbering hundreds of activists skilled in various types of combat (in addition to the thousands of fighters that the organization can mobilize in emergencies). The fighters have various types of weapons, including a large amount of sabotage means, light weapons, anti-aircraft missiles, anti-tank missiles (including Sager, TAW, Kornet, MATIS), as well as artillery including mortars, canons and rockets.

Hizballah entities that dealt in "mega attacks" – suicide attacks against American and French targets in Lebanon, the kidnapping of foreign citizens in Lebanon and terror attacks worldwide – acted under cover names like the Islamic Jihad, the Revolutionary Organization for Justice, and the Organization of the Oppressed on Earth. On the other hand, the organization that claimed responsibility for terror activities against the IDF and the SLA (the South Lebanese Army militia formed by Israel in South Lebanon) was the Islamic Resistance, which is another cover name for the Hizballah.[53] The use of various cover names spreads confusion regarding the identity of the party that perpetrate the terror attack and restricts the ability of the "terror victims" to retaliate or apply punitive measures.

The Hizballah acts as Iran's emissary in the power struggles in Lebanon and in terror directed against Israel, Western and Arab states in Lebanon and in the international arena. Two main types of attacks are characteristic of this organization: Suicide attacks against Western targets in Lebanon and Kuwait and against Israeli targets in Lebanon, and the kidnapping of foreigners on Lebanese soil. The entity in charge of these attacks is the Special Security Agency, which was headed, as noted earlier, by Imad Muraniya.

Israel as a target of Iranian Shiite Terror [54]

Israel was one of the most loathed states by Khomeini and his regime, although not the most despised. This approach stands – like in other policy areas – in complete contrast to the close and special ties that developed between the two countries during the Shah's reign. Suffice to say that from the early 1960s all Israeli prime ministers visited Iran. Also, there were strong military ties, including mutual visits paid by the most high-ranking officers, in addition to highly developed economic relations; Iran exported oil to Israel and in return acquired security equipment and technologies for industry and agriculture.

Khomeini had already expressed an anti-Israeli and anti-Zionist stand during his period of exile in the 1960s. At that time, his links with Arab and Palestinian nationalist circles grew stronger and his animosity towards Israel increased. Khomeini attributed gross injustices to Israel and Zionism which in his eyes turned it into the source of all evil on earth. His accusations relate to three main axes:

- Accusations pertaining to anti-Islamic policies adopted by Israel and Zionism: hostility towards Islam, joint attempts with the "Great Satan" (the United States) to cause dissension in the Arab world, invasion of the sites holy to Islam, and burning the Al Aqsa mosque.
- Accusations related to aspirations for expansion and Israel's imperialist nature – the invasion of Palestine, oppression of the Palestinians, the invasion of Lebanon, and perpetual wars against the Arabs with the aim of realizing the Zionist vision of a "world kingdom".
- Accusations against Israel that it is partner to economic exploitation of Iran and to a policy crafted to perpetuate Iran's dependency upon the United States and Israel.

Thus, it is not surprising that PLO chairman Yasser Arafat was the first foreign leader who came to congratulate Khomeini upon his victory on February 18, 1979. Khomeini responded:

> The Iranian revolution will reward the Palestinian revolution for the help that it gave in ousting the Shah, and Iranian volunteers will participate in the struggle to eradicate the Zionist conquest and liberate Jerusalem.

Subsequently, an official announcement was published regarding the severance of relations, and the cessation of oil exports and aviation ties, between Iran and Israel. Following that announcement – and in the presence of Prime Minister Bazargan, Foreign Minister Karim Sanjabi and member of the "Revolutionary Council" Dr. Ibrahim Yazdi – Arafat waved the "Palestinian flag" over the Israeli Embassy building in Teheran.

From the day that the Islamic regime came into power, its leaders have never missed an opportunity to condemn Israel and criticize most of the Muslim states for their lack of determination in the struggle against it.

Khomeini promised aid to anyone willing to fight Israel, and on June 8, 1981 the Iranian Majlis (Parliament) passed a resolution to allow Iranian "volunteers" to enter the war against Israel in South Lebanon. The resolution was approved by the Supreme National Security Council and by the Revolutionary Guards' headquarters. A year later, the Lebanon War presented Khomeini with a golden opportunity to demonstrate his dedication to the war against "imperialism and Zionism," and thus, despite the ongoing war with Iraq, Iran opened "another front" against Israel and the United States in Lebanon, and dispatched forces from the Revolutionary Guards which then positioned themselves in Lebanon.

The Hizballah, which was established in Lebanon under Iranian patronage, adopted the hostility and hatred towards Israel that characterized the Khomeinist ideology. One of the fundamental principles of the organization's ideology, which is derived from the vision of the leader of the Islamic revolution in Iran, is the ongoing and uncompromising struggle against the State of Israel until its eradication and the liberation of Jerusalem. On the basis of this fundamental principle, and in order to bring it to fruition, the organization believes that it is ideologically and practically obligated to strive for an ongoing struggle against Israel using any means and in any geographical location.

The Hizballah's terror activity is accompanied by malicious propaganda, which includes blatant anti-Semitism. For example, Hassan Nasrallah, secretary-general of the organization, stated in his speech on May 7, 1998:

> I wish to draw attention to the danger related to this entity growing in Palestine, an entity which has no boundaries, which spreads to any place where Israelis go, to any place where there are remnants of the Talmud or where a Jewish rabbi once lived. The hope to realize the divine promise regarding the destruction of this cancerous affliction grows in everyone.[55]

In another interview, which took place on April 9, 2000, Nasrallah said:

> The source of all of the great disasters that have troubled this region is the existence of Israel. As long as there is a state named Israel, these disasters will continue. This is a malignant body in the region. If we ignore the fact that our body has cancer, we may discover this when it is too late . . . there are those who view cancer as the flu . . . When cancer is found it must be dealt with bravely and extracted from the roots. Part of this body and its blood must be sacrificed so that the body will be healthy and whole.[56]

The hostility against the State of Israel is accompanied by a hatred for the Jewish people. The organization's leaders have often made sharp anti-Semitic statements that not only revile Israel as a state, but also the entire Jewish people, while using themes taken from classic and Muslim anti-

Semitism. This, for example, is how Hassan Nasrallah expressed himself in speeches delivered in Beirut:

- "What do the Jews want? They want security and money. Throughout history the Jews have been Allah's most cowardly and avaricious creatures. If you look all over the world, you will find no one more miserly or greedy than they are."[57]
- "This year, unfortunately, the tenth day of the month of Muharam (the Ashura holiday) falls near the fiftieth anniversary of that bitter and tragic historical disaster of the establishment of the state by the descendants of monkeys and pigs, meaning the Jewish Zionists."[58]
- "If we gathered the blood spilt and money spent in Iran, in Iraq and in the nation during eight years of war, they would suffice to liberate Palestine scores of times and to eradicate Israel dozens of times. Is that correct or not?"[59]

Based on the way it views Israel, the Hizballah negates any possibility of a future agreement with the former, which would include recognition of its existence as a national entity in the region and coexistence. The organization makes a point of expressing its unshakable Resistance to any efforts to reach an agreement in the region, and sharply criticizes those negotiating with Israel, with the aim of increasing pressure in the Arab street. During recent years special emphasis has been placed on the prevention of negotiations and agreements between Israel and Palestine, and on maintaining the level of violence and terror in Gaza and the areas of Judea and Samaria.

Iran's status in Lebanon, as it has developed over the last twenty years, is important to the regime in Teheran. Iran's ties with the Shiite community in Lebanon, the bolstering of this community's status within the Lebanese system, the use of the Lebanese arena for the struggle against Israel (and in the past the United States too), and most important the establishment of the Hizballah – all of these factors constitute the most successful model for exporting the Islamic revolution, Iran style. Iran's status in Lebanon is also important for the purpose of expanding its influence throughout the Middle East, particularly in connection to the Arab–Israeli conflict and the peace process.

The fundamentalist Islamic ideology which motivates the regime in Iran and Lebanon's importance dictate to Iran the following interests *vis-à-vis* the issue of South Lebanon:[60]

- Strengthening the status of the Shiite community in general, and the Hizballah in particular, in the Lebanese system. Although Iran has ties with other Shiite Lebanese organizations and entities, Hizballah serves as its main arm in Lebanon. On the ideological level, the forti-fication of the Hizballah is a stage in the realization of the long-term objective of establishing an Islamic arrangement in Lebanon.

• Preserving the alliance with Syria, while ensuring that controversies that erupt from time with that country regarding the Lebanese issue do not impair this alliance. Iran is aware of the fact that its status and influence are largely dependent on its cooperation with Syria. It also regards Syria as a central strategic ally in the Arab world. Therefore, if disputes develop between Iran and Syria regarding the Hizballah's modus operandi, Iran will prefer to acquiesce if it believes that the controversy may cause a rift in its ties with Syria. It appears that according to Iran's point of view, strategic alliance with Syria is more important than inflicting damage on Israel via the Hizballah.

• Ideological support for the struggle against Israel, until it is eradi-cated as a political entity.

To date there has been no essential conflict between Iran's various inter-ests pertaining to South Lebanon. The encouragement to act against Israel was in keeping with the strengthening of the Hizballah's status and with Syrian interests in Lebanon. Since 1982, the operational infrastructure of the Hizballah has mostly been built with extensive Iranian assistance, which included funding, the transfer of large amounts of weaponry (mostly through Damascus), and the training of the organization's activists – all this alongside Syrian political and military aid, which has grown signifi-cantly since President Bashar al-Assad rose to power.

From Iran's point of view, the Hizballah is the forerunner of the "terror weapon" in general and its focus against Israeli targets in particular. Iran also regards the Hizballah as a central source of inspiration for the armed Palestinian struggle against Israel, and in a broader connection – an impor-tant instrument in the Islamic struggle against Israel.

Iran regards the fortification of the Hizballah in Lebanon as its greatest success (and the only one to date) of the "export of the Islamic revolu-tion." Even after Israel's withdrawal from Lebanon, Iran continues to regard Lebanon as its most forward front against Israel, and the Hizballah as a key factor in leading the struggle. Based on this concept, Iran perse-vered in strengthening the Hizballah's military capabilities. Iran has consistently expressed its support for the continuation of Hizballah's terror activity along the border between Israel and Lebanon and calls for the "liberation" of additional Lebanese land, which it claims is still invaded by Israel.[61]

The "Al-Quds Force" ("Jerusalem Force"), which belongs to the Iranian Revolutionary Guards and is deployed in Lebanon, is an Iranian entity that leads Iranian activity in the region and its aid for the Hizballah.

The force deals in the channeling and provision of various forms of military and financial aid for terror activity against Israel, particularly that of the Hizballah and Palestinian organizations – both religious and secular.

Iran transfers airborne military aid to the Lebanese arena via the "Al-Quds Force". This aid passes through the international airport in Damascus and constitutes the Hizballah's almost single supply route of weapons. The Iranians, who are aware of the fact, are careful to maintain continuity of the aid, with Syrian consent, thereby perpetually enhancing the organization's operational and military capabilities. Over the years large quantities of qualitative weapons have been transferred: anti-tank missiles (Sager, TAW, Kornet, MATIS), short- (102 mm), medium- (improved Fajer 122 mm, 220 mm and 302 mm), and long-range rockets with ranges from 10 to 250 km; naval combat equipment including Zilzal anti-ship missiles (C-802); Ababil UAV; motorized hang-gliders; and advanced surveillance and intelligence equipment. [62]

The "Al-Quds Force" plays a central role in establishing the operational plans of the Hizballah in the event of scenarios of escalation with Israel, their realization in the field and the determination of the Hizballah's response levels in the course of operational developments. This means that the Iranians constitute a key factor in the organization's operational-terrorist guidance, and it is in their power to trigger a regional deterioration if they choose to do so.

The Hizballah enjoys not only Iranian aid, but Syrian aid as well. In the framework of the "Syrian arrangement" in Lebanon, Syria turned the Hizballah into the central Lebanese militia organization that is still armed, in blatant contravention of the Ta'if Agreement (1989). While other ethnic militias were disarmed, the Syrians enabled the Hizballah to maintain a broad military infrastructure and to conduct operational activity against Israel from South Lebanon without disruption.

Since Bashar al-Assad's rise to power (in July 2000) there has been a significant change in the pattern of relations between the Syrian regime and the Hizballah, which consists mainly of the organization's upgrading from an instrumental tool and aid in managing Syria's policy against Israel and Lebanon into a strategic partner ("a front arm") and a central actor which has significant influence on Syria's policy in this matter.[63] The setting for this change is rooted in the special and close relationship that has developed between the inexperienced Bashar al-Assad and the leader of the Hizballah, Hassan Nasrallah, which is particularly conspicuous when one recalls the distance and suspicion with which Assad Senior treated the organization. Two main developments have contributed to the rapprochement process between the parties and to the formation of the current relationship pattern:[64]

- A change in the balance of forces between Syria and the Hizballah due to the change of government in Damascus and Hizballah's success in forcing the IDF to withdraw from Lebanon in the summer of 2000. In the initial stages of the stabilization of Bashar al-Assad's government, Syria's position was weakened considerably, while the Hizballah was reaching the pinnacle of its glory and power due to its successes in Lebanon.

- A coinciding of Syrian and Hizballah interests due to the failure in the channel of the Syrian–Israel negotiations (March 2000), the Israeli withdrawal from Lebanon (May 2000), and the fear of what was interpreted as Israel's attempt to force new "game rules" by attacking Syrian targets in response to attacks in South Lebanon (April and July 2001).

Syria offers the Hizballah political support in the internal Lebanese and international arenas, as well as wide maneuvering space for its fortification in Lebanon and the continuation of its activities in South Lebanon: This activity is directed at preventing the Israeli Lebanese border from turning into a quiet one, and maintaining controlled tension. Expressions of this approach can be observed in the "Shaba'a Farm", in the firing of anti-aircraft shells at Israel Air Force flights, harassing and frightening the Israeli civilian population along the border, and attacks – sometimes under Palestinian cover – outside of the Mount Dov sector (such as the Matsuba incident on March 12, 2002).

On the propaganda and informational level, Syria and the Lebanese administration, under the former's control, act to create an international "defense umbrella" for the Hizballah, by presenting it worldwide as a legitimate "resistance organization" rather than a terror organization. Syria offers the organization military aid, which supplements the Iranian support, and is willing to deviate from the aid patterns that were customary during the period of Haffez Al Assad Senior. For example, during the years 2000–2006, Syria has given the Hizballah Syrian-made long-range 220 mm. and 302 mm. rockets.

As mentioned above, the Hizballah strives to preserve a controlled level of tension along the border with Israel, while finding various excuses for raising the tension level even in matters unrelated to the military. For example, when controversy arose between Israel and Lebanon regarding the drawing of water from the Vazani river, the head of the southern sector in the Hizballah Sheikh Kauk stated, "the issue is not open for discussion or negotiation." Similarly, the head of the Hizballah faction in the Lebanese parliament Naim Ra'ad stated, "the world is trying to force negotiations upon us regarding the waters of the Vazani springs . . . It is our right to use the water as we see fit, in any way that we deem appropriate, and no one has the right to interfere with this right."[65] This example illustrates Hizballah's uniqueness as a terror organization that takes upon itself the authority to represent the interests of the central administration in Lebanon and to state in its name whether negotiations will take place or not.

Aside from the Hizballah organization, Iran also directs Palestinian terror activity against the State of Israel. The Iranian aid to Palestinian terror is a central component of the overall use that Iran makes of the "terror weapon" as a tool that promotes its national interests. The Iranians strive to achieve a variety of goals by encouraging and helping Palestinian terror to emulate the "Lebanese model" in the "territories" (Judea, Samaria and the Gaza Strip); boosting the radical Iranian–Syrian axis in the Middle East; weakening Israel through a kind of war of attrition, forcing Israel to sink its resources into the Palestinian conflict, thereby diminishing Israel's ability to strike out at Iran; strengthening the radical Islamic forces in the Palestinian Authority and undermining even the slightest chance of an Israeli–Palestinian agreement or any momentum towards a political process.

Iran hosts gatherings which support continued terror and negate agreements or arrangements designated to put an end to terror. It opposes any attempt to redirect the course of conflict and terror to negotiations and discussion. It systematically calls for the destruction of the State of Israel.

Guiding the terror: The Iranians act regularly to prevent any kind of appeasement in the "territories" and to increase terror activities. They achieve this[66] in two ways: by manipulating the Islamic and secular Palestinian terror organizations to serve as "contractors" that perpetrate terror in the "territories"; and by operating the Palestinian terror organizations directly or through a Hizballah go-between.

Using monetary leverage: The funding leverage is a crucial tool when establishing terror infrastructures and motivating terror activity.

Training and practice: Iran aids the Palestinian terror organizations in the area of training as well. In addition to the Hizballah, members of the Iranian Revolutionary Guards' "Al Quds" force are active in the recruitment and training of Palestinian activists from the terrorist organizations under its wing and sometimes Fatah members as well. The latter undergo military training in Lebanon and some continue training in Iran. Subsequently they return to the territories and join the local terror infrastructure.

The transfer of advanced combat means to the territories: Iran offers additional aid in the form of the transfer of advanced combat means to the territories.

Links between Iran and Hamas

During 1988, in the aftermath of the Iraq–Iran war, the outbreak of the Palestinian Intifada, and the acceleration of the political process in the Israel–Arab conflict, Iran led the camp of those who opposed the peace process with Israel. In October 1991, regular meetings commenced between the heads of the Hamas and the Iranian leadership in the course of which it was decided to open a permanent Hamas representative office in Teheran, to provide Iranian financial aid to the organization and train its fighters in Iran.

On October 31, 1991, the "Conference for the Support of the Palestinian Jihad" was convened in Teheran in response to the "Madrid Conference". The former was attended by representatives of the Islamic and Palestinian terror organizations including the Hamas, the Palestinian Islamic Jihad (led by Fathi Shkaki), the Hizballah and others.

In the course of November 1992, one year after the Hamas opened an official bureau in Teheran, a delegation from that organization led by its spokesman Ibrahim Ausha arrived in Iran and met with its spiritual leader Ali Khameni and with the commander of the Revolutionary Guards, Muhsein Razai. Both parties signed a draft of an agreement for the establishment of a political and military alliance. Iran agreed to provide the Hamas with financial, military and political aid and to build a broadcasting station for the organization in South Lebanon. This agreement had long-term ramifications, and it appears that the intensification of the Hamas' military activity, which was aimed at disrupting the negotiations between Israel and the PLO, was an integral part of this agreement.[67]

According to reports, some of which are based on PLO sources, in 1992, Iran pledged $30 million annually to the Hamas with the aim of intensifying attacks against Israel and helping the families of the fallen.[68] But in 1993 Hamas sources claimed that Iran had reneged on its promise to grant the organization this money because the latter was disappointed with its approach to maintain its independence *vis-à-vis* Iran.[69] According to other reports the initial amount promised by the Iranians was lower and stood only at about $10–15 million.

In 1996, Iranian President Rafsanjani denied that Iran was providing material aid to the Hamas and claimed that the latter had never requested help. In contrast, the American Secretary of State estimated in 1996 that Iranian aid for the Palestinian organizations reached several million dollars per annum.[70] The media reported that US and Israeli intelligence agencies had accumulated reports according to which the Iranians conspired to influence the results of the elections being held that year in Israel by perpetrating terror attacks, and the suicide attacks in February and March of that year were carried out in this context. Secretary of State Warren Christopher stated that the United States also had information that prior to the elections Iranian-trained Palestinian terrorists had infiltrated Israel and the Palestinian Authority in order to carry out attacks.[71]

About a month before the Israeli elections, Palestinian security service exposed a secret military organization sponsored by Iran. The latter, which numbered 70 members, intended to perpetrate a series of serious terror attacks prior to the elections and target Palestinian figures, including Arafat. According to the Palestinian Authority's Minister of Justice and senior members of its security agencies, these detainees were not members of the Hamas' military arm, the Iz a-Din Al-Qasam, but rather were members of a separate mechanism called "the secret agency". They had undergone training in Iran and Sudan and received their orders from Teheran via messengers sent through the Hamas leadership in Amman. The arrest of the 70 suspects in 1996 raised the possibility in Israel (according to Ami Ayalon, head of the Israeli GSS) that Iran aspired to accelerate terror attacks in Israel not only through military and monetary aid and instigation of the Palestinian organizations, but also through the direct operation of terror perpetrators by the Iranian intelligence services.

A similar report surfaced prior to the Israeli elections in 1999. In February 1999, the chief of the Palestinian Police in Gaza claimed that his men had arrested a Hamas cell that was to have perpetrated a mass suicide attack in Gush Katif in order to stir up public opinion in Israel. He claimed that the police had confiscated documents stating that Iran had transferred $35 million to the Hamas for it to perpetrate this attack and others, and that Iran had allocated a sum totalling of $130 million for the perpetration of suicide attacks in Israel.[72]

These revelations focused attention on the military aid that Iran had been providing to the Islamic Palestinian organizations. Since the mid-1990s, the Israeli defense agencies and the Palestinian Authority have arrested a series of young men, mainly members of the Hamas and Islamic Jihad, who underwent military training in Iran, including in the use of firearms and explosives. The aim was to instruct them to build a terror infrastructure in the territories and perpetrate terror attacks in Israel. Some of them, who were arrested due to their connection to mega terror attacks in Israel, had undergone training in Iran.[73] One of the members of the Islamic Jihad detained in Israel in 1996 told his interrogators that he had undergone training in Iran with the aim of carrying out terror attacks in Israel together with two additional Palestinian terror cells numbering 17 individuals. There are no exact numbers regarding the number of Palestinians trained in Iran but it would be correct to assume that over the years several hundred Palestinians underwent training.[74]

The training of Hamas terrorists in Iran: The incident of Hassan Salameh[75]

Hassan Abd-al-Rahman Salameh is a Khan Yunis resident and a Hamas member who is serving a life sentence in Israel after having been found guilty of murdering 56 Israelis in various attacks. In an interview that he granted to the *Los Angeles Times* Salameh stated that he had traveled to Iran in 1993 via Jordan and Sudan. There he underwent training in firearms, sabotage, intelligence and setting up ambushes. In the interview he expressed no regrets, justified the suicide attacks and called for the eradication of the State of Israel. In his interrogation in Israel, Salameh divulged additional details about the training he underwent with other Hamas terrorists in Iran.

Hassan Salameh was behind two murderous attacks that took place in Jerusalem: The attack on the number 18 bus line (February 25, 1996), in which twenty-six of the bus passengers were killed and another fifty were injured, and an additional attack on the number 18 bus line (March 3, 1996) in which eighteen of the passengers were killed and nine others were injured.

During his interrogation, Salameh disclosed that in the course of his activities in the Hamas he settled in Sudan, where he worked in the organization's offices for about eight months. In 1993, he moved to Syria where he underwent training in a camp run by the "Popular Front for the Liberation of Palestine the General Command" (PFLP-GC), Ahmad Jibril's organization. He subsequently returned to Sudan where he met a group of eighteen Hamas fugitives who had fled the Gaza Strip.

The group's members placed pressure on the Hamas leadership in Sudan to allow them to undergo military training. Those in charge of the group in Sudan arranged a three-month military training course. The group members were flown to Syria and from there to Iran, on an Iranian aircraft. Salameh noted that upon their arrival in Iran they were met by Osama Hamdan, the Hamas representative in Iran. The group's members set out for a military base directly from the airport, along with two other Palestinians and an interpreter where they were trained by ten Iranian instructors in the following areas:

- Dismantling, assembly and the use of various firearms including RPG and LAW missiles, M-16 rifles, Dshk Russian machine guns, Uzi sub-machine guns, Gurianov machine guns and Beretta handguns.
- Laying explosive charges and landmines, and lobbing hand grenades.
- Preparing TNT explosive charges and bombs, dismantling land mines, and extracting explosive materials in order to prepare improvised bombs.

• Methods for gathering intelligence about military deployment and setting up ambushes against mobile and on-foot patrols.

Salameh returned to Sudan at the course's end and from there flew to Syria, where he began planning his return to the Gaza Strip, which by that time was already under Palestinian control. After returning to Gaza he was involved in vicious terror attacks perpetrated against Israeli civilians (as mentioned earlier).

Since the crisis of 2000 and the outbreak of the violent conflict with Israel, the scope of Iranian aid to Palestinian organizations has grown significantly – not only to the Hamas and the Islamic Jihad, but also to the Fatah and Tanzim. This aid expresses itself in the provision of training and funding. But the most prominent characteristic related to the intensification of Iranian aid is the accelerated Hizballah involvement in Palestinian military activity and Iran's direct involvement in operating Palestinian terrorist cells in the territories.

It is not clear to what extent the tightening of ties between the Hizballah and the terror organizations stems from Hizballah initiative, but there is no doubt that Iran is involved because this serves its interests. This development can be assumed to stem from several causes: The IDF's withdrawal in 2000 from Lebanon, which necessitated Hizballah's redeployment *vis-à-vis* Israel and the search for new ways to perpetuate the struggle against the accelerated Israeli–Palestinian peace process in the summer and autumn of 2000 (which Iran had its own good reasons to undermine); and the outbreak of the Al Aqsa Intifada, which gave Iran the opportunity to boost its involvement in Palestinian military activity. Iran's increased involvement in this activity was also reflected in attempts to forge ties with Israeli Arabs in order to perpetrate terror attacks. Moreover, since 2001 Iranian involvement in the armed struggle against Israel took a new direction: The beginning of weapon and sabotage shipments to the Palestinian Authority (such as the case of the arms ship *Karin A*).

Iranian orchestration of Palestinian terror (based on confiscated documents) [76]

Salient proof of Iran's orchestration of Palestinian terror can be found in documents confiscated during the Defense Shield Campaign (March–April 2002). The latter include intelligence reports produced by the Palestinian security agencies which were presented to Arafat for perusal. Thus, for example, an intelligence report dated December 10, 2000, which was prepared by the head of General Intelligence Amin al-Hindi, discusses the transfer of large sums to the territories by Iran ($400,000 to the Iz a-Din Al-Qasam Brigades; $700,000 to the Islamic organizations opposing the Palestinian Authority). According to this report, the funds were designated to support the military branch of the Hamas "inside" and promote suicide terrorism. According to the document, the Hamas leadership in Syria maintains links with activists in the Iz a-Din Al-Qasam Brigades in the territories in all matters related to the perpetration of military attacks against Israeli targets.

An intelligence report submitted by the head of the internal Palestinian Security Jibril Rajub on October 31, 2001, mentioned intensive meetings being held between members of the Hamas, the Islamic Jihad and the Hizballah in Damascus, with the aim of "increasing joint activities inside the area of Judea ans Samaria and the Gaza Strip with the help of Iranian funding." This followed "an Iranian message to the leadership of the Hamas and the Islamic Jihad that a lull must not be permitted at the present time." The document stated, "what is currently needed is to perpetrate suicide attacks against Israeli targets in Gaza, the West Bank and inside Israel."

Another intelligence report dated June 1, 2000, which was submitted to Arafat by the head of the General Intelligence, disclosed that a meeting had been held at the Iranian Embassy in Damascus on May 19, 2000. It was attended by the Iranian Ambassador and senior members of the Hamas, the Islamic Jihad and the Hizballah. The report stated that the Ambassador demanded of those present at the meeting "to perpetrate military attacks inside Palestine without claiming responsibility for them."

Another report dated September 11, 2000, which was presented to Arafat by the political department of the internal security agency, described a series of intensive meetings between the leaders of the Palestinian Resistance groups in Syria and Lebanon. Among others, these meetings were attended by representatives of the Islamic Jihad, the Hamas and the Hizballah in Palestine. Also present were Syrian, Iranian and Hizballah representatives. The objective of the meetings was to "formulate their action strategy for the upcoming period." During the meetings it was decided to escalate military activity in Jerusalem without claiming responsibility for the deeds.

Iran and the Palestinian Authority

Iran's willingness to transfer indirect financial aid to Fatah entities and its subsequent direct aid to the Palestinian Authority (the *Karin A* affair) constitutes a significant shift in Iranian policy. In the initial stages of the Intifada, Iran regarded the Palestinian Authority as a traitor aspiring to achieve a political agreement with Israel, but this approach underwent a transformation when the Palestinian Authority and its sponsored terror agencies gradually became leaders of the struggle and terror against Israel starting from the second half of 2001.

Iranian training aid to Palestinian terror organizations

Iranian aid to terror activists and to Palestinian terror organizations is also reflected in the area of training. The branch that serves as the conduit for this kind of aid is the Revolutionary Guards (Pasdaran) led by the "Al-Quds Force" ("Jerusalem Force"), an intelligence, military arm which is active overseas, including in the Baka area of Lebanon.

Since the outbreak (September 28, 2000) of the violent activities in the area of Judea and Samaria (the West Bank), the Revolutionary Guards' activity in Lebanon is characterized by a growing effort to recruit Palestinians for the battle against Israel. The Iranians were quick to identify the potential inherent in recruiting Palestinians from the "outside" (refugee camps) and from the "inside" (the area of Judea and Samaria – the West Bank). Thus, clear efforts to imbue these Palestinians with characteristics similar to those of the Hizballah are discernible. In the framework of the training aid, the Revolutionary Guards recruit Islamic activists who undergo training in Lebanon and sometimes continue their preparations in Iran as well. They subsequently return to the territories and become involved in terror activity.

An intelligence report submitted to Jibril Rajub by the head of the Palestinian internal security branch in Bethlehem addresses the issue of a fugitive Hamas cell planning suicide missions. The report mentions the names of two members of the cell who "underwent a training course in Lebanon at the Yahfufa camp (south of Baal Bek in the Lebanon Valley) under the supervision of an Iranian instructor named Abu Khaled. They underwent a three-month course in Lebanon and returned to Palestine."

The report also notes that it had just been learned that Iranian experts from the Revolutionary Guards in Lebanon were training Palestinians from the Fatah and Hamas to use individual ground-to-air missiles, apparently Russian SA-7 (Strella) missiles that can be launched from the shoulder. It further stated that the course was conducted at the Janta camp in the Baka Valley and attended by Palestinians from the Fatah and the Hamas who had undergone a basic military course in Lebanon sponsored by the Revolutionary Guards a year earlier. After completing the course, the "alumni" were to undergo another special course in Iran near the city of Qum and then return to Judea, Samaria and Gaza. The report also mentions a member of the Revolutionary Guards named Ali Rida Hamzi who handled coordinations, and Munir al Makdah, leader of a Fatah breakaway faction, who acts out of the Ein al Hilweh camp near Sidon.

The transfer of aid to "charitable associations," most of which are associated with the Hamas, serves the Iranians as an additional channel to assist the Hamas and is another way to influence the Palestinian arena. The Palestinian Authority is well aware of the secret motives behind the Iranian "humanitarian aid" but the PA does nothing to stop it due to its reluctance to confront the Hamas and Islamic Jihad.

The significance of this aid is reflected in a confiscated document dated June 2000 about a meeting held in Damascus between President Khatami, who was visiting Syria, and the Hamas leadership. According to the document, the meeting's goal was to attain Iranian aid for the Hamas. The document, which was sent to Arafat, describes the Hamas' extensive "Dawa" activity in the territories (preaching, propaganda, and religious political indoctrination) as it was presented to the Iranians. "The Hamas leadership addresses the Palestinian infrastructure (in the territories) in various areas: schools, universities, commerce, (various) public services for women and the growing generation of youth with the aim of recruitment. Thus it works in kindergartens – in order to prepare an entire generation of (Hamas) supporters in social clubs and centers . . . "

Hizballah Abductions against Israel

A central bone of contention in the prolonged conflict between Hizballah and Israel is the issue of the captives. The Hizballah grasps the sensitivity of Israeli society and of its decision-makers *vis-à-vis* its civilians and soldiers. Therefore, the abduction of soldiers has become a central target within the organization's modus operandi. The hostages become a "strategic asset" which the organization exploits to promote its goals in the conflict with Israel and to strengthen its position in Lebanon and the Arab world.

During the years 1986–2000, Israelis fell captive to organizations under Iranian sponsorship (Hizballah and the "Faithful Resistance") in four incidents:

- February 17, 1986 – In the course of a Hizaballah ambush two Israeli soldiers fell captive – Yosef Fink and Rahamim Alsheikh.
- October 16, 1986 – An Israeli Air Force plane fell in Lebanon. The plane's navigator, Ron Arad, was taken captive by the Amal organization. Subsequently, he was held hostage by Mustafa Dirani, head of the "Faithful Resistance," and subsequently was apparently handed over to the Iranians.
- On the night between September 4–5, 1997, an IDF force was ambushed by the Hizballah in the Antsaria area of South Lebanon. Eleven soldiers were killed in the attack and four were wounded. After its evacuation, one body was left at the site in addition to the body parts of two soldiers who were taken captive by the Hizballah.
- October 2, 2000 – Three IDF soldiers – Binyamin Avraham, Adi

Avitan and Omar Suwed – were abducted by the Hizballah in the Har Dov sector.

• October 2000 – Israeli civilian Elhanan Tannenbaum, who was lured to Dubai, was abducted by the Hizballah and transferred to Lebanon.

Israel left no stone unturned to free the captives: diplomatic channels, putting direct and indirect pressure on the Hizballah, and military operations.

During the years 1986–1991, the Hizballah consistently refused to divulge any reliable information regarding the number of soldiers that it was holding or their physical/mental condition, and was unwilling to enter negotiations regarding their return to Israel. The Hizballah leaders rejected negotiations with Israel due to their claim that they do not recognize its existence. The political and strategic changes that occurred in the region, and the new approach adopted by Hizballah's patrons Iran and Syria, forced the organization to change its position regarding the issue of Israeli POWs.

At the end of 1990, for the first time Hizballah leaders issued statements that appeared to constitute an attempt to prepare its supporters for a change of policy regarding the Israeli hostages. Spiritual leader Sheikh Fadallah called for the mutual release of Arab and Western hostages on a "humanitarian basis". In 1991, following the appointment of Sheikh Abbas Musawi as the Hizballah's secretary general, the organization agreed to enter negotiations with Israel for a prisoner exchange, parallel to negotiations that were being conducted at the time for the release of Western hostages being held by the organization.

After years of uncertainty Israel received verified information that two of the captives, Rahamim Alsheikh and Yosef Fink, were dead. In the course of the negotiations Israel and the Southern Lebanon Army released 91 Shiite prisoners in stages. In addition, the bodies of nine Hizballah members who had been killed during attempted terrorist attacks were returned to Lebanon.

The abduction of two IDF soldiers in Lebanon – February 17, 1986

On February 17, 1986 an IDF force set out on a military operation in Lebanon from Beit Jabil towards the roadblock at Beit Yahun in a convoy that included three cars. At 12:10, when the convoy reached a curve on the northern road at Kfar Kunin, it encountered a Hizballah ambush.

The ambush had been well planned. It included a cell that shot at the convoy and carried out the abduction, as well as two other cells positioned to the north which opened immobilizing mortar fire at a nearby Southern

Lebanon Army stronghold to serve as a diversion. The Hizballah ambushers opened fire at the two cars at the rear after the first car had taken the curve. The driver of the second car in the convoy was killed and the car went down a ditch at the side of the road.

An officer and soldier jumped out of the car into the ditch and immediately opened fire at a nearby house where they thought the shooting had originated, however they were unable to clearly identify the source of the gunfire. A few minutes later the officer got into the car and attempted to make radio contact but was unsuccessful. Subsequently, the officer attempted to see what had happened to the third car but due to the gunfire could not approach it.

At about 12:45 an IDF force arrived at the site, but the Hizballah had already withdrawn. A search of the area revealed that two Israeli soldiers – Rahamim Alsheikh and Yosef Fink – had been abducted from the third vehicle.

An investigation of the incident indicated that the abductors had fled via Wadi Alka to east Barashit and then traveled down a dirt path parallel to the road. It appears that in the vicinity of the Shakra petrol station the abductors got into an ambulance and continued towards the Jamijama intersection. The ambulance's destination was never verified, nor is it known where the hostages were taken.

Immediately after news of the soldiers' abduction had been reported at the headquarters of IDF Division 91, steps were taken to block off the area of activity and close off the roads in that sector in order to prevent the abductors from fleeing the security zone. These activities were carried out by combat helicopters and IDF forces active in the IDF Division 91 sector, as well as SLA soldiers.

The IDF carried out an extensive search (the "Electric Pipe" campaign) for several days in the security zone in order to try to locate the abducted soldiers. At the same time the Israeli navy took action to prevent the removal of the soldiers from Lebanon via the sea. But the soldiers were never found.

During the "Electric Pipe" campaign, two IDF soldiers were killed, as well as 18 terrorists. Some 184 men suspected of belonging to terrorist organizations were arrested and numerous combat means were confiscated including land mines, 50 RPG launchers, 147 Kalachnikov rifles, one hundred and fifty 122 mm. rockets, fifty 107 mm. rockets, two SA7 shoulder missiles and more.

Ten years later, the bodies of Rahamim Alshaich and Yosef Fink were returned to Israel after prolonged negotiations with the Hizballah through intermediaries on July 21, 1996.

The Ron Arad Affair[77]

On October 16, 1986, Ron Arad bailed out of his plane due to a technical problem during a flight mission in Lebanon and was taken captive by the Amal Organization. At the time of the incident, Nebiya Beri stood at the head of Amal. Beri claimed responsibility for Ron Arad's capture on various occasions, as will be elaborated below, and even declared, "Not even a hair on Ron Arad's head will be touched as long as he (Beri) headed the organization."

At the time when Ron Arad was taken into captivity, Mustafa Dirani served as head of Amal's security agency under Nebiya Beri's command. Beri appointed Dirani security director in 1985. In the framework of this role, he was also responsible for Maadushiya, the village near the site where Ron Arad parachuted after bailing out of his Phantom aircraft.

A short time after falling captive, Ron Arad was handed over to Dirani as Amal's representative. The latter held him hostage. At first, Dirani held him in his headquarters in west Beirut and subsequently moved him frequently from one hideaway to another in west Beirut so that Israel would not be able to track him down.

A short time after Ron Arad was taken captive, Beri left his headquarters in Beirut and moved to Damascus. The move was initiated by Beri's cohorts, the Syrians, for his personal security and in order to protect him from the long arm of the State of Israel due to his involvement in the affair. After Beri's departure, Ron Arad remained under Dirani's complete control. On October 18, 1986, for the first time Israel officially announced that it regarded Amal as solely responsible for Ron Arad's well-being.

During the first two months of his captivity Amal enabled Syrian interrogators to question Arad and possibly allowed the Russians access as well. At the beginning of 1987, tension escalated between Amal and the Hizballah, against the background of a dispute between the Shiite organizations regarding control over South Lebanon. At the same time that fighting broke out between Amal and the Hizballah, on February 8, 1987, the Israeli navy imposed a naval blockade on Sidon and Al Uzai, which were under Amal's control, in order to clarify to Ron Arad's captors that they were responsible for his safety, among other reasons due to the fear that he might be hurt in the skirmishes. In response to the blockade, Beri announced that if the blockade was not lifted, he would not be responsible for Arad's life. Beri's response served as additional confirmation that Ron Arad was being held by Amal under Dirani's control.

In 1987, Beri returned to Damascus, leaving Ron Arad in Dirani's hands. Dirani continued to move Ron Arad frequently from one safe house to another. During the transfers, Ron was placed in the car's boot bound up, and without food and water for several days. During this period Dirani continued to abuse, attack and humiliate Ron Arad while preventing any contact with his family.

At a press conference held in April 1987, Beri proposed that the Red Cross serve as an intermediary in an exchange deal – Ron Arad for Shiite prisoners incarcerated in Israel and Israel's withdrawal from South Lebanon. During the negotiations between Israel and Amal regarding the exchange, organization members disclosed information several times about Ron Arad and the state of his health. In September 1987, as part of the negotiation process between Israel and Amal, letters and two pictures of Ron Arad were handed over to his family. These letters and pictures were the last signs of life received from Ron Arad to this very day.

At that time Dirani founded an independent radical Islamic organization called the "Faithful Resistance," which he headed. Upon the establishment of this new movement, Dirani and his men left Amal in favor of the new organization.

On October 20, 1987, following the establishment of the new organization, which cooperated with Hizballah and the Iranians, Dirani "abducted" Ron Arad from Amal, where he had previously served as its security director, and resumed full control over him in the framework of the new organization. Over a period of 18 months following Ron Arad's abduction from Amal by Dirani, he was again moved from place to place. During this time Ron Arad was deprived of the basic rights granted to a POW by the Geneva Convention, and the Red Cross was not allowed to visit him.

Dirani's ties with the Iranians and his organization's affiliation with the Revolutionary Guards led Dirani to search for an opportunity to hand Ron Arad to the Iranians as a "deposit". Immediately after Dirani's "abduction" of Ron Arad, the former initiated negotiations with the Iranians regarding the terms for holding the "deposit". Towards the end of 1987, Ron Arad was held in Dirani's house while the latter negotiated with the Iranians regarding the transfer. In mid-1988 Beri informed Israel that Ron Arad was in Dirani's hands. He claimed that Dirani had announced his intention to transfer the captive to Iran or the Hizballah.

At the beginning of 1988, Israel contacted Dirani. The latter demanded the release of hundreds of prisoners incarcerated in Israel. Despite Israel's agreement in principle to release prisoners, its efforts to gain progress in the discussions ended in no releases. On May 4, 1988, Dirani "sold" Ron Arad to Iranian entities (apparently the Revolutionary Guards) and since that day, the captive has disappeared without a trace. On May 21, 1994, Dirani was captured at his home in Lebanon by Israeli security forces. He was brought to Israel and incarcerated in a prison facility of the Israeli security forces.

The "Poplar's Whistle" Campaign (the Navy Seals' Débâcle)

The "Poplar's Whistle" campaign took place on the night between September 4–5, 1997. The Israeli Navy Seal's force no. 13 participated in this campaign with a total of 16 soldiers. While making its way towards the target, the force encountered an ambush in the form of explosive devices (in the first moments of the encounter two explosions detonated near the force). Some three minutes after the beginning of the skirmish, and as a result of the initial explosions, an explosive device that Sergeant Major Itamar Iliya was carrying on his body detonated. With the exception of one soldier, all of the other members of the force were hit as a result of the shooting and explosions. Eleven fighters, including the force's commander, Lieutenant Colonel Yosef Kuarkin, were killed and four wounded. A rescue force from the air was summoned in order to extricate the soldiers and it exchanged fire with the enemy at the site of the ambush. The rescue force's doctor was killed during the exchange of gunfire. The injured and dead were evacuated from the site but following an exact count of the evacuees at the Nahariya hospital it became clear that Sergeant Major Itamar Iliya's body had been seized and body parts belonging to Sergeant Major Tebi Raz and Staff Sergeant Golan Guy had been left behind.

The initial contact for the return of the bodies was launched the day after the débâcle on September 5, 1997. Ya'akov Peri (former head of the GSS) was the State of Israel's representative in the negotiations. He transferred an appeal to the Lebanese government through the Red Cross. Initially it was unclear who was holding Iliya's body but three days later it was decided that negotiations would be conducted *vis-à-vis* the Lebanese government.

The initial Lebanese demand was to release all of the prisoners at the El-Hiyam prison and all of the bodies of Lebanese terrorists buried in Israel. Israel rejected this demand and stated that it would only return the terrorists' bodies. When it became clear that the deal did not stand a chance if live terrorists were not returned, Israel agreed to a gesture which would include the release of live terrorists. Lebanon was not satisfied with Israel's promise to carry out the gesture and demanded a third-party guarantee that the deal would take place. The letter of commitment signed by Prime Minister Netanyahu was accompanied by a guarantee from the French president.

On May 29, 1998, the French president visited Lebanon. Israel decided to take advantage of this trip to break the deadlock in the negotiations. Israel President Weizmann sent a personal letter to the French president stipulating Israel's final offer – 40 terrorists' bodies and 60 prisoners, 10 from Israeli prisons and 50 from El-Hiyam. Several days later the Lebanese government announced that the proposal had been accepted. A short time later, Sheikh Nasrallah announced that Israel and Lebanon had reached an agreement regarding the exchange of bodies and added that his son's body would be included in the deal. On June 5, 1998, the Lebanese government officially approved the deal and requested another letter of guarantee in all matters related to the exchange arrangements and the schedule. On June 25, 1998, at the end of prolonged negotiations, the body of Israeli navy seal Itamar Iliya was returned together with the body parts of Tubi Raz and Golan Guy. As noted earlier, it was agreed to transfer 60 prisoners and 40 bodies of terrorists interred in northern Israel (including the body of Sheikh Nasrallah's son, who was killed during IDF activity in Lebanon). On June 26, the 59 prisoners included in the deal were returned to Lebanon. One of the prisoners refused to leave the Israeli prison, claiming that his life would be endangered if he returned to Lebanon. Sheikh Nasrallah defined the deal as "a great achievement for the Hizballah and the Lebanese people."

The abduction of three IDF soldiers at Mount Dov – October 7, 2000

On Saturday morning, October 7, 2000, a motorized patrol was driving a patrol vehicle near the border security fence in the Mount Dov sector. The patrol included three soldiers – commander Binyamin Avraham, Adi Avitan and Omar Suwed. When the patrol arrived at a gate in the fence, which enabled crossing over into Lebanon, two explosive charges were detonated, causing injuries to the soldiers. The gate itself was detonated by another explosive device. A vehicle with Hizballah members entered Israeli territory and abducted the three wounded soldiers.

An investigation indicated that the operations room of the Hermon brigade received an electronic warning regarding the intrusion through the security fence, but the abduction was only discovered 15 minutes later when the squadron's commander was unable to reach the soldiers on the two-way radio and went out to see what was happening.

Due to a large-scale bombardment of artillery fire and anti-tank missiles along the sector which took place simultaneously as a cover up for the abduction, precious time passed before the commander could approach the burning patrol vehicle and declare the incident an abduction. When the abduction was verified, IDF forces pursued the abductors inside Lebanon. IDF helicopters strafed roads and bridges in order to prevent the abductors from fleeing up north deep into Lebanese territory, but the abductors got away.

The Hizballah planned the abduction meticulously and in the morning hours had already initiated a distraction. Near Zarit, people gathered together, threw stones at IDF soldiers and demonstrated against them.

Thus they distracted the attention of the Mount Dov command, where the abduction was to take place. Around noon, the Hizballah began bombarding the Mount Dov sector, the Hermon and its strongholds with hundreds of mortar shells and dozens of missiles. This extensive bombardment prevented the rescue force from responding immediately.

Israel invested considerable effort in its attempts to find out what had happened to the abducted soldiers and negotiated with the Hizballah via a German intermediary. The bodies of the soldiers and civilian Elchanan Tannenbaum were returned to Israel on January 29, 2004. Israel released 400 political prisoners in exchange, including 29 prisoners from Arab countries and the bodies of 60 Hizballah terrorists. Among the terrorists who were returned to Lebanon were Sheikh Obeid and Mustafa Dirani.

Israel's efforts to bring about the release of IDF POWs from the Hizballah

Since the abduction of IDF soldiers Yosef Fink and Rahamim Alsheikh, followed by the capture of navigator Ron Arad, Israel made tremendous efforts to bring about their release. The Hizballah refused to divulge information about the fates of Fink and Alsheikh. In Ron Arad's case, information was available up to the time he was transferred by his captors to the Hizballah and Iran.

Due to the fact that until 1989 all efforts to force the Hizballah to release the prisoners proved to be futile, it was decided to try to promote their release by obtaining "bargaining chips" which would serve as an incentive for the Hizballah (detailed in full in the next section) to enter negotiations for their release. The first step of this policy *vis-à-vis* the Hizballah was carried out in September 1989 when an IDF force abducted Sheikh Karim Obeid and brought him to Israel. Obeid was one of the senior Hizballah members in Southern Lebanon. After this move failed to bring about the desired results, Israel initiated another operation in May 1994 and caught Mustafa Dirani, leader of the "Faithful Resistance" who had held Ron Arad hostage until turning him over to the Hizballah and the Iranians. Dirani's abduction to Israel had three goals:

- An attempt to acquire information about Ron Arad.
- The use of Dirani as an additional "bargaining chip" for Ron Arad's release.
- Punishing Dirani for his cruel and humiliating treatment of Ron Arad when he was being held hostage by him, and for turning the prisoner over to the Iranians.

Mustafa Dirani's interrogation in Israel clarified certain issues regarding Ron Arad's fate after falling captive in Lebanon but it did not provide up-to-date information about his location. Dirani's incarceration in an Israeli prison did nothing to contribute to Iran or Hizballah's willingness to enter negotiations for Ron Arad's release.

The Abduction of Sheikh Abd al Karim Obeid

In July 1989, the Israeli security authorities decided to try to promote a move that would force the hand of Iran and the Hizballah to return POW Ron Arad. The goal was to create a high-level bargaining card by abducting one of the Hizballah leaders. The security authorities decided that the prime candidate was Sheikh Abd al Karim Obeid, who since 1983 was considered a key figure in the South Lebanon Hizballah.

Sheikh Karim Obeid was born in the village of Jibsheet in South Lebanon and was one of the followers of the Hizballah's spiritual leader Sheikh Muhammad Hussein Fadallah. In 1980, in the aftermath of the successful Islamic revolution in Iran (1979), Sheikh Obeid departed for the city of Qum in Iran (where Ayatollah Khomeini resided) in order to continue his Islamic studies in a religious seminary. While studying in Iran, Sheikh Obeid also underwent firearms and sabotage training, as well learning various terrorist attack methods. In 1982, after the War of the Galilee, he returned to his village Jibsheet in South Lebanon and was appointed an Imam.

Sheikh Obeid maintained his close ties with Iran and even compared the relationship between the Muslims in Lebanon and Iran to the relationship between Christians throughout the world and the Holy See at the Vatican.[78] During the period that he served as one of the Hizballah leaders in South Lebanon, Sheikh Obeid received funds from Iran. In 1986, he hosted the Iranian Ambassador to Damascus at that time, Ali Akbar Mukhtashemi Pur. The latter was one of the founders of the Hizballah and was in charge of Iran's ties with the organization.

Sheikh Obeid's interrogation in Israel indicated that he was involved in the planning, management and support of many terror events including:[79]

- The abduction of IDF soldiers Yosef Fink and Rahamim Alsheikh in February 1996.
- Multiple attacks against IDF forces in South Lebanon.
- The abduction of the American Lieutenant Colonel William Higgins and his transfer to Beirut, in addition to providing the abductors with a safe haven (his home in Jibsheet).

Sheikh Obeid stated that the plan for Higgins' abduction took shape in his house and that the Mercedes in which the victim had been abducted was kept hidden near his home for about a month. He claimed that two additional cars were used during the abduction, a Mercedes and a Volvo estate car. He divulged that he had turned Higgins over to Hizballah members in south Beirut.

The plan to abduct Obeid was prepared by the IDF and presented to and approved by the security cabinet. On Friday, July 28, 1989 at about 2:00 a.m., helicopters carrying members of the elite general headquarters' reconnaissance unit landed near Sheikh Obeid's village Jibsheet, seven kilometers from the security zone's border. The special force members stealthily made their way towards Obeid's home at the village's eastern end. Obeid was taken from the house together with another four Shiites who were in his company and they were transported to Israel by helicopter. The next day the State of Israel admitted that it was responsible for Sheikh Obeid's abduction.

The Sheikh's interrogation in Israel indicated that he lacked concrete information about Ron Arad. He believed that Ron Arad was still alive and was being transferred from place to place by his captors who maintained strict compartmentalization even *vis-à-vis* the organization's leaders. In the aftermath of Obeid's abduction by the IDF, Defense Minister Yitzchak Rabin proposed an exchange of prisoners:[80]

> Israel once again calls for the release of the Israeli POWs and the other hostages being held by Shiite organizations in Lebanon. Israel proposes an exchange of prisoners, detainees and hostages. According to this proposal, the Israelis and the foreign hostages being held by the Shiite organizations will be exchanged for all of the Shiite prisoners being held in Israel, including Sheikh Abd al Karim Obeid, Juad Katsfi and others.

The Israelis hoped that the abduction would elicit a positive response from the Hizballah regarding the prisoner swap. Instead, the Hizballah declared that "we will not negotiate with Israel. He who was abducted forcefully will be returned by force."

Iranian and Hizballah steps to release Sheikh Karim Obeid

In the aftermath of Sheikh Obeid's abduction, Iran and its sponsored organizations in Lebanon took various steps in order to release him. Among Iran's political and propaganda related moves was a statement made by the Iranian Foreign Minister Ali Akbar Waligat that "we condemn the abduction of Sheikh Obeid and ask the international community to exert pressure on the Zionist regime to release him." Iran also appealed to the UN, holding Israel responsible for Sheikh Obeid's well-being and safety.[81]

Iran and the Hizballah also threatened to attack Israeli and American targets in Lebanon and execute hostages if Sheikh Obeid was not released. In 1989, when Sheikh Obeid was abducted, his friend Ali Akbar

Muhtashemi-Pur was Iran's Minister of Interior. It therefore came as no surprise that Muhtashemi-Pur immediately placed himself at the head of the list of those demanding Sheikh Obeid's immediate release. Pur appealed to Muslim militia fighters in Lebanon to increase their attacks against Israeli and American targets in that country.

Pur also accused the United States of playing a role in Obeid's abduction.[82] He stated, "The American and Israeli criminals must be held responsible for any reaction of faithful Muslims." And he added: "As long as the regime that conquered Jerusalem is in control of Palestine, it is forbidden for Muslims to strip off their combat uniforms, and they must exact revenge from the United States and the Israeli criminals."

The Hizballah threatened to execute American citizen Lieutenant Colonel William Higgins if Sheikh Obeid was not released. The related manifest, which was published by "the Organization of the Oppressed on Earth" and titled "In the future it will be even worse,"[83] was distributed by the Associated Press representative in Beirut. The full text of the organization's manifest about Lieutenant Colonel Higgins' hanging is as follows:

In the name of merciful Allah

"As criminal America and the Zionist enemy did not take our decision seriously to execute the American spy Higgins, and due to the fact that Sheikh Obeid and his two brothers were not released on the designated date, out of disdain for our ultimatum, Higgins' life and everything that we hold holy, and out of a desire to carry out Allah's righteous will, the American spy Higgins was executed by hanging today, Monday afternoon. He will serve as an example and model for those who fear Judgment Day.

"We renew our demand that the virtuous Sheikh (Abd al Karim Obeid) and his two brothers be released immediately, otherwise it may be even worse in the future, and American and Israel will take full responsibility for this. Death for America and Israel, for those who are arrogant and their agents.

"Glory and immortality for our nation's heroes and righteous martyrs. We vow that we will continue our struggle along the path they outlined with their weapons and blood to uproot the Israeli cancer and to cut off the hands of the arrogant people who play in our land, particularly America, in order to magnify and glorify the Muslim faith and Muhammad's nation, until the banner of Muslim unity will wave proudly over the entire world."

The Organization of the Oppressed on Earth

The Hizballah also threatened to execute the hostage Joseph Cicippio.[84] A leader of the Hizballah in Lebanon, Hussein Mussawi, threatened: "We will execute one of the Israeli soldiers being held captive if it serves Islamic interests." And he added, "Even if all of the Hizballah leaders, including myself, are abducted, we will not negotiate with Israel." In actual fact, Iran and the Hizballah did not carry out their threats. The pictures showing

Higgins' hanging were fake – Higgins had been executed by his captors much earlier. In addition, hostage Joseph Cicippio was not murdered by his captors.

In contrast to the line of a threatening and hostile tone adopted by most of the Hizballah leaders, the organization's spiritual leader Sheikh Muhammad Hussein Fadallah stated the following in an interview at the Muslim radio station 'The Nation's Voice':[85]

> Let us agree and search together, each of us with his own means and influence, for the way to put an end to the crisis of the hostages, all of the hostages, and the ways to put an end to the question of Arab prisoners inside and out.
>
> "The issue will move toward a realistic solution, something that will take a good deal of time. But it will not be possible to push the issue forward due to the American activity.
>
> "The military activity will only exacerbate the danger to the hostages' well-being and increase the possibility that something that the Americans define as terror will happen. The deployment of the American navy constitutes preparations for a coordinated military operation between the United States and Israel.

Nevertheless, Iran and the Hizballah refused to participate in negotiations with Israel for the release of Ron Arad and the other POWs that the organization was holding (Fink and Alsheikh). During Nachshon Wachsman's abduction five years later (1994) another attempt was made by the Hizballah and Iran to bring about Sheikh Obeid's release, this time through an abduction perpetrated by the Hamas organization in the Palestinian arena.

The abduction of Mustafa Dirani [86]

Mustafa Dirani, who held Ron Arad prisoner, was marked as a candidate for abduction for a prolonged period. Israel believed that Dirani could effectively fill in the intelligence blanks regarding Ron Arad's fate.

Mustafa Dirani was a Shiite Muslim who served as Amal's security officer from the mid-1980s. In the framework of this role, in October 1986 he was responsible for the capture of Ron Arad. Following a process of religious radicalization which Dirani and some of his associates underwent, he and his followers left Amal at the beginning of 1988 and established a new organization called "the Faithful Resistance", which was affiliated with Iran and the Hizballah. For a year and a half Dirani held Ron Arad hostage and controlled his life until May 1988 when Dirani handed him over to Iranian factions and he disappeared without a trace.

Both in his role as Amal's security officer and as the leader of "the Faithful Resistance", Dirani was responsible for attacks against IDF forces in Lebanon.

Mutafa Dirani was caught on May 21, 1994 during an intricate military operation carried out by an IDF force that raided his home in the village of Kafar Kaser, whence he was transferred to Israel.

Documents confiscated in Dirani's home were also brought to Israel. Among the documents was a letter written by Dirani to the secretary general of the Hizballah, Sheikh Abas Musawi, in which he protested the fact that Ron Arad had been abducted from his possession without any kind of compensation. During his interrogation in Israel, Dirani claimed that Ron Arad had been kidnapped from him by the Iranians, and that he had not willingly handed the POW over or "sold" him.

In Israel the authorities believed that the letter was an "insurance document" that Dirani had prepared for a "rainy day" in order to shirk any responsibility for Ron Arad's fate. In any event, Dirani was interrogated thoroughly in Israel and divulged everything he knew up to the day that he handed Ron Arad over to the Hizballah and Iranians. The assumption was that Dirani would be able to provide up-to-date information about Ron Arad and that his abduction would help (together with the prior bargaining chip – Sheikh Karim Obeid) to convince the Hizballah and Iran to enter negotiations for the release of Ron Arad as well as other IDF POWs, but similar to the instance of Sheikh Obeid, the abduction failed to bring about the desired breakthrough.

Reciprocal links between Hamas abductions and Iranian/Hizballah abductions

Previous chapters discussed the reciprocal ties between Iran and the Hamas as well as other Palestinian organizations, which were reflected in financial, military and propaganda-related aid to these organizations. During the 1980s, the violent struggle *vis-à-vis* Israel was fought on two fronts simultaneously, the Lebanese front and the Palestinian front. As a result of the fighting in these two arenas and Israel's thwarting activities, hundreds and sometimes thousands of Lebanese and Palestinian prisoners involved in terror activity were incarcerated in Israel at various times. The release of these prisoners, particularly the more senior ones such as the head of the Hamas Sheikh Ahmad Yassin, constituted a main goal for the terror organizations.

The strategic Iranian concept which regards the struggle against Israel as a joint battle of the entire Muslim world – Shiite and Sunni alike – was also adopted by the Hizballah and the Palestinian organizations, which regarded the merging of the forces as a vital component capable of swaying the struggle against Israel. As a result of the adoption of this approach by terror entities in both the Lebanese and Palestinian arenas, operational cooperation developed which was reflected in the abduction-bargaining attacks perpetrated by the terror organizations. In exchange for the release of Israeli hostages, the Hizballah consistently demanded the release of prisoners from Palestinian terror organizations in addition to the release of their own imprisoned members, particularly the Palestinian Islamic Jihad and the Hamas.

A similar phenomenon is identifiable in the Palestinian organizations – during the abduction of Nachshon Wachsman, the Hamas demanded the release of Sheikh Obeid, Mustafa Dirani and twenty additional Hizballah prisoners.

A study of the abductions perpetrated by the Hizballah and the Hamas indicates that they involve a consistent and systematic policy regarding the demands to release prisoners from these organizations. An analysis of Nachshon Wachsman's abduction points to the possibility of Iranian and Hizballah involvement in guiding the Hamas in the perpetration so as to promote the joint interest of both organizations, i.e., to bring about the release of their prisoners. Moreover, Iran and the Hizballah, much like the Hamas, had a salient interest in hampering the political process between Israel and the Palestinian Authority via the abduction.

It is impossible to unequivocally prove that the Hizballah and Iran were involved in the abduction but the following facts support these claims:

- The "external" headquarters of the Hamas in Jordan, Lebanon and Syria were apparently partners in the planning of the abduction although they were not privy to the details. In various interviews with the media, senior Hamas members in Gaza claimed that the abduction had been perpetrated according to instructions issued by the organization's "external leadership" and they had no part in the kidnapping.
- Commanders and Hamas activists who had close links with Iran and the Hizballah, including some of those who were deported to Lebanon in 1992, were in charge of the abduction and its perpetration.
- Muhammad Def, military commander of the Hamas in Gaza who was behind Nachshon Wachsman's abduction, had close ties with Sheikh Az a Din Subhi Khalil in Damascus and personally visited Iran.[87]
- Salah a-Din Nur a-Din Rada Drawza, one of the commanders of Wachsman's abduction, was among those deported to Lebanon.[88]
- Salah Jadallah, son of the Imam Jadallah Jadallah (who was deported to Lebanon), was one of Wachsman's abductors.[89]
- Ahmad Jadallah, son of the Imam Jadallah Jadallah, was involved in the preparation of the video cassette of the abducted soldier.[90]
- The claiming of responsibility for the abduction and the presentation of the organizations' demands were announced both in Gaza

and in Lebanon as well as over the Al Quds radio broadcasted from Syria.

- In exchange for Wachsman's release, as top priority the Hamas demanded the release of Hamas leader Ahmad Yassin, the organization's military leader Salah Shehada, Sheikh Karim Obeid (Hizballah), and leader of the "Faithful Resistance's" Mustafa Dirani.

Clearly, the declaration of priorities in Hamas' demands attests to the extreme importance which the organization attributed to the release of Sheikh Obeid and Dirani, as well as its close ties to Iran and its obligation to promote that country's goals.

Israel's Policy Regarding Captives and Hostages

The matter of the release and/or return of the Israeli POWs, MIAs and hostages is one of the most sensitive issues faced by Israeli society and its leadership. The sensitivity in this regard stems from several main reasons including the value of human life and personal freedom in the eyes of Israeli society; the religious aspect, namely the obligation to redeem prisoners; the religious and moral importance attributed to returning the bodies of Israeli civilians and soldiers for Jewish burial; the state's moral obligation to preserve the life and safety of its citizens; and the obligation to protect IDF soldiers and members of the security forces who act on behalf of the State of Israel and fall captive into enemy hands.

In contrast to Jewish law, the commandment to redeem captives or bodies of the fallen is not a religious obligation in Islam. A study of the Koran and the "Hadith" (Islamic tradition) reveals that the only issue under discussion is that of a captive (prisoner) who falls into Muslim hands and his fate, and not a Muslim captive or his redemption. There is a dispute in the "Hadith" regarding how the captive should be treated, and two alternatives are raised – either accepting ransom money ("Fida'a") or executing the prisoner. As to the bodies of fallen Muslims in the enemy's hands, there is no religious obligation to bring them home.

Hassan Nasrallah addressed the issue of Lebanese bodies in Israel's hands several times, including the body of his son Hadi, stating that there was no obligation to return them to their families because they were buried in the holy earth of Palestine.[91] Thus, the Islamic terrorist organizations' interest in the issue of the captives and prisoners does not stem from religious doctrine but rather from practical (political, social and humanitarian) considerations. The difference between the religious and normative approaches held by Jewish/Israeli society as opposed to Muslim values imparts the Islamic terror organizations with significant bargaining space which they fully exploit. Over the years, Israel's policy in the matter of negotiations *vis-à-vis* terror organizations has reflected two polarized approaches – adamant refusal to succumb to terror as opposed to a more flexible policy.

As a rule, when Israel had the opportunity to release hostages or captives through a military operation without succumbing to the terrorists' demands, the decision makers preferred this alternative. In other cases, when a military operation was not an option, Israel generally demonstrated flexibility and endeavored to bring about the hostages' release via negotiations, meeting the terror organizations' demands either partially or fully.

By its very definition, the "flexible policy" was adapted to the negotiations and the price that Israel was willing to pay given the political, defense and social circumstances in Israel; to the type of terror organization that was partner to the negotiations; and to the quality of the bargaining chips in Israeli hands. Yitzchak Rabin, who served as Israel's Minister of Defense in 1989, shed light on Israeli policy *vis-à-vis* the handling of hostages in an interview following the abduction of Sheikh Karim Obeid. He stated[92]

> In the framework of the war on terror, and regarding the issue of Israeli hostages, Israel has chosen two courses of action: When there is the possibility of rescuing the prisoners through a military operation, we prefer this course. That is what we did in the Entebbe Operation. We have a special responsibility to IDF soldiers who were sent to war in Lebanon and are missing or fell into the hands of Shiite organizations. We are willing to negotiate for their return and exchange them for Shiites who were abducted for this purpose and are being held by us.

The Nachshon Wachsman affair is another example that reflects Israeli policy regarding the handling of the extrication of hostages being held by terrorists. At the weekly cabinet meeting held on October 16, 1994, Prime Minister Rabin, the Chief of Staff Ehud Barak and the acting head of the GSS reported on the IDF's operation to rescue Nachshon Wachsman.[93] Rabin and the Chief of Staff stated that they had believed that the rescue mission could work. They noted, "In operations of this kind, the gap between success and failure is hair-breadth." They added that "the soldiers had been phenomenal but they encountered technical obstacles – the house was fortified and the explosive devices failed to blast the entrance."

At the meeting all of the ministers justified the military operation. Some criticized Rabin, who had decided to launch the operation on his own, without convening the cabinet. In response to the arguments that he had approved the operation alone, he said that the circumstances were unique. A cabinet meeting had been held on Friday morning. "It is possible to prevent leaks about the meeting's content, but not about the meeting's existence. Reconvening the cabinet so soon after the first meeting might have compromised the operation,"[94] he stated. He added that he hadn't told the ministers that Wachsman was being held in the West Bank because this fact was verified only at 11:00 a.m.

Rabin explained the considerations that led him to the conclusion that "there was no other choice but to go for the military option." He noted that he had considered "the character of the people we were facing, keeping in mind that all of the previous abductions had ended in death. There was no true partner for negotiations, no possibility to make contact technically or essentially. No one could tell whether Arafat's proposal to exchange Wachsman for Sheikh Yassin was serious."

The Prime Minister added that it was unclear whether the demand document published by the Hamas on Thursday regarding the postponement of the ultimatum in exchange for the release of Sheikh Yassin and 40 female prisoners actually came from the abductors. He noted that his emissary, Yossi Genosar, was also unable to make contact with the abductors' representatives. "Time was running out and Wachsman's execution was almost certain – there was no other alternative." And he added, "Accepting their demands would have constituted the State of Israel's total capitulation – a terrible possibility which no government would even consider. And even this was not insurance that they wouldn't kill him because they had stated that they were willing to negotiate over a body too."

Foreign Minister Shimon Peres stated during the discussion:[95] "The Hamas not only attempted to abduct the soldier but also to kill the peace. The discontinuation of the peace process would be a reward for the Hamas." He called for the renewal of talks with the PLO and for Israel to call off the encirclement of the territories. The Foreign Minister expressed full support for the military operation and noted that previous operations to release hostages had not ended without casualties, whether these were among the rescuers or the hostages. He noted, "There was no option other than to take the decision to execute the mission and to carry it out."

Prime Minister Rabin praised the Palestinian Authority and its head, Yasser Arafat, and declared, "Their behavior was admirable. The moment we told them that the soldier was being held in Gaza they did their utmost, carried out searches and took a stand *vis-à-vis* the Hamas. We hope this will continue, but the future is an enigma."

An announcement was made at the end of the cabinet meeting as follows:[96]

The government received a full and detailed report about the IDF operation against the terror cell that abducted sergeant Nachshon Wacshman and the steps taken in this matter from the moment the abduction became a known fact until the end of the operation. The government sends its condolences to the Wachsman and Poraz families, and shares their deep mourning at the passing of their loved ones. It wishes the wounded a speedy recovery. The cabinet is united in its conviction that under the prevalent circumstances, there was no other choice but to initiate the military operation in an attempt to rescue the hostage.

Former Israeli prime minister Benjamin Netanyahu described his worldview in the matter of handling terror in general and abductions in particular in his book, *Terrorism: How the West can Win.*[97]

> The taking of hostages forces the government in charge of their welfare to face a difficult dilemma: If it prefers the use of force to release the hostages over capitulation there is the possibility that the number of casualties will rise. On the other hand, if you cave in to the terrorists' demands they will emerge victorious.
> Sometimes the terrorists themselves resolve this dilemma when they execute some of the hostages and threaten to kill the rest if their demands are not met. In some cases these demands are simply unacceptable and at other times, it is unclear whether the capitulation to their demands will not cause additional casualties. In this event, the government may argue that as the terrorists will undoubtedly kill additional hostages, it must take immediate action. But how should the government act if the terrorists have not begun to execute the hostages? In such circumstances, has the need for military action diminished? The answer is: no. Terrorists need to be under no illusion that a government would be willing to take determined action against the abductors, regardless of the fact that hostages have not been executed. The very act of abducting hostages justifies this policy. It is a grave error to allow the terrorists to think that in certain situations they are immune to a military operation. The terrorists' fear of a military operation serves as a significant deterrent *vis-à-vis* their actions, which causes a decrease in the number of abductions. This is clearly reflected in Israel's case. There is no other country that has suffered more from this type of attack.

Summary: Responding to the Challenges of Negotiation, Leverage, and Intelligence

The State of Israel was forced to respond to challenges in which Israeli captives or hostages were being held by terror organizations in two main scenarios: Israeli hostage/s that were held inside Israeli territory; Israeli captives or hostages that were held by the terror organization outside of Israeli territory. In a third scenario, the State of Israel was forced to deal with a situation where the terror organization was holding foreign hostages but demanded the release of prisoners incarcerated in Israel.

In scenarios where Israeli hostages were held by a terror organization inside Israeli territory, the State of Israel has consistently adopted a strategy of taking a firm stand. In some instances, such as the abduction of Nachshon Wachsman, the Israeli government expressed willingness to enter negotiations with the terror organization in order to release him, but when intelligence was received about his whereabouts, and it became operationally possible to bring about his release in a military offensive, Israel preferred this option.

Moreover, a study of the goal of Hamas abductions indicates that in most cases the hostage was murdered a short time after the abduction and that negotiations initiated by the organization began after the hostage was no longer alive. In the course of negotiations, the Hamas generally maintained a certain vagueness regarding the hostage's fate in order to force Israel to "pay a higher price" for his release due to the assumption that he was still alive.

In all of the incidents that captives or hostages were held by the Hizballah (as well as by other organizations such as Jibril's Front), the conditions prevented the possibility of conducting a military operation to release them. Israel was forced to negotiate, mostly through intermediaries, and to pay a price for their return.

Israel also tried to apply indirect military leverage in the Lebanese arena, by abducting "bargaining chips" designated to boost Israel's negotiating power and force the adversary to agree to prisoner exchanges. It subsequently became evident that the various abductions of "bargaining chips" failed to bring about any kind of breakthrough in negotiations *vis-à-vis* the adversary, but rather became a way to legitimatize additional abductions and attempted abductions by the Hizballah, who explained that the terror act was perpetrated in order to release the entities abducted by Israel.

Israel's capitulation to the Hizballah's demands in the framework of prisoner exchange negotiations did not stem from consent in principle to negotiate with a terror organization holding hostages but rather as a consequence of the circumstances.

It appears that during all of the years of conflict with the Hizballah and Palestinian terror organizations in the Lebanese arena, the State of Israel has been unable to develop intelligence capabilities that would meet the operational needs for the planning and conduction of a rescue mission. In cases where sufficient intelligence was gathered, unfavourable operational conditions prevented a military attack.

Thus, it is clear that in the case of abductions that took place inside Israeli territory, Israeli governments did not give in to the abductors' demands and whenever it was possible to carry out a military operation they chose to do so. In contrast, in every instance that Israeli hostages or captives were held by the Hizballah, the State of Israel was forced to enter negotiations with the organization and to release Palestinian, Lebanese and other prisoners in exchange for the release of the Israelis.

4

The Abduction of Foreign
Hostages in Lebanon

Imad Muraniya and the Attack Mechanism[1]

Imad Muraniya was born on July 12, 1962, in the village of Tir Daba in South Lebanon, some fifteen kilometers from Tyre. He is the eldest of three sons and a daughter. His father, who was a religious Shiite, died in 1979. He spent most of his childhood in Bir al-Abed – one of the disadvantaged sections of Beirut. His family was poor, but the Muraniya clan is considered to be of top lineage in Shiite society, and in the 1970s one of its leaders, Sheikh Muhammad Muraniya, was considered a "marja taklid", a senior religious title in the Shiite community.

In the late 1970s, after dropping out of high school, Muraniya joined the Fatah and underwent training in guerrilla warfare. He subsequently joined Force 17 – the Fatah's security unit – and was among Abu-Iyad's bodyguards. In 1982, during the Lebanon War, when the Fatah was about to evacuate Beirut, Muraniya decided to stay in Lebanon and joined the Islamic al-Dawa organization, and consequently became a member of its successor, the Hizballah.

In 1983, Muraniya married his cousin Sa'ada Bader a-Din, and the couple had two children – Fatma (August 1984) and Mustafa (January 1987). In contrast to other young leaders of the Hizballah such as Abas Musawi, Subhi Tufeili or Hassan Nasrallah, Muraniya had no religious or political authority: his activity focused in the operational area. Muraniya's first role in the Hizballah was to serve as the bodyguard of Sheikh Fadallah – the Hizballah's spiritual leader. Shortly afterwards he transferred to another job, but his brother Jihad inherited his place, so that Imad Muraniya continued to be responsible for Fadallah's security by "remote control".

In 1983 a decision was made by Iran and the Hizballah to take action to remove the American and French presence in Lebanon through the perpetration of terrorist attacks. Imad Muraniya volunteered to execute the attacks, while aspiring to boost his status within the Hizballah and in the eyes of his patrons in Teheran. Muraniya did indeed orchestrate the series of terror attacks against the US Embassy in Beirut and against the Marines headquarters and French forces in Beirut. Due to his "successes" he was appointed head of the "Special Security Agency" of the Hizballah, or to go by its other name – "the Islamic Jihad".

"The Special Security Agency" under Muraniya's command was responsible for a series of attacks in Kuwait against US and Kuwaiti targets. On December 12, 1983, his men detonated the US Embassy in Kuwait and attacked other targets, including a shopping center in Shueiba and the control tower at the Kuwaiti airport. Five people were killed in these attacks and eighty-six were injured. The Kuwaiti authorities arrested seventeen suspects and sentenced seven of them to death. One of the condemned men was Mustafa Bader a-Din, Muraniya's brother-in-law and friend; another was Hassan Musawi, cousin of the Hizballah's secretary-general, Abas Musawi, who was killed in a targeted attack by Israeli helicopters in 1992.

Imad Muraniya regarded the liberation of the accused as a central goal and used every means at his disposal to achieve their release. After the Kuwaiti royal family refused to release them, Muraniya initiated an assassination attempt against Emir Jaber a-Sabah, via a Shiite suicide attacker who detonated his car near a convoy in which the Emir was traveling in Kuwait City on May 25, 1985. Both of the Emir's bodyguards were killed but he emerged unscathed. Subsequently, Muraniya's people hijacked a Kuwaiti passenger plane (flight 211 from Dubai to Karachi), forced it to land in Teheran and killed two American government employees before turning themselves in to the Iranian authorities in exchange for political asylum.

Starting from the mid-1980s, Muraniya's agency was involved in the abduction of Western nationals in Beirut in order to apply pressure on Kuwait through these countries to release the condemned men, and for the purpose of achieving additional objectives *vis-à-vis* the Western countries according to the interests of the Hizballah and its patrons in Teheran. In June 1985, Muraniya was responsible for the hijacking of TWA flight 847 from Athens to Rome. The airplane landed in Beirut, and in the course of the hijacking an American soldier was killed onboard. On April 5, 1987, Muraniya's henchmen hijacked a Kuwaiti airplane on a flight from Bangkok to Kuwait and forced it to land in Mashad in north Iran. From Mashad the hijackers flew with their hostages to Larnaca, Cyprus, and the incident finally ended in Algeria where the hijackers reached an agreement with the authorities, released the aircraft and its passengers, and "disappeared".

As stated earlier, since the 1980s Muraniya has been behind most of the Hizballah's terror attacks against Western targets inside and outside of Lebanon. To this day there is no clear picture of the hierarchical structure and relationships of subordination of Muraniya and the agency that he heads, in relationship to the parent organization of the Hizballah and Iran. Within the Hizballah there is an entity that coordinates the attacks called "Shurat al-Jihad" which is comprised of two agencies: One is responsible for gathering information, and the second, the "Islamic Jihad", perpetrates the attacks. The agency headed by Imad Muraniya is part of the attack mechanism of the Hizballah, but due to Muraniya's status and importance, there exists a direct link with Iran. Therefore, there is a certain vagueness regarding the hierarchical subordination in "Muraniya's agency".

Muraniya constitutes an important target for intelligence services worldwide, particularly in Israel and in the US. The United States has placed him on the list of the twenty-two most wanted terrorists, alongside Osama Bin-Laden. Although over the years several opportunities have arisen to arrest him during his travels around the world under false identities, he has not been caught, and he continues to direct the terror activities of the Hizballah and Iran. (In 1988 he was almost arrested at Charles de Gaulle Airport in Paris, and in April 1995 he was almost caught during a stopover of the airplane in which he was traveling in Riyadh, Saudi Arabia.)

The Kidnapping of Foreign Nationals [2]

Hizballah and entities identified with the organization or associated with it have made extensive use (sometimes with Iranian guidance and at other times at the organization's initiative) of abducting foreign citizens (as well as local Jews) and holding them hostage. Between 1984 and 1989, ninety-six foreign citizens were kidnapped in Lebanon, most of whom were Americans and Frenchmen. About fifty-five of them were kidnapped by the Hizballah and entities linked with the organization.[3]

At the heart of these attacks against the West, including the abduction of foreigners, stood ideological hostility towards the United States and Israel, and towards any foreign presence in Lebanon. But there were also other motives, sometimes even stronger ones:[4]

- Obtaining a bargaining chip for the release of imprisoned Shiites worldwide. The most prominent targets of terror attacks for this purpose were the United States, Kuwait, France, Britain and Germany. Among the leading activists in this type of terror attack were relatives of the imprisoned Shiites abroad.

- The implementation of the Iranian terror policy, which believes in activating terror to achieve political goals (including as a means to place pressure on countries that supported Iraq during the Iran–Iraq war).

The first Western hostage to be abducted in Lebanon was the President of the American University in Beirut, David Dodge, who was abducted in Beirut in July 1984. From July 1984 and onwards the hostage-taking activity continued up until 1992. Some of the hostages were executed by their captors, others died from the lack of medical care and miserable conditions, and still others were released in exchange for the liberation of Hizballah prisoners, firearms supplied to Iran or ransom money. Some simply "disappeared" and their fate remains unknown. The abduction of foreign nationals in Lebanon stopped in 1989, apparently against the backdrop of the conclusion of the Iran–Iraq war and Iran's desire to improve its relations with the United States and other Western countries. The last of the hostages were released in 1991–1992 thanks to the intervention of a special UN envoy.

The abduction of foreign hostages in Lebanon as a political bargaining tool mainly characterizes the Shiite organizations in that country, although Palestinian organizations, such as Abu-Nidal's organization, made successful use of this tactic as well. Between 1982 and 1988, ninety-six foreign citizens of various nationalities were abducted in Lebanon, mainly citizens of Western countries, in sixty-seven different kidnapping incidents. The Hizballah was responsible for fifty-five kidnappings, Amal for eight, and the remainder was perpetrated by various organizations, some of which were probably Palestinian. The Hizballah, much like other terror organizations worldwide, justified the use of terror against the West by claiming that terror constitutes a self-protection measure against the greater power of imperialism. As an organization with a religious orientation, the Hizballah needed moral arguments to justify the abduction of innocent civilians according to Muslim religious law, because from the moral aspect there is a difference between terror attacks against Israeli, American or French military targets, which are defined as part of the struggle against foreign forces, and the abduction of hostages. The basic justification for abductions was generally the accusation that the hostages had been spying for a Western country.[5]

In any event, the issue of religious justification for abducting hostages remained controversial: radical leaders, like Hussein Musawi, supported the abductions while the Hizballah's spiritual leader, Sheikh Fadallah, publicly condemned them and claimed that they contradicted the spirit of Islam and are detrimental to the Muslim image. Nevertheless, Fadallah himself never took any steps to prevent the abductions, probably due to his fear of a confrontation with Khomeini and radical circles within the Hizballah.[6]

Hizballah turned the abduction of hostages (mainly of Western origins) into a central bargaining tool to achieve political and military goals set by the organization and its patrons in Iran. The organization's leaders knew how to exploit Western sensitivity regarding the welfare of its citizens as well as the fanfare of the media and public opinion in these countries in order to apply pressure on decision-makers in those states.

An example of shrewd exploitation and an attempt made by the Hizballah and Iran to influence the political system in a Western country in order to promote their interests is discernible during the presidential election campaign in France in 1987. President Mitterand declared that he was opposed to negotiating with the abductors of hostages, and that France would continue supplying weapons to Iraq despite the terror threats.[7] The response of the Hizballah abductors was dispatched to Jacques Chirac (who had been a resistance leader during World War II. The kidnappers demanded that Chirac publish an announcement expressing his concern regarding the President's declaration about terror within forty-eight hours. In addition, the message stated that if Chirac failed to do so, a French hostage would be executed. By preferring Chirac over Mitterand and by fanning the internal political struggle in France, the Hizballah kidnappers served Iranian interests, as the latter preferred to negotiate with Chirac rather than Mitterand.[8]

The Hizballah consistently denied any connection to the abduction of hostages, and instead placed the blame for the perpetuation of the problem and its complications upon the United States and the West, while calling for the release of all of the abducted Lebanese, Palestinians and Iranians incarcerated in Israeli prisons. On May 3, 1990, in response to an announcement made by the US administration, the organization claimed:

> The American attempt to blame the Hizballah in the matter of the foreign hostages and to conceal the real reasons for this problem will not prevail . . . It is the United States that supports the method of holding civilians in captivity by covering for the crimes perpetrated by the Zionists against the Palestinian people and supporting them . . . the Zionist entity was founded on the basis of kidnapping innocent civilians and massacring them, and it still adheres to this method. The kidnapping of Sheikh Obeid from his home is the most prominent example of this Zionist method, a method which is protected, supported and covered up by the American administration.[9]

These examples and others indicate that alongside the Hizballah's ideological–religious motives, the organization is also motivated by practical and rational considerations, and is equipped with full knowledge of the weaknesses and vulnerabilities of Western democracies. Recognition of the sensitivity of these regimes to the media and public opinion, familiarity with the various political entities in these countries and awareness of the crucial timing within internal political frameworks in various countries (elections, political crises and more) – all of these factors are shrewdly manipulated by the organization to increase its bargaining leverage and to derive propaganda-related benefits by maneuvering the "bargaining chip" of the hostages that it was holding.

The different approaches of various countries to the hostage issue, and how these states contended with the Shiite/Iranian entities in this matter, are detailed below.

The United States

The US approach to the hostage issue avers that under no circumstances should there be any surrender to the abductors' demands.[10] In actual practice, the administration was often forced to take into account the various power factors, which made it difficult to implement its declared policy, such as hostages' families who generated public pressure for their release, as well as the extensive influence of the media. At times, the public pressure was directed towards political channels by Resistance entities that criticized the administration's policies. For example, in June 1986, in contrast to the declared policy of the administration at that time, 247 congressmen sent a letter to President Assad in which they prevailed upon him to use his influence to liberate the American hostages.

In fact, during most of the hostage situations, the United States conducted secret negotiations with the kidnappers through Syrian, Iranian or Algerian mediators; the public pressure was harmful to these delicate contacts and made it difficult for the administration to take action.

One of the prominent examples of the use of hostage-taking was the seizure of the American Embassy in Teheran.[11] The Iranian regime evinced a basic ideological hostility towards the United States, "the Big Devil". The desire to strike out at the United States took on momentum due to the fear that the Americans would act to oust the Islamic regime which had only recently ascended to power (1979). The Shah's hospitalization in the US for medical treatment merely cemented the Iranian regime's fear that America posed an immediate threat to its existence.

In a speech that Khomeini delivered on November 1, 1979, he called on the public to increase its attacks against the United States and declared that November 4 – a memorial day for students who had been killed in demonstrations against the Shah a year earlier – was the most appropriate day to take action. That day, "students following the Imam's line" carried out Khomeini's instructions and seized American diplomats (defined as spies) at their embassy. The hostage incident at Teheran went on for 444 days, and exposed American weakness as well as the Islamic revolution's "triumph". This incident constituted a central milestone for the regime in Iran and encouraged it to make use of terror in the future as well.

- The seizure was ostensibly perpetrated by "students" (actually members of the Revolutionary Guards), but there is no doubt that the act was planned and perpetrated according to instructions issued by the authorities.
- The definition of the attackers as "students" motivated by ideological reasons supposedly absolved the Iranian regime of any responsibility for the incident, and enabled Iran to claim the neutral stance of an "intermediary" capable of "understanding the students' feelings" while aspiring to resolve the problem.
- During the incident, particularly in light of US responses including demands that the Iranian government put an end to the siege as well as the threat of American retribution, a gradual erosion took place in Iran's purportedly neutral stance until it was ultimately exposed to be identical to that of the perpetrators.
- The incident itself constituted a mortal blow to the most basic international "rules of the game" as it invalidated the immunity granted by international law to foreign embassies and diplomats.

In negotiations towards the end of the affair, official Iranian conditions were set to end it: The Shah's extradition; the return of Iranian funds frozen in the United States; cancellation of American monetary claims *vis-à-vis* Iran; an American promise to refrain from interfering in internal Iranian affairs in the future.

The American capitulation to some of the Iranian demands (the return of some of the funds and its promise not to get involved in the country's internal affairs) was perceived by the Iranian regime as an Iranian victory and as evidence that America could be "brought to its knees". It appears that this precedent is what encouraged the Iranians to make terror and hostage-taking key tools in the achievement of their political goals. The realization of the threat to seize embassies became a means that the Iranians wielded several times during crises with Western countries (although in actual fact incidents similar to the US Embassy siege never recurred).

Since the mid-1980s, Iran began to promote its interests by abducting Western hostages in Lebanon through the Hizballah. Four examples of US handling of incidents in which American hostages were held by the Hizballah are detailed below: The abduction of William Buckley; the "Irangate" Affair; the hijacking of TWA flight 847; and the abduction of Colonel Higgins.

The abduction of William Buckley

On March 16, 1984, William Buckley, head of the CIA branch in Beirut, was abducted by the Hizballah (the Islamic Jihad).[12] Buckley was held under dreadful conditions, including torture and withholding medical treatment. He died in captivity, apparently on June 3, 1985, as a result of the lack of medical treatment for his illness.

During his captivity, Buckley was interrogated by Iranian intelligence entities. According to the testimony of David Jacobsen, a hostage who was held together with Buckley and was subsequently released, the person in charge of the guards was an Iranian called "Ali". The United States spared no effort to bring about Buckley's release (see the "Irangate" Affair), but to no avail.

The "Irangate" Affair

A prominent example of American willingness to conduct covert negotiations for the release of hostages is the "Irangate" affair. At its center stood the issue of selling American arms to Iran through Israeli involvement in exchange for releasing the hostages.

There were two main reasons for America's participation in weapon shipments to Iran. First, the United States wanted to liberate seven American nationals who had been abducted in Beirut between March 7, 1984 and June 9, 1985. As stated earlier, one of the seven was William Buckley, head of the CIA branch in Beirut, who was abducted on March 16, 1984. Information discovered by American intelligence indicated that most, or perhaps even all of the captive Americans, were being held by Hizballah, which acted in cooperation with Iran.[13]

Secondly, the United States had a hidden interest in renewing relations with Iran due to its strategic importance and American fears of Soviet intervention in this country during "successor struggles" after Khomeini's death. (In actual fact Khomeini died only in 1989 and his successor was appointed without any crisis.) In secret talks via intermediaries between the United States and Iran an agreement was reached regarding the provision of combat means to Iran (which was in dire need due to the Iraq–Iran war) in exchange for the release of American hostages being held by the Hizballah in Lebanon.

According to the agreement, at the end of August 1985 and at the beginning of September of that year Iran received shipments of TOW anti-tank missiles and in exchange the Hizballah released American hostage Benjamin Weir on September 14, 1985. The United States waited for the release of additional hostages according to the bargain but this failed to take place.

On July 26, 1986 an additional hostage was freed in Lebanon, Lawrence Martin Jenco. The Islamic Jihad (a name for the Hizballah) published an announcement stating that this was an act of goodwill, but in actual fact it is known that on June 3–4, 1986, a short time before the captive's release, Iran had received an additional shipment of combat means. According to some sources – and this information was never verified – the release of the two hostages also involved the payment of an unknown amount in ransom money.

The final shipment of combat means reached Iran in October 1986, after which David Jacobsen was released on November 2, 1986. He was the third and final hostage to be released in the framework of the "weapons in exchange for hostages" deal. The United States concealed the details of the deal until its exposure as the "Irangate" Affair at the end of 1986. While the deal was being closed with the Iranians, a British Church envoy named Terry Waite acted in Lebanon as an intermediary for the release of the Western hostages. Initially, it was thought that the hostages were released thanks to Waite's efforts. Only later did it become clear that they had been released in the framework of the arms deals between the United States and Iran.[14]

Ostensibly, the arms deals with Iran, which had brought about the release of the hostages, were successful; but the findings of the inquiry committees discussing the matter (such as the Tower Committee) described this approach as an utter failure *vis-à-vis* basic policy and long-term American interests in the war on terror and international relations.

The Tower Committee pointed out that only three hostages were actually released although the basic purpose of the negotiations was to liberate all of the foreign hostages. It turned out that William Buckley, who constituted a central reason for the American consent to the deals, had been murdered a long time before the negotiations began for his release. Moreover, during September/October 1986, in the course of the negotiations between Iran and the United States, the Hizballah abducted three additional American nationals in Beirut – Frank Reed, Joseph Cicippio and Edward Tracey. These abductions ultimately demonstrated that submission to blackmail and the willingness to supply Iran with weaponry in exchange for the release of hostages were not the right way to handle this issue, even in the short term. Moreover, this approach had grave negative impact on the campaign that the West formulated against terror and states that support terror.

The Tower Committee stated:[15]

> The Iranian initiative contravened the American administration's policy regarding terror, the Iran–Iraq war and military aid for Iran. The committee believes that the inability to face these contradictions was the basis for the erroneous decisions that were made. No acceptable ongoing examination of the initiative was

made, nor was it studied properly by the sub-cabinet levels. No proper use was made of intelligence sources. Legal restrictions were not taken into account. The entire issue was discussed too informally, without leaving records regarding discussions and decisions.

Although the initiative was under the jurisdiction of the CIA, the State Department and the Defense Department, these entities did not intervene. The initiative depended on a private network of operators and intermediaries. The operation was not subjected to a serious discussion at any stage nor was there a periodical assessment of the initiative's process. The consequences were an unprofessional operation, lacking in satisfactory results.

The report continued:

The Iranian initiative was a covert operation which contradicted declared policy. But the initiative itself was made up of contradictions. Two goals were clear from the start – opening a strategic dialogue with Iran and freeing the hostages in Lebanon. It would appear that the sale of weapons to Iran provided a means to achieve these goals. The concept played into the hands of others who were moti-vated by different considerations, including profitable gain.

In actual fact, the selling of arms was not the appropriate means to achieve any one of these goals. Iran needed arms. The United States wanted to free the hostages. Thus, the arms deal in exchange for the hostages was the best way to achieve the goals of both sides. But if the US goal was more extensive, then the arms sale should have been postponed until after establishing strategic relations. The arms deal in exchange for hostages would have interfered with the achieve-ment of this goal.

In addition, the release of the hostages necessitated contact with elements in Iran that influence the Hizballah, which are the more radical elements in Iran. The opening of a strategic dialogue, as the United States desired, could only have been achieved with entities that appeared to be more moderate.

American officials that handled the affair had three different outlooks. For some, the main goal was to initiate a strategic dialogue with the Iranians. For others, the strategic dialogue was an excuse for the arms sale in order to release the hostages. There were still others that clearly viewed the affair as an arms deal in exchange for hostages.

The hijacking of TWA Flight 847 to Lebanon[16]

On June 14, 1985 four Shiite members of the Islamic Jihad (the Hizballah) hijacked TWA Flight 847 on a flight from Athens to Rome. Imad Muraniya stood at the head of the hijackers. The members of the cell that hijacked the plane belonged to a unit that dubbed itself "the Sader Brigades", after the Imam Mousa Sader, the Shiite leader from South Lebanon who had disappeared during a visit to Libya. There were 152 passengers and crew members on the plane, 139 of which were American. On June 18 the hijackers released most of the passengers in order to make it easier to control the hostages, but continued to hold 36 passengers and crew members. The hijackers demanded the release of 766 Shiites imprisoned in Israel in exchange for the passengers' release. In order to prove their determination they murdered an American passenger and dumped his body on the runway. But Israel refused to meet the hijackers' demands and the United States did not press Israel to give in. The hijacking was meant to test US President Reagan's declarations regarding the war on terror. During the months prior to the hijacking the president had made several references to the American intention to activate a policy of "determent, prevention and reprisal" against Iran. Now the time had come to "settle the debt." While constantly conferring with Amiram Nir, the Israeli prime minister's advisor on the war against terrorism, Colonel Oliver North planned a rescue operation for the airplane's passengers.

The counter-terror Delta Force was sent to Europe and the aircraft carrier *Nimitz* was stationed opposite the Lebanese coastline. But due to the fear of an American military rescue operation, the hijackers spread the hostages out in private homes in west Beirut and its suburbs, thus thwarting the mission. The timing of the hijacking had the power to disrupt Iranian efforts to obtain American weapons – directly or through Israel (see "Irangate" affair), therefore Iran apparently decided that it was preferrable to resolve the crisis. On June 24, 1986, in the middle of the crisis, the chairman of the Iranian parliament Hashemi Rafsanjani arrived in Damascus. At a press conference held in the Syrian capital, Rafsanjani denied his country's involvement in the hijacking and said, "If we had known the identity of the hijackers, we would have thwarted the hijacking." Rafsanjani met with Hizballah leaders in Damascus and "mediated" for the release of the passengers and crew.

The day after Rafsanjani's visit, on June 25, Syrian President Hafez Assad raised the equation that brought about the release of the TWA passengers. Assad proposed that Israel release Shiite prisoners from the Atlit prison, but in order to prevent it from looking like capitulation to terror the prisoners would not be released at the same time as the passengers but rather at a later date. Assad asked the United States if this concept was acceptable. The United States turned to Israel, which replied that as it was about to release some of the Shiite detainees in any case, it did not object to helping the US in this matter. Iran also accepted Assad's formula and instructed the Islamic Jihad (Hizballah) to accept it. On June 29 the hostages were taken by bus to Damascus and from there they were flown to Europe on a special flight. On July 3 Israel released 300 Shiite terrorists, thus meeting its obligation to the United States.

The Iranian involvement in the hijacking of the TWA aircraft confirmed assessments that the Iranian government stood behind terrorist acts in Lebanon and Europe. It would be reasonable to say that a very important by-product of the deal for the release of the TWA passengers was the exposure of evidence regarding Iran's involvement in terror abductions as well as its ability to control its sponsored organizations.

The abduction of Colonel William Higgins[17]

Colonel William Higgins served in the UNIFIL Force in southern Lebanon. On February 17, 1988 Colonel Higgins met with one of the commanders of the Shiite Amal organization in the city of Tyre. Quite ironically, the agenda of the meeting was to coordinate activities of UNIFIL and the south Lebanese militias during a hostage situation.

After finishing the meeting, Higgins called the UNIFIL headquarters, noted that his way back would pass through areas where armed Hizballah members were located, and asked that the headquarters keep track of his movements and maintain contact with him until his return. Colonel Higgins and his escorts traveled in a two-car convoy. Colonel Higgins was alone in the second car. During the drive, after one of the turns in the road, the driver of the first car noticed that Colonel Higgin's car was missing. He stopped, reversed and discovered Colonel Higgins' jeep standing empty at the side of the road.

Colonel Higgins' men in the first car immediately notified UNIFIL headquarters about his disappearance. An abduction alert was declared immediately. Roadblocks were set up and searches were conducted, but the efforts were futile. Five days later a group identifying itself as the "Oppressed on Earth" (a name the Hizballah had used in previous abductions) claimed responsibility for the abduction and aired a video cassette in which Colonel Higgins appeared with his abductors.

On April 21, 1988, the organization released a photograph of Colonel Higgins in captivity. This was the last message that his family received. From that time on his fate remains a mystery. During the ensuing months, the organization occasionally released announcements in which it threatened to bring him to trial for espionage or execute him. In 1988, the UN's peacekeeping forces in Lebanon were awarded the Nobel Prize for Peace and the UN General-Secretary took advantage of the opportunity to call for the Colonel's release, but to no avail.

In July 1989, when Colonel Higgins had already been held in captivity for 18 months, IDF forces abducted Sheikh Obeid, a Hizballah leader in southern Lebanon. Two days after the abduction, the Hizballah demanded the Sheikh's immediate release and threatened that if its demands were not met it would hang the Colonel. On July 31 when its demand was not met, the Hizballah aired a video cassette in which Colonel Higgins was seen hanging by his neck. The video cassette was transferred to CNN and broadcast all over the world. The United States was outraged by the cassette and started preparations for a military operation in Lebanon in order to prevent the execution of other hostages.

Two years later, in 1991, Colonel Higgins' body was returned and flown to the United States. A post-mortem clearly indicated that he had been killed by his captors before the production of the video cassette in which they had ostensibly hanged him.

US policy on terror and abductions

The United States' declared policy regarding its handling of terror in general, and the abduction of US citizens in particular was not to give in to the terrorists' blackmail. In the framework of this policy, the United States activated its covert agencies as well as special units in order to apprehend terrorists wanted by the US authorities, even those located outside US territory, with the aim of bringing them to justice there.

In this framework efforts were made to apprehend Imad Muraniya, whose name surfaced as the individual responsible for many of the abductions of hostages in Lebanon, but they met with no success. On the other hand, US intelligence agencies and special forces succeeded in apprehending another Shiite terrorist named Awaz Yunis, who had been involved in several abductions, and in bringing him to trial in the United States. In practice, the United States – much like other countries that fell victim to abductions – was forced to negotiate with the abductors, usually through a third-party mediator and to meet the abductors' demands either directly or indirectly.

France's policy on hostage-taking

France dealt with the hostage problem via two parallel channels: The first, through direct talks with Iran, the Hizballah's patron; and the other, through mediators *vis-à-vis* the Hizballah itself, with the help of Syria, Algeria and Saudi Arabia.

One of the mediators who acted in the service of France was Dr. Ra'ad, a French doctor of Lebanese origin who had maintained close contact with the Shiite community in Lebanon. In the course of 1985, Ra'ad made two trips to Lebanon and Syria in an attempt to liberate the four French hostages who had been kidnapped in March and November 1985, but his efforts were unsuccessful.[18]

In 1986, following the abduction of four members of a French TV crew in Lebanon, another mediator was sent to Damascus – a Syrian businessman named Amran Adham, in order to deal with their release. At the same time Prime Minster Jacques Chirac, who had just recently been elected, began to contend with the issue of the hostages through other emissaries including Dr. Ra'ad.

In June 1986, two of the kidnapped TV crewmembers were released. The French Prime Minister thanked Syria, Algeria and ironically enough – Iran – for their assistance in freeing the hostages.[19] Two weeks after the release of the hostages France expelled several hundred activists of the anti-Iranian underground Mujahidin Khalq, including the organization's leader Masoud Rajavi; this was France's form of payment to Iran for releasing the hostages.[20]

In November 1986, another French hostage was released in Lebanon, and this time as well the French Prime Minster thanked Syria, Algeria and Saudi Arabia for his release. A short time later France announced its intention to return part of the Iranian loan given to France during the Shah's reign, of about a billion dollars, while the French actually paid Iran a sum of approximately 330 million dollars. A short time after the transfer of the money to Iran another hostage was released.[21]

Through these actions, Iran not only succeeded in causing Iranian Resistance members to be deported from France but also regained the Iranian funds frozen in France since Khomeini's Revolution.

The release of the two remaining TV reporters on November 27, 1987 was also the result of the French capitulation to Iranian demands: France agreed to withdraw all of the charges against Wahid Gorgi, an Iranian terrorist involved in a terror network that had perpetrated a series of attacks in France in the course of 1986. Gorgi found asylum in the Iranian Embassy in Paris, and the French authorities surrounded the Embassy and demanded that he be turned over to them. The Iranians took similar action in Teheran: They accused the French Consul Paul Toure of espionage and placed a siege on the French Embassy. The French surrender in the matter of Gorgi put an end to the "Embassy War" between the two countries. France repeated its declaration regarding its intention to continue paying back the country's financial debts to Iran, and the third gesture towards Iran was the deportation of additional Iranian Resistance members from France. Some sources claimed that France had also agreed to supply Iran with spare military parts, but the French authorities denied this accusation emphatically.[22]

On May 4, 1988, the last French hostages were released, and subsequently, on June 16 the countries renewed diplomatic ties. France undertook to act for the release of Anis Nakash (the terrorist who had assassinated Shahfur Bakhtiar, the prime minister during the Shah's reign who was in exile in France), and agreed to pay the Hizballah a ransom of about 30 million dollars. There were several reports regarding the intention to reduce the scope of arms consignments to Iraq and renew weapon supplies to Iran via Syria. The release of Muhammad Mukhajar, a

Hizballah activist arrested in France a year earlier, was apparently also connected to the deal relating to the release of the hostages in Lebanon.

Regarding the deal between Iran, the Hizballah and France, it is interesting to quote Sheikh Fadallah, who stated in March 1986 that "their release was the outcome of the deal between France and Iran," and "only a similar deal between Iran and the United States may bring about the release of the US hostages."[23] The meaning to be derived from this declaration is that Iran is the entity that stood behind the Hizballah's activities, and it was Iran that could bring about the release of the hostages in exchange for achieving its political objectives.

In summary, it is obvious that France's repeated acquiescence to Iranian demands encouraged Iran and the Hizballah to activate terror against it until realizing of most of Iran's political, economic and military demands *vis-à-vis* France.

Britain's policy to kidnapping

For the most part, the British approach was refusal to submit to the kidnappers' demands or even to enter negotiations with terror organizations for the purpose of liberating hostages.[24]

The Hizballah was involved in a relatively small number of abductions of British citizens in Lebanon, and most were released within a relatively short time. An exception was the abduction of Church envoy Terry Waite, who was visiting Lebanon in a mediation attempt to release the hostages and was himself kidnapped in 1986. Britain refused to meet the ransom demands posed by the kidnappers and condemned France and Germany for their surrender to the kidnappers' demands in order to free their hostages. According to information which was never officially verified, it appears that in late 1987 Britain conducted talks with Iran in order to achieve Waite's release, but the discussions were discontinued when Britain refused to pay a ransom. Waite was finally released together with other Western hostages in 1991.

Switzerland's policy to kidnapping

Eric Werley, who was kidnapped by the Hizballah on January 3, 1985, was released in exchange for the release of a Hizballah member, Hussein Talaat. The latter was arrested at Zurich airport on November 18, 1984, in the possession of explosives designated for an attack against the US Embassy in Rome.[25] Additional abductions perpetrated in order to free the hijacker of the Air Africa airplane, Ali Muhammad Hariri, who is imprisoned in Switzerland, were to no avail. Subsequently, the kidnapped Swiss citizens were released during the years 1991 and 1992, in the framework of Iran and Hizballah's resolution to release all of the Western hostages.

Germany's policy on kidnapping

The first kidnappings of German citizens in Lebanon occurred in 1987. These kidnappings were connected to the arrest of two Shiite terrorists – the Hamadi brothers – in Germany. A few days after their arrest a German citizen was abducted in Lebanon, and several days later another one was abducted. As mentioned above, the objective of the abductors was the release of the Hamadi brothers. Shortly after the kidnappings, Germany appealed to Syria and Iran to help obtain the release of the hostages. The German Ambassador in Beirut even met with the Hizballah's spiritual leader, Sheikh Fadallah, in the knowledge that the latter had consistently opposed the kidnapping of foreign hostages. The dilemma faced by the German government was that on the one hand, the Americans were demanding the extradition of Muhammad Ali Hamadi on the charge of hijacking a TWA plane in 1985 and murdering an American passenger, while on the other hand, the abductors had declared that if Hamadi were extradited to the US the hostages would be executed. The German resolution was that Hamadi would not be extradited to the United States, but would be brought to trial in Germany and charged with hijacking and murder. On September 7, 1987, the Hizballah freed one of the hostages – Alfred Schmidt – and announced that his release was in exchange for the release of the Hamadi brothers in Germany.

Germany thanked Syria and Iran for their assistance in liberating the hostage but denied any kind of deal with the abductors. British sources claimed that Schmidt's release had been part of a deal according to which Muhammad Ali Hamadi would be sentenced to a short prison term after which he would be deported to Lebanon, while his brother would be liberated after serving an even shorter sentence.[26]

The second German hostage, Rudolph Kords, was also released shortly afterwards. There were reports in the press according to which Germany had paid the Hizballah three million dollars through the mediator Rashid Makrum, a German businessman of Lebanese origin. The German Siemens Company, which employed Kords, was also involved in the deal and it appears that the company closed the deal in Damascus with Syrian arbitration.[27]

On May 16, 1989, two German citizens were abducted in Lebanon – Heinrich Sturbig and Tomas Kamptner. No organization claimed responsibility for the kidnapping. On May 30 Hussein Musawi, one of the leaders of the Hizballah in Lebanon, was interviewed by the German *DPI* News Agency in Baal-Bek, Lebanon.[28] In the interview, Musawi stated,

"Germany has no conflict with anyone in Lebanon, not even with the Hamadi family. The government in Bonn agreed to release Hamadi in exchange for the two hostages Alfred Schmidt and Rudolph Kords." However, when this promise was rescinded, and Hamadi was sentenced to life imprisonment, the Hamadi family apparently carried out the abduction in a renewed attempt to achieve his release. In the early 1990s the German hostages were released along with the rest of the Western hostages.

Kuwait's policy on abductions

Many incidents of abductions of Western hostages were perpetrated in Lebanon in order to apply pressure on Kuwait to release seventeen Shiite terrorists who were incarcerated there, some of whom had been sentenced to death. Kuwait's unyielding policy not to give in to the abductors' demands under any circumstances stood firm during the entire period, despite the considerable pressures under which it was placed, probably due to the Kuwaitis' understanding that the abduction of hostages in Lebanon was only a single component of an overall and broader Iranian threat against Kuwaiti interests.[29] Fifteen terrorists were released by Iraq when it invaded Kuwait in August 1990 and were transferred to Iran.

The end of the Western hostages affair in Lebanon

During the series of hostage abductions in Lebanon, at least eight of the hostages were executed by their captors, but most were released over the years following negotiations that the countries conducted with Shiite terror organizations in Lebanon and with Iran. The hostage abduction affair finally ended with the release of the last of the Western hostages in December 1991, apparently due to Iran's desire to improve its ties with the West. As Iran was the one to create the problem, it also had the key to its resolution.[30]

Benjamin Netanyahu eloquently summarized the principles connected to this phenomenon in his book.[31]

> The roots of the problem of international terror lie in the involvement of hostile governments. Similarly, the roots of the solution lie in the counter-actions of the governments under attack. Terror countries are influenced by a sober calculation of profit and loss, no less than the terrorists. They rely on the terrorists to attack their opponents without having to take the risks involved in overt warfare. As long as they succeed in denying their involvement, they find it easy to evade punishment. But when their support of terror is exposed to everyone, in a way that the victims can no longer pretend to believe their denials, the rules of the game will change dramatically.

Over the years, the Hizballah attempted to form a linkage between the liberation of Lebanese/Hizballah detainees in Israel and the release of the Western hostages. The Hizballah claimed that Israel's refusal to release the Lebanese detainees was the main reason for the prolonged suffering of the Western hostages. .

The Links between Abductions of Foreign Hostages and Israel

The incident	Demands of Israel	Result
Hijacking of the TWA airplane by Hizballah (June 17, 1988).	A demand to release Shiite prisoners in Israel.	• Hostages released on June 19, 1986. • Israel responded positively to an American request to release Shiite prisoners in exchange for the Western hostages, July 3, 1986.
Abduction of seven Americans, including the head of the CIA branch William Buckley, and their captivity under the Hizballah, 1984–1985.	The supply of combat means to Iran in exchange for the release of Western hostages.	• August 1985 – November 1986, three Western hostages were released. • Several arms shipments delivered to Iran. • Contacts severed and sharply criticized in the United States (the Tower Committee).
Abduction of Sheikh Karim Obeid by Israel, July 28, 1989.	The Hizballah demands the release of Sheikh Obeid and threatens that if he is not released Colonel Higgins will be executed.	• Sheikh Obeid was not released. • The Hizballah "staged" the execution of Colonel Higgins (in actual fact he had been killed much earlier by his captors).

A study of the examples presented in the above table, discussed in depth earlier, indicates that at least in several instances Iran and the Hizballah succeeded in achieving their goals *vis-à-vis* Israel by leveraging Western (particularly US) pressure. Processes that took place on the global and regional levels (the collapse of the Soviet Union and the Gulf War of 1991), as well as adjustments in the Lebanese power balance, triggered changes in the priorities of each of the parties involved in the issue of hostages and captives: Iran, Syria and the Hizballah.

The recognition that prolonging the matter would turn it into a burden rather than an asset is what finally triggered a breakthrough and the beginning of negotiations for the release of the Western hostages through the intercession of the UN General Secretary in August 1991.[32]

From the Iranian aspect, the end of the Iran–Iraq war in the summer of

1988 and Khomeini's death in June 1989 paved the way towards greater openness regarding the West, with the aim of rehabilitating the country's economy. In the new reality of dialogue between Iran and the West, the issue of the hostages in Lebanon became an obstacle in the path of renewed economic links and full diplomatic ties with some Western countries. Iranian President Rafsanjani took vigourous action to promote Iranian ties with the West and in this framework aspired to resolve the hostage crisis. The Iranian willingness to end the hostage crisis grew in the wake of the Iraqi invasion of Kuwait on August 2, 1990, based on the claim that the hostages had "lost their value".[33]

At the same time, Damascus expressed a growing interest in ending the affair. For years Syria had played a central role in the matter of the Western hostages: As part of its political and military influence in Lebanon, Syria indirectly encouraged the continued existence and activity of the Hizballah, the organization responsible for the abductions; but Syria presented itself as the entity that brought about the release of the hostages for purposes of world public opinion. From the Syrian point of view, the liberation of the hostages could also serve as a means to demonstrate that country's ability to control Lebanon.[34]

The Iraqi invasion of Kuwait in August 1990 cancelled out an additional reason for holding on to the hostages: The invasion brought about the release of 15 Shiite terrorists incarcerated in Kuwaiti prisons for perpetrating terror attacks against Western and local targets in December 1983. Since their arrest, the Hizballah had acted to liberate them, among other ways through the abduction of Western hostages.

After the invasion, the 15 terrorists were transferred to Iran as part of Saddam's efforts to obtain Iranian support against the Western Coalition, and from that time on no longer constituted a stumbling block on the path to releasing the Western hostages.[35]

After the Gulf War (1991) many Arab states joined the peace process with Israel, which began with the Madrid Conference. However, Iran opposed the process and became the leader of the remaining hardline states. As a result of the Iranian hostile attitude, the Hizballah refused to negotiate with Israel.

During the negotiation process for the release of the Western hostages, talks began for the release of the IDF POWs under the UN's auspices. Western governments called on Israel to accelerate the process by making the gesture of releasing Lebanese prisoners even without a reciprocal release of the IDF prisoners. But by spring 1993, the bodies of Yosef Fink and Rahamim Alsheikh still had not been returned. In addition, there was no new information regarding Ron Arad or the three IDF MIAs from the first war in Lebanon (1982): Zecharya Baumel, Yehuda Katz and Zvi Feldman. Israeli hopes that the end of the Western hostages affair would also trigger a resolution of the IDF prisoners problem were dashed. The MIA issue was partially resolved only later, following negotiations that took place between the Hizballah and Israel.

5
Abductions in the Iraqi Arena

Hostage-Taking and Decapitations, 2003–2005

In the framework of the ongoing conflict between the Coalition forces and terror/guerilla organizations in Iraq, the phenomeon of abducting local and foreign hostages has become prominent. Some of these abductions end with the decapitation of the hostages in front of a video camera. The video cassettes are subsequently distributed to the media worldwide.

It would appear that the abduction of hostages, negotiations for their release and the occasional execution if the captors' demands are not met, do not constitute a new phenomenon – the current innovation lies in the continuous media coverage on television which broadcasts the "drama" to the homes of millions of viewers up to its horrendous climax, thus intensifying the psychological effect that the terrorists strive to achieve. Over 200 foreign nationals have been abducted since the US-led Coalition invaded Iraq in 2003. Although over 35 Western hostages were executed, most of the hostages were released by their captors.[1] Due to the unstable security situation, many of the foreign nationals working or serving in Iraq live in the "Green Zone," a complex of residential buildings and services on the bank of the Euphrates River in Baghdad which is secured by US military forces. As of August 2005, 40 hostages from 25 different countries were being held by various terror organizations in Iraq. Shiite and Sunni Islamic terror organizations as well as criminal gangs have turned the issue of hostage abductions in Iraq into a "thriving industry". Dr. Mustafa Alani of a Dubai research center claims that some ten Iraqi citizens are abducted daily for criminal reasons.[2] Most of the victims are middle-class professionals whose families are forced to pay a ransom for their release. Dr. Alani points out that children from middle-class homes constitute relatively easy prey for the abductors.[3]

Most of the victims are Iraqi citizens but foreign nationals have also become a "popular item" in the Iraqi "abduction industry". There are strong links between local criminal elements and terror organizations in the Iraqi arena. When criminal elements succeed in abducting foreign nationals they sometimes "sell" them to Islamic terror organizations.

While the local criminal gangs deal in the abduction of local and foreign residents in order to extort as much ransom money as possible, the Islamic terror organizations in the Iraqi arena make political stipulations in addition to demanding the ransom money. For example:

- The removal of military forces or presence of humanitarian and/or economic organizations of the country whose citizens are being held captive.
- The release of prisoners.
- Political statements condemning the invasion and the Coalition's presence in Iraq.
- A combination of several of the above-mentioned demands.

In many cases, the hostages are tortured by the captors and/or executed, sometimes during a horrifying and well-documented decapitation ceremony. Local terror organizations as well as entities affiliated with the global Jihad and Al Qaida are active in Iraq. The most prominent terror organization *vis-à-vis* the abduction and decapitation of foreign nationals was the entity run by Abu Musab Zarqawi (the most senior Al Qaida commander in the Iraqi arena until he was killed by US forces in 2006). Zarqawi's men acted under the name "Tawahid al Jihad" (The Union of Jihad) until he was appointed the Al Qaida commander in Iraq.

Other organizations that have claimed responsibility for the abductions of foreign nationals are: The Ansar al Sunna Organization; the Mahdi Army under the command of Muktada Sader (a Shiite militia); the Islamic Army, the Khaled Bin al Walid Brigade; the National Movement for the Land of the Two Rivers; the Islamic Army of Iraq; the Abu Baker al Sidik Brigade; the Green Brigades; and the Black Flags

As a rule, it is accurate to state that a Muslim hostage has a better chance of surviving an abduction and being released than a foreign national, but this statement must be qualified: citizens of Muslim states that are identified with the Coalition are sometimes vulnerable to harm no less than the nationals of Western countries. Among the citizens of Muslim countries who were murdered are Turkish, Egyptian and Jordanian nationals.

Sometimes the victims of the abduction/decapitation incidents who are chosen as targets by the terror organizations are specific foreigners. At times the terror organizations abduct relatively large groups of victims. The largest group of foreign hostages abducted by a terror organization in Iraq was a group of 12 workers from Nepal (August 31, 2004). A video cassette distributed by the abductors showed the decapitation of one of the hostages as well as the bodies of the remaining 11 hostages who were executed by a gunfire shot in the head.[4]

The largest abduction/decapitation attack took place in the Al Kaim area in western Iraq (March 9, 2005). The bodies of 26 people (one of them a woman) were found in Al Kaim, some 500 kilometers west of Baghdad. A hospital to which the bodies were taken announced that the victims had been shot two days earlier. Another 15 bodies, some bullet-riddled and others decapitated, were found in the "death triangle" south of Baghdad, an area under Sunni control. This massacre of 41 people carried the "signature of the rebels" – a gunshot in the neck or decapitation. This modus operandi was mainly the characteristic of Abu Musab al Zarqawi.[5]

The city of Faluja served as a central focal point for the activity of Zarqawi and in the course of an extensive operation conducted by the American forces in the city and its surroundings, several buildings were found where the hostages had been held by the organization.

Faluja as a center for holding hostages[6]

Following the American takeover of the city of Faluja (November 2004), which for months had served as a major focal point for Islamic terror activity in Iraq, an infrastructure that served for holding hostages in captivity was also exposed there. At one house, the US Army showed reporters a black banner bearing a yellow sun and the words "Tawahid al Jihad" (The Union of Jihad), the name of the organization run by the senior Al Qaida commander Abu Musab a-Zarqawi.

This banner was familiar because it appears in many of the video cassettes of hostages' decapitations in Iraq. In another house, the US Army showed the media a wire cage for holding hostages. Both houses were opened to the press after all objects belonging to the Iraqi rebels were removed. The US Army presented the latter in a detailed photo album: handcuffs, propaganda material, and bloody javelins and knives.

According to American sources, Faluja was one of the main bases where hostages were held by the rebel forces. One of the Iraqi informers that helped the US forces find the houses claimed that he had been held captive himself; he stated that during his incarceration he heard the voices of at least three other hostages who were held in nearby rooms. He believes that one of them was the British engineer Kenneth Bigley, who was later decapitated.

American officers stated that during the takeover of the city almost 20 sites were discovered where atrocities had been committed against the hostages. Two houses displayed by the army reflected the most detailed picture to date of the lives of the abducted hostages. The American officers noted that the hostages had been held in two rooms located in one of these houses. Many legcuffs and handcuffs were found, which were used to shackle the hostages. In one of the rooms there were manacles attached to metal rods which apparently served as neck shackles. Black masks and black tennis shoes generally worn by the rebels were found at the site. US forces found a small room in the basement where the hostages were apparently interrogated and tortured. The cage found in the other house, which was made out of metal and barbed wire, could just barely accommodate a human being; it was 2.1 meters high, two meters wide and about one meter deep, leaving the hostage very little space for movement.

The Coalition countries' approach to the hostage issue in Iraq

As noted earlier, the citizens of 25 different countries have fallen victim to abductions in Iraq. Some of these countries are part of the US-led Coalition; a number of them maintain military forces in Iraq, while others contribute to that country's rehabilitation. These countries did not advocate a uniform policy when their citizens were abducted in Iraq. Their responses can be depicted on a scale: at one end of the spectrum are the United States and Britain, which refuse to negotiate with the terrorists; in the middle are countries that negotiate with the terrorists generally through a middleman; and at the other extreme are countries that capitulated almost immediately to the terrorists' demands.

The countries' response to the terrorists' demands was significantly influenced by the nature of the demand. When the terrorists' demands were for a ransom, which could be met secretly without any damage to the country's image, the response was more expedient than when the demand stipulated that military forces must be withdrawn or that the country's nationals be removed from Iraq.

Examples of abductions and countries' responses are detailed below:

- On September 16, 2004, two American citizens were abducted, Eugene Armstrong and Jack Hensley, along with a British national named Kenneth Bigley. The three were abducted by al Zarqawi's men. The United States and Britain adhered to their policy not to negotiate with the terrorists, as expressed by the spokesman of the US Administration in Iraq, Dan Snor: "The United States will not negotiate with terrorists holding the hostages. The FBI and CIA, as well as the Coalition Forces and Iraqi security agencies, are acting to locate the captors and their captives in Iraq." The two Americans and the British hostage were executed in a gruesome decapitation "ceremony" documented on video tape.
- On July 20, 2004, a Philippine truck driver named Angelo de Cruz was abducted by a terror organization in Iraq. The abductors demanded that the Philippine military force withdraw from Iraq.

The Philippine government, which maintained a force of 51 soldiers in Iraq who were to complete their tour of duty in August 2004 in any case, agreed to the abductors' demands and brought forward their departure to July 16, 2004. The Philippine captive was released.

- On August 20, 2004, two French journalists were abducted on their way to the city of Najaf in Iraq. France is not a member of the Coalition and opposed the war in Iraq. Following negotiations that France conducted through various intermediaries with the abductors, the two journalists were released on December 22. The French government denied that it had paid a ransom for their release.

- A "complex" affair, which attests to the considerable sensitivity prevailing among the Coalition countries *vis-à-vis* the issue of abductions and the liberation of hostages in Iraq, is reflected in the abduction and release of the Italian journalist Juliana Zagarna who was kidnapped on February 4, 2005, in Baghdad.[7] In a video cassette distributed by the abductors, they demanded the withdrawal of Italian forces from Iraq (some 3,000 Italian soldiers were serving in Iraq at that time). They threatened to execute the journalist if their demands were not met.

La Republica reported that several weeks after the abduction, the Coalition Forces in Iraq believed that they had located the place where Zagarna was being held. They proposed to Rome that an attempt be made to liberate her in a military operation by elite units with a "75% chance that no harm would come to the hostage." The Italians felt that the risk was too great and the operation was shelved. At this point, so the newspaper claimed, the negotiations for ransom money were entering the final stage. An Italian intelligence agent named Nicola Kalipari agreed to meet the terrorists unaccompanied and without a GPS tracker in a rented car at a predetermined site. He also promised to refrain from contact with the Americans. Once the ransom money had been handed over, the hostage was released and Kalipari rushed to Baghdad Airport in an attempt to evade the Americans and prevent the hostage's interrogation by the latter and the Iraqis.

While the agent was driving with the released captive to the airport, he circumvented an American roadblock. US forces opened fire, killing Kalipari.

According to the newspaper, the Italian Foreign Minister also did not deny that a ransom was paid for the journalist's release. In a reply to a question in this matter he stated: "We adopted diplomatic and political directions as well as the aid of the secret services."

The American military headquarters in Baghdad announced that it had invited official Italian entities to join a high-ranking investigation of the incident. *La Republica* called for a public debate in Italy to discuss whether ransom should be paid to terrorists. It further demanded a public discussion as to whether this type of procedure wouldn't expose its citizens to further abductions and whether the state could undertake the financial burden of paying out ransoms, which it believed could reach $15 million for one person.

• On the night of July 2, 2005, the designated Egyptian Ambassador Ihab a-Sharif, who was serving as acting ambassador to Iraq,[8] was abducted near his home in Baghdad. Previously, the emissary had served as the acting Egyptian Ambassador to Israel since September 2000. He was abducted shortly after the announcement that the Egyptian Foreign Ministry was planning to upgrade his status to official ambassador. If a-Sharif had been appointed, he would have been the first Arab ambassador in Iraq following the ascent of the Iraqi government after the toppling of Sadam's regime.

A-Sharif was abducted when he went out to buy a newspaper. According to eyewitnesses, as he started back towards his home, armed men grabbed him and pushed him into a vehicle. The abduction was part of the opposition's struggle against the Iraqi government to prevent the granting of international, and particularly Arab, legitimacy for Ibrahim al-Ja'afri's government. The rebels had already declared in the past that they would take determined action against the presence and activity of Arab diplomats in Iraq due to the fact that through this activity Arab governments bestow legitimacy upon the Iraqi government, which according to the terrorists is sponsored by the United States and obeys American orders.

Several days after the emissary's abduction, Zarqawi's organization claimed responsibility for his abduction and execution (the announcement claiming responsibility is detailed in Appendix 5).

Abductions/decapitations and the media

Terror organizations in Iraq make extensive use of the media, television and the Internet in order to intensify the impact of the abductions and occasional decapitation of their victims. Most of the abductions perpetrated by Islamic terror organizations are accompanied by video cassettes that are dispatched to the media and distributed worldwide.

Three "scenario" stages are discernible in the majority of the abductions:

• The distribution of a video cassette of the hostage in the hands of the captors, who present their demands in exchange for the hostage's release.

- If the captors' demands are not met, an additional video cassette is distributed of the hostage pleading for his life and appealing to his country to act on his behalf.
- If the captors' demands are not met, the abduction sometimes draws to a tragic end with the hostage's execution at the hands of his captors, at times by decapitation.

Most of the state media refrain from airing the horrific filming of the execution or else choose to broadcast censured sections of the incident, but the Internet enables uncontrolled distribution of these cassettes. Jihad websites serve as the main channel for the distribution of these video cassettes, but Western websites also make use of these tapes.

According to an article published in Asharq al Awsat, research indicates that the Internet is one of the most influential factors in connection to the recruitment of young men for the Jihad movement.[9]

In an article in *Ha'aretz*, Shahar Samoha describes the problematic handling of the issue of abductions by Western websites:[10] "South Korean citizen Kim Il Sun was abducted in Iraq. The kidnappers delivered an ultimatum to the South Korean government to withdraw its forces from Iraq, or else Kim Il Sun would be executed. The ultimatum appeared on several Western websites. The South Korean government refused to respond to the kidnappers' demands and Kim Sun-Il was executed. His decapitation was documented on a home video."

The horrific video clip was uploaded onto several websites identified with the Al Qaida terror network. Shortly afterwards two versions of the clip also appeared on various Western websites that presented both versions – the first of Kim's heartrending pleas, and the second featuring the brutal murder. Thus, Al Qaida's psychological assault was accomplished, and the clip's real target audience – Western citizens who could not access it on the Arabic websites – joined the terror "theater". It is clear that the Internet provides terror organizations like Zarqawi's with a free and significant platform, thus intensifying the psychological impact of the struggle that the Islamic terror organizations are fighting against the Coalition states.

The Islamic Tradition of Decapitation

Decapitation is not a new phenomenon in Islamic culture. It has been a part of Islam since the latter spread throughout the Arabian Peninsula, during the Islam's "Golden Age" in the Middle Ages, and from the time of the Spanish conquest to date.

The amputation of limbs – including decapitation – as a death sentence is part of the Islamic penal arsenal. The punishment of amputating limbs is still applied in Saudi Arabia. According to an Amnesty International report, up to 2003 (over a period of twenty years), 1100 people were executed by decapitation in Saudi Arabia. In 2003 alone, 52 people were decapitated there (based on the verdicts of Saudi Arabian courts).[11]

The Koran specifically refers to decapitation, and Al Qaida and its supporters exploit this fact to justify the decapitation of Jews, other infidels and people who have betrayed Islam. The Koran describes an incident whereby a tribe of Jews that signed a pact with the Prophet Muhammad reneged on the agreement and joined Muhammad's enemies. When the Jewish tribe had been routed, Muhammad instructed his followers to decapitate the 600 male members of the tribe and sell the women and children into slavery. Radical Islamic entities (Mujahidin) decapitated their captives during the conflicts in Afghanistan, the Balkans, Chechnya, Algeria and elsewhere. In Bosnia, for example, a video cassette documenting the decapitation of Serb captives was distributed in the thousands among the Muslim population in the Balkans and radical Islamic followers worldwide.[12]

The first victim of an abduction/decapitation was the journalist Daniel Pearl who was abducted by a radical Islamic organization in Pakistan in 2002 and decapitated by his captors.

Justification through Religious Doctrine[13]

On November 18, 2004, a two-day conference of the Trustee Council of the International Federation of the Muslim Ulama (religious scholars) was held in Beirut. The federation had been established in July 2004 in London. At the end of the conference, a document was published bearing the signatures of the Federation's director, Sheikh Dr. Yusuf al-Qardawi and its secretary-general Sheikh Dr. Muhammad Salim al-Awa. The declaration, which appeared on a website close to Sheikh al-Qardawi, stated that the resistance in Iraq against the Coalition forces is the personal obligation of anyone who can undertake it, whether or not they are Iraqi residents.

The declaration opened with a theological introduction regarding the behavior of Muslims during war. It stated:

> The International Federation of the Muslim Ulama (believes) that in light of the situation prevailing in the world in general and among Muslims in particular, it must bind the (believers) of the monotheistic religion (Islam) to several moral and religious principles regarding how Muslims should behave, and to clarify to people the rules of behavior among Muslims and between Muslims and those who are not Muslim . . .

It is forbidden to attack those who are not fighting even if they are part of the aggressive countries. The human soul is holy and an attack against it can be likened to an assault against all of humanity. (As it says in the Koran 5.32), 'He who kills one soul which is not weighed against another, or not due to the dissemination of corruption in the land, it is as if he killed all of the people.' The Prophet Muhammad banned the killing of women and children, stating 'do not kill a child,' and added, 'do not kill progeny and workers with ease,' meaning all those hired to carry out services who are not connected to the fighting. Also, Islam forbids the murder of hostages and monks that dedicate themselves to God. It does not permit the taking into captivity of those who are not involved in the combat. If those who are not involved in combat are taken prisoner, Allah instructed Muhammad his emissary to treat them well (as stated in the Koran 76.8): 'Out of their love (for Allah) they feed the poor, orphans and prisoners,' (so says Muhammad) 'treat prisoners compassionately'.

It is forbidden to hold hostages and threaten the lives of those who are not in combat due to actions that others took or did not take. The hostages are not responsible for this action and could not prevent it. Allah said: 'One soul will not carry the burden of another soul,' (Koran 6. 164) and the Prophet (Muhammad) says, 'a criminal will be punished only for his own deeds'.

Following the theological introduction regarding the proper religious behavior of Muslims during wartime, the manifest of the International Federation of the Muslim Ulama moves on to discuss developments in the world in general and the fighting in Iraq in particular. As noted earlier, the statement declares that the resistance in Iraq is a (personal) religious obligation and that this is a Jihad of self-defense. The statement attempted to create the impression that it distinguishes between fighters and civilians who must not be hurt. But in actual fact, the statement diminished the definition of "civilian" when it explained who is included in this term – "women, children and the elderly". This definition omits men but from the declaration it is clear that only those "who do not take part in hostilities, especially men who deal in humanitarian or communications activity, are protected." Anyone who does not meet this category is to be considered an enemy and therefore harming him is permissible. On November 19, 2004, a day after the publication of the manifest, al-Qardawi honed the differentiation between fighters and civilians, stating that foreign engineeers, laborers or technicians working in Iraq are not considered protected civilians and are therefore fair prey: In an interview with Al Jazeera, al-Qardawi stated: "I have banned killing Americans. When asked a question in this matter I said that it is forbidden to kill civilians. I explained that it is permissible to kill only those involved in the fighting. Islam forbids the killing of women and children, etc. I have stated this openly but at the same time I posed the question, 'who is a civilian?' Are engineers, laborers and technicians coming into Iraq with the American army considered civilians? Is a fighter only someone in a tank or is it also someone who provides services to the army? I refer to the interpretation of the word civilian. If it is clear that someone is a civilian then it is forbidden to kill him. We, at the Federation of the Muslim Ulama, published a manifest yesterday stating that the resistance in Iraq must adhere to the Laws of the Sharia: It is forbidden to kill a civilian, only a fighter."

The manifest stated:

"The International Federation of the Muslim Ulama cannot stand by and watch the oppression and aggression against the weak taking place all over the world as well as the massacres that occur time and again, particularly in Muslim countries. (These things happen) in order to ignite the fire of the destructive wars for no reason other than to sate the avaricious appetite of the minority that profits from these wars, lethal arm dealers, and others whose interests link them to war and agitation. Thus, the International Federation of the Ulama wishes to clarify the following:

I   The resistance of the Iraqi people fighting a Jihad against the foreign occupation, which is aimed at liberating Iraqi land and reinstating its national sovereignty, is a Sharia obligation which falls on anyone who belongs to the Muslim nation inside or outside of Iraq, and who has the ability to achieve this.

Allah permitted this when He said, "We will give them permission to fight because they were oppressed" (Koran 22.39), and so he said to the Muslims, "Fight on behalf of Allah against those who fight you" (Koran 190.2). This fighting is a Jihad for the purpose of defense, which does not necessitate the instruction of general leadership (that would declare a Jihad), but rather it is implemented according to the personal capability (of each Muslim individual). In addition, it is recognized that the resistance to occupation is a legitimate right ratified by international conventions and the UN pact.

2   The acts perpetrated by the foreign armies invading Iraq are unprecedented atrocities. The US's justification for the invasion of Iraq was the claim that the latter was concealing non-conventional weapons and aiding terrorism. In actual fact non-conventional weapons were not found in Iraq; this is a gross violation of the Geneva Convention and other pacts addressing the (handling of) civilians during wartime and (the handling of) the providers of medical treatment and POWs: The use of internationally banned weapons; the destruction of homes, buildings, mosques, churches, other houses of worship and (the destruction of) infrastructures; the death of the wounded in mosques and the prevention (of the delivery of) emergency aid and rescue from those hit by disaster; the bombardment of hospitals and preventing medical teams from carrying out their humanitarian duty towards the injured – all this is a mark of disgrace on the foreheads of the states that perpetrate (these deeds).

The International Federation of the Muslim Ulama calls on the governments of each and every one of these countries to change their ways, resume humanitarian behavior and withdraw from Iraq immediately, after temporarily handing over control to a recognized international entity that will supervise free and untainted elections, which will enable the Iraqi people to run their country independently.

3   No Muslim is allowed to support (the deeds of) the invaders against the Iraqi people and its noble resistance. This is because this type of support is a way of abetting (the invaders) in their crime and aggression against the oppressed Islamic people. If the situation and conditions necessitate some Iraqis to work in the army or the police they must try to avoid causing damage to their civilians (the Iraqis). The resistance will not inflict any harm on them as long as they do not (actively) fight their people and do not form an alliance with the enemy.

4   The distinguished resistance fighters must adhere to the commandments of the Sharia during their Jihad against the occupiers and refrain from injuring civilians who are not involved in the fighting, women, children and the elderly, even if they are nationals of the invading forces, if they do not perpetrate hostile acts, especially if they are involved in humanitarian or communications activity. Because Allah directed us to fight those who would fight us and forbade acting aggressively. If some of the enemy forces are taken captive they must be treated kindly during their captivity and be brought to fair trial in order to release the innocent among them.

5   It is forbidden to hold hostages and threaten to kill them in order to apply pressure during an interrogation for a certain purpose, because as it says in the Koran (6.164): "A soul shall not carry the burden of another soul," and Muhammad said, "A violator will be punished for his deeds alone." If a person is held in this way then he is a prisoner of war and it is forbidden to kill him or harm him. Moreover, he will certainly be released as Allah said, "Whether to mercy and whether to ransom" (Koran 47.7).

6   The distinguished resistance fighters must take note of the existence of many (groups of) fifth columns interested in inflicting damage upon Islam and Muslims that carry out acts that would appear to be resistance. However, these (acts) are actually a continuation of the aggression and a distortion of the noble resistance. It is possible that these fifth column (groups) are connected to the Zionist and world intelligence agencies. The noble resistance must condemn the acts (of these groups) and expose their collaboration (with foreign intelligence entities) and their infiltration (to Iraq). Particularly because many of the crimes (that these groups) perpetrate become apparent due to the exposure of the invaders' barbaric behavior. Thus, they perpetrate even more barbaric acts in order to cover up the occupiers' behavior and make the world forget their atrocities.

7   Today there is a dangerous plot against Iraq whose aim is to rip its social texture . . . by encouraging hostility on a religious or national basis as well as emphasizing controversial issues. All Iraqis must feel that they are one people united by Islam as a religion and by "Arabism" as a language and culture. (They must understand) that their religious and national obligation is to cease all controversy and stand together in order to banish the conquest and build a united Iraq for all its residents . . .

In contrast to the relatively moderate approach adopted by the International Federation of the Muslim Ulama and by al-Qardawi himself in this forum, on other opportunities he took a far more radical stand. Several examples are detailed below:

- At a conference addressing "pluralism in Islam" that took place in August 2004 at the Egyptian Journalists' Association in Cairo, he stated: "All Americans in Iraq are fighters, there is no difference between a civilian and a soldier, and they must be fought because American citizens come to Iraq in order to serve the invasion. The abduction and execution of Americans in Iraq is a (religious) obligation so that they will be forced to leave Iraq immediately. But (in contrast) the mutilation of the dead bodies is forbidden in Islam."
- In September 2004, al-Qardawi published a religious precept permitting the abduction and murder of American citizens in Iraq in order to pressure the American army to withdraw its forces.
- Additionally, the manager of Sheikh al-Qardawi's office, Atsam Halima, confirmed that the Sheikh had published a religious declaration according to which it is obligatory to fight American citizens in Iraq because they are invaders.

In summary, al-Qardawi supports abduction attacks against foreign forces in Iraq while his seemingly moderate declarations are designed to inform media sources in the Western world of his radical program.

6
Abductions in Yemen

Yemen and Islamic Terror[1]

Yemen's demographic and social structure, its tribal division, the perpetual civil wars and the lack of an effective central government have turned the country into a convenient arena for the development of radical Islam. The British colonial rule in South Yemen also left its mark *vis-à-vis* the population's approach to the West and constitutes a source of hostility and hatred. Until South Yemen's union with North Yemen, the Marxist South Yemen Republic served as a haven for a wide range of Palestinian and other terrorist organizations that established a terror infrastructure which enjoyed government sponsorship. This tradition of supporting subversive organizations also continued after the confederation of Yemen's north and south, but Islamically oriented organizations came to replace the Palestinian and radical left-wing organizations.

Yemen, which subsists in the shadow of affluent and western-oriented Saudi Arabia, traditionally served as a refuge for entities opposing the Saudi Arabian monarchy and sought regional allies that would balance the asymmetry between its own status and that of its rich and large neighbor. Thus, Yemen has always been a potential ally for Saudi Arabia's adversaries such as Iran, Iraq or Egypt in the past.

Since the early 1990s, Yemen has gradually became a refuge and transit area for radical Islamic entities, including Osama Bin Laden, whose father came to Saudi Arabia from Hadramawt in Yemen. In addition, one of Bin Laden's wives is of Yemenite descent. *Jane's Intelligence Review* estimates that during the years of the Jihad against the Soviets in Afghanistan, about 3,000 volunteers from Yemen participated in the war. The majority returned to Yemen at the end of the Jihad and became the spearhead of radical Islam there. Bin Laden opened accounts at Yemen's central bank where he deposited some $200 million at one point. Some of the money was deposited in the bank account of Sheikh Abdul Majid Zandani, a prominent Islamic leader in Yemen.[2] Bin Laden developed a widespread financial infastructure in Yemen while simultaneously developing strong links with the radical Islamic leaders, some of whom were familiar to him from the Jihad in Afghanistan. The first terror attack to be initiated by Bin Laden in Yemen with the aid of the local infrastructure took place in 1992.[3]

Throughout the 1990s, Yemen continued to serve as a focal point and transit area for Islamic terrorists, due to the tolerant – and indeed enthusiastic – support of the Yemenite authorities. In early 1988, during Al Qaida's preparations for the attacks against the American embassies in Eastern Africa, and as part of the Global Jihad that Bin Laden had declared against the United States, Bin Laden established organizational "frontal headquarters" in San'aa, Yemen. Bin Laden himself was also seen at that time in Yemen. Al Qaida's newly established infrastructure enjoyed the sponsorship of Abdul Majid Zandani, one of the senior leaders of radical Islam in Yemen.[4]

During 1998–1999, Yemen also served as a base for the activities of Al Qaida and other organizations, including the Islamic Army of Aden and Abyan, which was established at that time. Subsequently, Yemen itself became an arena for terrorist attacks, some of which were thwarted, while others "succeeded" such as the abduction of Western hostages and the attack against the *USS Cole*. In the past and even today, Yemenite citizens have been active partners in Bin Laden's terror network:[5]

- At least seventeen of the Al Qaida prisoners transferred to Guantanamo in Cuba are Yemenite citizens.
- Several Yemenite nationals were involved in the attacks against the American embassies in Kenya and Tanzania.
- One of the hijackers in the September 11 attacks was a Yemenite named Khalid al Midhar.
- Yemenite Al Qaida members were involved in the attack on the *USS Cole*.

During the past decade, the American administration, Britain and Saudi Arabia have acted to convince the authorities in San'aa to refrain from offering support to terror organizations, and to cooperate with them in the struggle against Bin Laden.

A real turning point in Yemen's approach to terror came in the aftermath of the terror attacks of September 11, 2001 and America's declaration of "global war on terror". Due to Yemen's fear that it would become a target of the US and suffer a fate similar to that of the Taliban regime in Afghanistan, it decided to at least formally side with the Coalition fighting global terror.[6]

In the framework of these steps, Yemen established a special counterterror unit within its Ministry of Interior and began to cooperate with international entities in the war against terror. However, the Yemenite government's steps are only marginally successful:

- The government's control in remote areas that are distant from the capital is limited and the tribal structure of Yemenite society precludes the existence of an effective central government.
- Strong tribal leaders operate their own policy and support radical Islamic entities for financial and ideological reasons.
- There are strong radical Islamic circles that enjoy widespread popularity.
- Corrupt and ineffective administration and control systems impair the government's control of what takes place in the country.

The Abduction of Foreign Residents

One of the most prominent expressions of the ongoing ineffectiveness of Yemen's central government is the phenomenon of the kidnapping of foreign residents and holding them as hostages by tribal entities, usually with the aim of furthering their interests in the struggle against the San'aa authorities. Since 1991 there have been over one hundred incidents of kidnapping of foreign residents, generally by tribal entities that demanded ransom money for their release. When the ransom is paid, the hostages are usually released unharmed.[7] During the years 1996–2000, the Yemenite kidnappers held 150 hostages, including 122 foreign residents.[8] Examples of kidnappings of foreign residents in Yemen include:[9]

- January 26, 1996 – Seventeen elderly French tourists were kidnapped by tribal members in the Maareb area. The kidnappers demanded the release of one of their tribal members who had been arrested. The kidnappers released the hostages on January 29.
- October 20, 1996 – A French diplomat was kidnapped in San'aa and was released on November 1, after the Yemenite authorities capitulated to the kidnappers' demands.
- March 4, 1997 – Seven German tourists were kidnapped, and the kidnappers demanded twelve million dollars for their release. The hostages were released on March 12.
- March 27, 1997 – Four German tourists were kidnapped and the kidnappers demanded three million dollars for their release. They were released on April 6.

In the first week of December 2001, a German citizen employed at the Mercedes dealership in San'aa was kidnapped by armed men. The kidnappers, apparently from the Zubian tribe, transferred the victim to a hiding place in a mountainous area some 170 kilometers east of the capital. The Yemenite security forces pursued the kidnappers and conducted a manhunt.[10] On December 6, the security forces surrounded the village of al-Muhgiza and engaged in a gunfight against the tribe members, who they believed were involved in the kidnapping. In the exchange of fire three tribe members were killed as well as two policemen; many more were injured.[11]

The Arrest of the "British" Terror Network in Yemen (December 23, 1998)

On December 23, 1998, three terrorists were arrested in a car loaded with explosives. They were on their way to perpetrate a terror attack against the British Consulate in Aden. As the result of their interrogation another three cell members were arrested and a safe house was located which contained mines, rocket launchers, computers, encrypted communication means and many cassettes belonging to the SOS (Supporters of Sharia). Subsequently, the SOS organization, which had been planning a series of attacks against British and American targets,[12] was apprehended in Yemen.

Five of those arrested were carrying (authentic) British passports, and the sixth was carrying original French documentation. Questioning revealed that they were members of SOS in London, headed as mentioned earlier by Abu-Hamza al-Mitsri, a radical Islamic leader associated with Bin-Laden.[13]

Among the cell's members were two relatives of Abu-Hamza — his cousin Muhsein Gailan, who was arrested in Yemen, and his son Muhammad Mustafa, who succeeded in eluding capture.

The network's members arrived in Yemen in mid-December, and according to the testimony of at least one of the arrested suspects, they met with Abu-al-Hassan (one of the leaders of the Islamic Army of Aden-Abyan), who provided them with weaponry and instructions for perpetrating attacks.[14] Their intention was to carry out a series of attacks on Christmas Eve against Western targets in Aden including the British Consulate in Aden, an Anglican church, and a group of Americans dealing in the removal of mines from Yemen who lived at the "Movenpick" Hotel in Aden.

Abu-Hamza denied any connection with terror activity in Yemen and claimed that the detained suspects were not members of the "Supporters of Sharia" organization. Abu-Hamza also claimed that his organization deals with religious studies and adheres to the laws of Britain.[15]

The abduction of tourists on December 28, 1998[16]

On December 28, 1998, sixteen tourists from various countries were kidnapped (twelve British, two American and two Australian citizens) while they were touring the Abyan region in Yemen. A convoy of five vehicles in which the tourists were traveling was attacked about 60 kilometers northeast of Aden by a group of armed people who kidnapped the tourists and held them hostage. The tourists were transferred to a hiding place in a remote mountainous area that served as a camp for the terror organization's members. On the night of December 29, 1998, a spokesman for the terror organization known as the Islamic Army of Aden-Abyan stated that members of his organization had kidnapped the tourists, and he made several stipulations for their release:

- The release of the "British" network's members (sent by Abu-Hamza), and members of the Islamic Army of Aden-Abyan.
- Cessation of US and British aggression against Iraq.
- Banishment of the British and US presence in the Arabian Peninsula.

The Yemenite authorities refused to accept the kidnappers' demands, and the Yemenite security forces trailed and surrounded them and their victims at their place of hiding. In the course of the Yemenite forces' rescue attempt several hostages were killed and others were wounded. At least three of the kidnappers were killed in the incident and three others were caught, including Abu-al-Hassan.

During his interrogation, Abu-al-Hassan confessed that the kidnapping was to have brought about the release of the organization's members and that of the "British" terror network members incarcerated in Yemenite jails. According to the testimony of one of the kidnapped victims, during the kidnapping Abu-al-Hassan held a telephone conversation with General Ali Muhsan al-Ahmar, a relative of President Salah of Yemen, in an attempt to get the latter to agree to the abductors' demands, but the Yemenite authorities had already made the decision to take action to release the hostages. During the 1990s, there were over 100 incidents of abductions of foreign residents in Yemen, but this particular incident was the broadest in scale and one of the few that ended in the death of hostages.

The phenomenon of abducting foreigners did not cease even after the Yemenite government joined the Coalition against terror in the aftermath of the September 11, 2001 attacks. Thereafter, abductions continued in Yemen, including:

- In 2004, an Australian oil engineer was abducted together with his two escorts from Oman. The three were subsequently freed by their abductors. It is not known whether a ransom was paid for their release.

- In November, 2005, two Austrian tourists were abducted. The two were subsequently released. It is not known whether a ransom was paid for their release.
- In December, 2005, a senior German diplomat was abducted together with his family. The abductors demanded that the Yemenite government release prisoners from a certain tribe in exchange for the captives' release. The German hostages were released following negotiations. It is unclear whether the Yemenite government kept its promise to release prisoners.
- At the beginning of 2006, five Italian tourists were abducted. The latter were subsequently released. Two of the abductors were arrested by the Yemenite authorities.

In summary, despite Yemen's decision to join the global war against terror led by the United States, the regime in Yemen has encountered difficutly in controlling the subversive entities and the Global Jihad in that country. As a result, Yemen still constitutes an arena of activity for Islamic terror, including abductions of foreign citizens.

7

The Confrontation Arenas, Western Governments' Policy, and Crimes Against Humanity by Offending States and Organizations

This study has examined aspects of abductions perpetrated in four arenas in the Middle East, including the involvement of Islamic terror organizations in these attacks, the reciprocal relationship among the organizations, and the ties between the latter and Iran as a state that supports and promotes terror.

The Israeli–Palestinian Confrontation Arena

Despite the prolonged duration and intensity of the Israeli–Palestinian confrontation, the Hamas perpetrated a relatively small number of abductions (13 attacks) between the years 1988 and 2005. The organization's attacks can be divided into three periods:

- The period of the First Intifada (1989–1993): During this period the Hamas perpetrated six abductions. Most of the attacks ended in the hostage's murder and an Israeli refusal to capitulate to the organization's demands.
- The period of the Oslo Agreements (1994–2000): During this period the Hamas perpetrated six abductions. Once again, during this time most of the abductions ended with the hostage's execution and an Israeli refusal to capitulate to the organization's demands.
- The period of the Al Aqsa Intifada (2000–2006): During this period

the Hamas planned several abductions which were thwarted, with the exception of the abduction of a civilian named Sason Nuriel, who was abducted and murdered in September 2005.

The abduction of Nachshon Wachsman was the only incident in which the Israeli security forces succeeded in locating the place where the abductors and hostage were hiding while the latter was still alive, and for whom a military operation was conducted in a rescue effort. In all of the Hamas abductions, a single hostage was taken. In most of the cases the victim was a member of the security forces (a soldier or a Border Guard policeman). The Hamas never held more than a single hostage at any given time in contrast to other abduction arenas in the Middle East (Lebanon, Yemen and Iraq), where the abductors held several hostages simultaneously. The relatively small number of Hamas abductions and the relatively low number of hostages can be attributed to several causes:

- Effective intelligence work in the Israeli–Palestinian confrontation arena.
- The difficulty that the Hamas encountered when holding a hostage in the area controlled by the Palestinian Authority.
- The decisive policy adopted by successive Israeli governments not to capitulate to the abductors' demands and the preference for a military attack (when there was operational feasibility) in order to try to bring about the hostage's release.

A study of the abductions indicates that in the majority of cases the Hamas murdered the hostage. This can be explained by the difficulty that the Hamas experienced when holding a hostage for a prolonged period without exposure by Israeli intelligence or the Palestinian Authority's intelligence organizations, as well as the perception that there was little likelihood that Israel would meet the abductors' demands. Thus, most of the abductors preferred to kill the hostage and attempt to negotiate with Israel while hiding the fact that the hostage was dead; and after the subsequent discovery of his death to barter over the return of the body. In all of the instances of abduction in which the Hamas presented stipulations to the State of Israel, it focused on liberating prisoners linked with this organization or others (including Shiite Lebanese organizations) in exchange for release of the captive.

Following 1992, which marked the growing alliance between the Hamas on the one hand and Iran and the Hizballah on the other, there have been reciprocal operational links *vis-à-vis* the perpetration of terror attacks in general and abductions in particular. This fact is reflected in the mutual demands posed by the Hizballah and the Hamas to bring about the release of both organizations' prisoners when negotiations for hostage exchanges are entered with Israel.

The Lebanese Arena

During the entire period relevant to this study (1980–2006), Iran constituted a central factor in the leverage and encouragement of terror in the Middle East against Israel and Western targets whose countries were perceived as Iran's foes, with the United States – "the Great Devil" – at the top of the list.

Abductions of American, British and French civilians in the Lebanese arena were first and foremost directed at promoting salient Iranian interests such as:

- The cessation of arms supply to Iraq (during the Iran–Iraq war).
- The attainment of combat means in exchange for the release of hostages (Irangate).
- The prevention of support for Iranian opposition entities.
- The return of Iranian money frozen in Western states (France and the United States).

Abductions perpetrated by the Hizballah against Israeli targets in Lebanon were intended to serve several goals:

- To damage Israel's image and its presence on Lebanese soil (in the Security Zone).
- To undermine Israeli national morale, and trigger public and political pressure in that country to withdraw its forces from Lebanon.
- The release of prisoners from the Hizballah as well as Palestinian and Lebanese organizations incarcerated in Israeli prisons.

Iran and the Hizballah often attempted to create linkage between holding foreign hostages in Lebanon and Israel's policy regarding the Lebanese issue due to the desire to exert pressure on Israel. Several examples offered in this study indicate that this pressure did indeed yield results: Israel acquiesced to Western (mainly American) requests and released Lebanese prisoners in order to facilitate the release of Western hostages.

Several behavior patterns were adopted by countries when their citizens were abducted and held by Islamic terror organizations in Lebanon. Some espoused a declared policy of non-capitulation to terror (such as the US) but actually entered negotiations, which in some cases culminated in the release of the hostages. Other countries preferred to openly adopt a policy of negotiations with the terrorists, usually through intermediaries. Following negotiations and meeting the terrorists' demands the hostages were released (France, Germany).

The State of Israel was forced to deal with a different challenge in the Lebanese arena; for prolonged periods, mainly at the end of the 1980s and at the beginning of the 1990s, the Hizballah refused to enter negotiations with Israel for the release of the captives. Israel was the only country that tried to bring about the release of its prisoners by snatching a "bargaining chip", such as Obeid and Dirani, who were abducted in order to provide information about the POWs and serve as an incentive for the Hizballah and its patrons in Teheran to enter negotiations with Israel.

In retrospect, it is clear that the abduction of these indivduals failed to yield the desired results, and the demand to release Obeid and Dirani became a regular component in abductions perpetrated by the Hizballah and Hamas.

In both the Lebanese and the Palestinian arenas it is clear that these attacks are regarded as strategic tactics orchestrated by the senior leadership of the Hamas and the Hizballah, and sometimes with Iranian direction and involvement as well.

Negotiations *vis-à-vis* countries that fell victim to abductions were always conducted with the most senior political and security echelon. Thus, through a "tactical" act, the terror organizations succeeded in leveraging processes and achieving strategic goals.

It is noteworthy that as a rule, in contrast to the Hamas' complete failure to achieve any goals through the abduction of Israelis, abductions perpetrated by the Hizballah in Lebanon almost always culminated in the achievement of part or all of the organizations' demands.

In the Lebanese arena, the Hizballah and Iran succeeded in perpetrating abductions and hiding the hostages in a way that prevented their opponents from locating the captors and the hostages through intelligence, which effectively neutralized the possibility of a military rescue operation. In these circumstances, the only choice left to the countries whose citizens had been abducted was either to abandon the hostages or cave in to the abductors' demands through negotiations. In the Lebanese arena Israel was also unable to create intelligence conditions that would enable locating the place where the hostages were being held in order to conduct a military operation. Thus, it too was forced to give in to Hizballah demands.

Abductions were perceived as "strategic attacks" both in the Palestinian and Lebanese arenas. Therefore, when the strategic circumstances changed, the abductions ceased and the hostages were released. The Lebanese arena was affected by the end of the Iraq–Iran war and Khomeini's death, as well as by the Iranian government's desire to improve relations with the West. Therefore, the abduction of Western hostages in

Lebanon ceased in 1989, and by 1992 all of the hostages had been released.

However, the situation was different when it came to Israel. The intensity of the Iranian hostility did not abate, and Iran declared itself the leader of the rejectionist camp, whose declared aim was to undermine the peace process between Israel and Arab or Palestinian states. Additionally, the continued presence of the IDF in Lebanon served as a backdrop for an unrelenting struggle in Southern Lebanon, including abduction attempts of IDF soldiers by the Hizballah.

From 1992 onward, Iran and the Hizballah increased their involvement, influence and aid on behalf of the Palestinian terror organizations, including the Hamas. Thus, while the problem of Western hostages in Lebanon had been resolved, the issue of the Israeli hostages being held by the Hizballah remained insoluble. In the Palestinian arena, the Hamas joined the struggle to undermine the Israeli–Palestinian peace process. Abductions and suicide attacks perpetrated during the years that the Oslo Agreements were implemented were aimed at sabotaging the agreement. This was also the background against which Nachshon Wachsman's abduction took place in October 1994.

Due to the intensified implementation of the Oslo Agreements and internal political shifts between the Hamas and the Palestinian Authority, abductions ceased in 1996 for several years but were subsequently renewed during the Al Aqsa Intifada (2005–2006).

Yemen

In Yemen, abductions of local and foreign hostages constitute a "traditional" criminal activity, and most of the hostages were released in exchange for a ransom. The Islamic radicalism that claimed roots in Yemen, under the influence of the "Afghanistan alumni" and the Global Jihad, and the establishment of infrastructures by local Islamic terror organizations and Al Qaida, triggered a change *vis-à-vis* the issue of abductions in Yemen. From 1998 onward, parallel to the continued criminal abductions, came the abduction of Western hostages with the aim of releasing imprisoned members of Islamic terror organizations.

This was a new threat that the Yemenite authorities had to face. Here, the prevalent "arrangements" with the tribal leaders regarding the release of hostages in exchange for ransom were irrelevant. These abductions, which were perceived by the Yemenite authorities as part of the radical Islamic threat against the government's stability, were fought with military operations that generally ended in failure; while the abductors were killed, so were many of the hostages. The abductions decreased significantly in the wake of the 9/11 attacks, following a resolution taken by the Yemenite authorities to join the US-led counter-terror Coalition and take a tougher stand against radical Islamic entities in their country. Nevertheless, due to the Yemenite government's limited control in peripheral areas, its steps to mitigate terror, including abductions, were only partially successful.

The Iraqi Arena

Iraq became the "Jihad arena" and the most prominent focal point for abductions in the world following Iraq's invasion by the US-led Coalition in 2003. Islamic terror organizations in Iraq, mainly the organization operated by Abu Musab Zarqawi (Al Qaida's most senior representative in the Iraqi arena), turned abductions into a central component of the struggle against Coalition forces.

The Iraqi arena, in which many military and civilian entities from the Coalition countries are active, supplies a plethora of abduction targets, and media representatives are not immune to abduction. A dramatic and horrifying addition to the terror repertoire of Islamic terror organizations in Iraq is the execution of the hostage in front of a video camera, the preferred method being decapitation. The drama of the abductions that goes on for weeks and sometimes even months, during which negotiations are conducted between the terrorists and the countries whose citizens were abducted, and the dramatic and appalling culmination of executing the hostages when negotiations fail, constitute an important component of the psychological pressure applied on Western public opinion and leaders.

The Iraqi arena undoubtedly serves as the most significant and intensive focal point in the development of abductions in the Middle East. Between 2003 and 2005, over 200 foreign hostages were abducted in Iraq (almost double the number of foreign hostages abducted in Lebanon). Moreover, the number of abductions in Iraq – over 100 in the relatively short period of two and a half years – turned the Iraqi arena into the most dangerous in the history of the Middle East from the aspect of abductions. The number of hostages who died as the result of abductions as well as those whose fate is unknown by far exceeds the statistics in Lebanon, and certainly surpasses the number of abduction victims in the Israeli–Palestinian arena.

The behavior pattern adopted by the various countries whose citizens are being held as hostages by Iraqi terror organizations does not differ from that advocated by the same countries in the Lebanese arena during the 1980s. The United States and Britain espouse a declared policy that prohibits capitulation to terror. Due to the presence of significant US and British forces in Iraq, limited military operations which brought about the release of the hostages were conducted during the relevant period. The aim of larger military operations (such as the capture of Faluja in November 2004) was to get to the root of the Islamic terror problem, including the release of hostages and the apprehension of the captors.

In contrast to the American–British approach, many countries demonstrated weakness when their citizens were abducted in Iraq and openly or covertly caved in to the terrorists' demands, whether by withdrawing their forces from Iraq (the Philippines) or agreeing to pay a ransom (France, Italy and others).

Points of Emphasis and Lessons to be Drawn

The examination and comparison of abduction arenas detailed in previous chapters indicate the following:

- In most of the arenas, periods or "waves" of abductions of foreign citizens (many of whom are Westerners) are apparent.
- "Waves of abductions" cease when local, regional or strategic circumstances change.
- The abductions are generally regarded as strategic attacks whose aim is to extract demands from various countries.
- "Waves of abductions" take place in regions where there is no effective central government and the terror organizations enjoy relative freedom.
- A state that supports terror, such as Iran, constitutes a central factor in the initiation and encouragement of the "waves of abductions", as well as its ability to put a stop to the attacks when it so chooses.
- Since the late 1990s, the Global Jihad and Al Qaida have served as a central factor *vis-à-vis* the encouragement and initiation of abductions.
- Abductions that take place in an arena where there are restricted intelligence capabilities, and the ability to launch a military operation by the country whose citizens are being held is limited, usually culminate in victory for the abductors.
- Capitulation to the terrorists' demands sometimes prevented additional abductions of citizens from that country but at the same time encouraged the abduction of other countries' citizens based on the assumption that they too would give in to the abductors' demands.
- It is impossible to unequivocally determine whether taking a firm stand based on the principle of withstanding terror extortion has brought about a decrease in the number of abductions because sometimes these countries' refusal to capitulate has triggered repeated attempts to abduct their citizens in order to bring about the

desired capitulation. Nevertheless, it is reasonable to assume that a broad and coordinated consensus shared by as many countries as possible that would advocate a uniform policy of refusal to give in to the terrorists' extortion would diminish the phenomenon.

- There is no "magic formula" for the resolution of the issue of abductions but there is no doubt that international action involving the formulation of a treaty defining abductions as "crimes against humanity" (which in fact they are), and bringing the perpetrators and the leaders of the organizations behind these acts to justice would certainly contribute to the eradication of this phenomenon.

Epilogue: Abductions of Israeli Soldiers and Civilians

June and July 2006

During 2006, the Israeli security forces became aware of many warnings regarding the intentions of Palestinian terrorists to kidnap Israelis. On July 16, 2006, *Yediot Aharonot,* a daily Israeli newspaper, quoted security entities as follows:[1]

> We have recently gathered evidence that the Fatah, Hamas and Palestinian Islamic Jihad are eager to abduct Israelis, as they claim that Israel will not release Palestinian prisoners and abduction is the only way to force it to do so. Palestinian prisoners incarcerated in Israeli prisons have called for their headquarters and comrades in arms to abduct Israelis in order to ensure their release. We recently arrested several terror cells planning abductions. Abductions do not necessitate extensive planning. A pistol and a car suffice to perpetrate the deed. It is commonly known that Israelis all over the territories regularly wait at hitchhiking stations for a lift.

Between 2005 and 2006 Hassan Nasrallah, general-secretary of the Hizballah, issued several statements regarding his organization's intention to kidnap Israeli soldiers in order to bring about the release of all Lebanese and Palestinian prisoners incarcerated in Israel. A Hizballah attempt to kidnap soldiers near the village of Rajar was thwarted on November 12, 2005.

In June and July 2006, there was an unprecedented wave of abduction attempts against Israeli soldiers and civilians in Judea and Samaria, the Gaza Strip and the Lebanese border. A record of the events that occurred in June and July 2006 is detailed below:

On June 10 armed Palestinians attempted to kidnap two girls who were hitchhiking near the settlement of Rehelim. The two struggled with the kidnappers and were rescued thanks to an Israeli officer who happened to be passing by at the time.

On June 25 a joint terror attack was perpetrated against an IDF force near Kerem Shalom. In the course of the attack, two soldiers were killed, four were injured, and one soldier, Gilad Shalit, was kidnapped and taken to Gaza.

On June 25 eighteen-year-old Eliyahu Asheri was kidnapped by the "Popular Resistance Committees." The kidnappers murdered him shortly after his abduction. The perpetrators were captured on July 4 by the Israeli security forces.

On July 12 a combined terror attack was carried out in the Avivim area. Four soldiers were killed, two were injured and another two were abducted to Lebanon by the Hizballah.

On July 28, 2006, Dr Danny Yaakobi, from the settlement of Yakir, was abducted and murdered. His body was found in the shell of his car after it had been torched by the killers. The Al Aqsa Brigades claimed responsibility for the deed.

The attempt to kidnap the two girls near Rehelim

On June 15, 2006, an attempt was made to abduct two girls who were hitchhiking near Rehelim. The armed abductors were driving a white Chevrolet Cavalier on the road between Nablus and Jerusalem. Around 15:00 they saw two girls waiting at the hitchhiking station near Rehelim. The girls, Emuna Shahar (15) from Jerusalem and Hadas Mann (15) from Beit El, had finished their studies for the day at the Ma'ale Levona religious high school and were trying to get a lift home.

In an interview to *Yediot Aharonot* they stated:[2] "'A white car drew up. We began to approach the vehicle but when we saw they were Arabs we returned to the station. Suddenly, two armed men jumped out of the car.' The girls did not lose their cool; Hadas fled and hid in the bushes. The other girl, Emuna, attempted to escape but the abductors lunged at her and began dragging her towards the car. Emuna struggled and screamed for help. Luckily, a captain in the IDF Nahal company happened to be driving by and he drove away the attackers. The captain reported the abduction attempt to IDF troops in the area and a manhunt was launched. IDF forces managed to stop the vehicle with the three terrorists, who attempted to flee. A loaded gun and handcuffs were found in the possession of the abductors, all residents of Jenin."

The Kerem Shalom incident

On June 26, 2006, a combined attack was launched against IDF forces at Kerem Shalom. In the course of this incident, seven terrorists penetrated Israel via an underground tunnel dug from Palestinian territory. The terrorists attacked several IDF targets including an observation tower, an empty armored personel carier (APC) and a tank.

As a result, two soldiers who were in the tank, Lieutenant Hanan Barak and First Sgt. Pavel Slutsker, were killed. Another soldier was injured and the fourth soldier, Corporal Gilad Shalit, was abducted. Three other soldiers were injured when the terrorists attacked the observation tower. Two of the terrorists were killed in this incident and the rest fled back to Palestinian territory.

Modus operandi of the attack   The terrorists penetrated Israel through a tunnel dug under the security fence from Palestinian territory into Israel.[3] The hatch was found in a house inside Palestinian territory and the tunnel spanned a distance of over 400 meters. At 4:45 a.m., seven terrorists penetrated Israel via the tunnel. They launched their attack from behind the observation tower. The IDF sentries were facing the opposite direction, specifically the security fence surrounding Gaza. The assailants split into three squads – one aligned itself behind the observation tower, another behind an APC and a third behind the tank. They opened simultaneous fire with rocket propelled grenades (RPGs), light arms and grenades. As a result of the RPG shooting, an empty armored vehicle caught fire. The tank was hit and penetrated, as was the watch post.

After the RPG shootings, two of the terrorists approached the tank and killed the commander and driver. The terrorists threw a grenade into the tank hatch, and grabbed the gunman – Gilad Shalit. Dragging him along, they moved towards the fence, blew it up and crossed the border into Rafah. The squad's third terrorist was positioned near the road and ambushed an IDF jeep driven by a captain who rushed in to provide assistance. After the terrorist's attempt to shoot an RPG, the captain returned fire. The assailant fled west towards a tunnel dug along the fence. An IDF armored vehicle attempted to shoot him, but the terrorist lobbed grenades and fled back to Rafah.

The third team of terrorists approached the watch tower, opening RPG and gunfire. One of the terrorists crept towards the tower and placed an explosive charge next to the bottom door – the ensuing explosion damaging the building's communication cables. One of the terrorists remained where he was to serve as backup, while the other climbed the stairs shouting "Allah Akbar". The force in the tower opened gunfire. Eventually the terrorist was hit and fell in the upper part of the stairway.

The second terrorist began returning west and crossed the fence. He was identified by an IDF lookout and IDF forces opened fire, eventually killing him. Only 20 minutes had passed from the moment that the terror squads opened fire until their retreat.

Claiming of responsibility and the abductors' demands   The three Palestinian organizations claiming responsibility for the Kerem Shalom attack announced their terms for the release of Gilad Shalit on June 26, 2006.

The statement, which was signed by three military arms – Iz a-Din Al-Qasam of the Hamas, Salah a-Din of the Popular Resistance Committees and Islam's Army – demanded the release of all female prisoners and all prisoners who are minors from Israeli prisons in exchange for information about the soldier's fate.[4]

A spokesperson from the Popular Resistance Committees, who identified himself as Abu Mujahed, confirmed to the *Ha'aretz* daily newspaper that the manifest had been sent by the organizations holding Shalit captive.

The manifest, written by the Iz A Din Al-Qasam Brigades, quoted verses from the Koran and lauded the 'heroic act' which was named "The Shattering of Illusions". The declaration stated:

> The occupiers will receive no information regarding the missing soldier until they agree to release all of the female prisoners and incarcerated minors.

In a second manifest published on July 3, 2006, the three organizations repeated their demand for the release of the female prisoners and incarcerated minors, as well as 1,000 additional prisoners, promising nothing in return.[5]

The third pamphlet declared:

> About the missing Zionist soldier . . . because of the obstinacy of the enemy, and its insistence on ignoring all humanitarian values and due to its persistence in perpetrating military actions and aggression, we issue an ultimatum to the Zionist enemy to be met by tomorrow, Tuesday, July 4 at 6:00 a.m. If the enemy does not respond to our humane demands as stated in the previous pamphlet regarding the terms in the case of the missing soldier we will launch the first stage – we consider the case closed due to the obstinacy of the enemy's leadership. The enemy will be held fully responsible for any future outcome.

The Hamas Government, Abu Mazen and Kidnapping

The attack near Kerem Shalom and the kidnapping of Gilad Shalit aroused internal disputes within the Hamas between proponents and opponents of the ceasefire, and exposed the lack of effective leadership within the Hamas. Disputes arose not only between the external Hamas leadership, headed by Khaled Mash'al and exiled Hamas representatives on the one hand, and the homeland Hamas on the other, but also between various factions inside the Iz A-Din Al-Qasam Brigades and the force's main faction that continued to be loyal to the political leadership.

Hamas sources indicated that a breakaway faction of the Iz A-Din Al-Qasam brigades had joined up with an organization called the Resistance

Committees as well as family gangs, including a band run by the Abu-Samahadane family (one of whom – Jamal – had been killed in a skirmish with IDF forces), alongside splinter factions of organizations that control various quarters in Rafah.[6] These elements were responsible for digging the tunnel, and the attack was planned over a period of several months.

It appears that Ismail Haniyeh, his assistants in the political leadership of the Hamas and some of the Iz A-Din Al-Qasam Brigades officials, did not have prior information about the intent to carry out the attack and the kidnapping.[7]

On June 26, Palestinian President Abu Mazen, assembled the commanders of the security services in Gaza and instructed that a manhunt be launched to locate the soldier.[8] Abu Mazen also met with an Egyptian delegation. The night before his representative had met with Prime Minister Isma'il Haniyeh. The former reported that Haniyeh was not a partner to the kidnapping scheme. Khaled Mash'al, head of the political Hamas branch, had ensured Haniyeh's isolation and the latter had no contact with the kidnappers, who refused to talk to him. According to Haniyeh's party, Mash'al made use of the attack and kidnapping to confront Haniyeh. Even Hamas officials, including cabinet members, estimated that the attack was meant to thwart the agreement formulated in the "Prisoners Paper". (The "Prisoners Paper" addresses the regularization of the relationship between the Hamas and Fatah and it is thus called because it was formulated by the two organizations' leaders currently incarcerated in Israeli prisons.) Senior Hamas members claimed that the tunnel had been ready several days prior to the attack, but the order to carry out the mission was issued by Khaled Mash'al on the day that the paper was signed and the unity government was formed.[9]

On June 26, Abu Mazen and Haniyeh met again to discuss the release of the kidnapped soldier. During the meeting, which was described as extremely tense, Abu Mazen flung harsh accusations at Haniyeh. The meeting ended in stalemate. The Hamas government spokesperson, Razi Hamed, reiterated that the government was eager to resolve the crisis as soon as possible.[10]

The reaction of the Israeli government

In response to the kidnapping, Israeli Prime Minsiter Ehud Olmert instructed the security forces to prepare a "broad military operation in the Gaza Strip."[11] At a security cabinet meeting convened in the wake of the Kerem Shalom incident and the kidnapping of Gilad Shalit, Olmert stated: "The period of restraint is over. Up to now we have acted with restraint due to Israeli interests connected to political issues. Today's event has effectively curtailed this restraint."[12] Olmert added that "Israel holds

President Mahmoud Abbas solely responsible. We do not take sides in connection to their internal problems." Olmert emphasized that Israel would not release Palestinian prisoners in exchange for the IDF soldier, and warned that it would "take forceful action over a period that would exceed a day or two, and would be implemented in several steps and phases."

The Israeli cabinet's statement combined aggressive rhetoric against the Palestinian Authority, while abstaining from immediate military action, due to the fear for the kidnapped soldier's life. The aim of the threat was undoubtedly to place pressure on the Palestinians so they would refrain from harming Shalit and release him. The cabinet resolution reflected Israel's position that the soldier's release constituted a top priority. The IDF was to prepare for a lengthy military operation, and help prevent Shalit from being smuggled outside of Gaza. In addition, diplomatic efforts were to continue in order to exert additional pressure on the Palestinian Authority.[13]

The cabinet's announcement stated as follows:[14]

> The Palestinian Authority will be held responsible for any harm that comes to the soldier, and no person or organization will be immune to Israeli retaliation. The cabinet approves the recommendation of Israel's security forces to prepare the appropriate forces for urgent military action, which is unavoidable due to the hostile actions and intentions of the Palestinian Authority. The Prime Minister and the Minister of Defense will approve activities against terror targets and the Palestinian Authority based on the advice of the security forces.

Cabinet ministers Shimon Peres, Eli Yishay and Meir Shitrit urged restraint. Justice Minister Haim Ramone pointed out the risks of cowardly behavior, and demanded that Israel refrain from bombing tents and empty structures. Minister of Internal Security Avi Dikhter suggested that an ultimatum be issued to the Palestinian Authority with a final date for releasing the kidnapped soldier. Foreign Minister Tzipi Livney reported to the cabinet regarding talks with her counterparts abroad. Prime Minister Olmert predicted that an Israeli military offensive across the border would win international sympathy.

The ministers were informed that Israel lacked intelligence as to the whereabouts of the kidnapped soldier, and that military operations rely on accurate intelligence. They were also told that the Hamas leadership in Damascus was involved in the attack, and that it had been planned by Jamal Abu-Samhadne, who was killed in an IDF strike ten days prior to the attack.

At a meeting between Prime Minister Olmert and Defense Minister Amir Peretz held prior to the cabinet meeting, heads of Israel's security agencies and the IDF recommended a forceful response.[15] These elements averred that Israel could not stand idle following the attack initiated within its territory by the Hamas, which is the ruling party in the Palestinian Authority. Their suggestion was to destroy the organization's infrastructure. They also claimed that Israel could use the ground invasion as n pretext to release Shalit. According to one political source, all of the proposals were unanimously approved without a vote.

At a press conference in Tel Aviv, Defense Minister Amir Peretz noted that, "As far as we are concerned, anyone causing injury to the soldier should be aware that he will be held responsible, as well as his leaders. All those involved will discover that a high toll will be exacted. If things continue as they are – it will be tenfold more painful." Peretz also accused the Palestinian Authority of being "riddled with terrorism from head to toe."[16]

On June 26, 2006, Prime Minister Ehud Olmert took a tough stand against Hamas demands regarding negotiations over the kidnapped soldier, Corporal Gilad Shalit, and announced that no negotiations would be conducted for the release of prisoners incarcerated in Israel. In a speech at the Jewish Agency Conference held that same day, Prime Minister Olmert stated:[17] "The question of the release of prisoners is not on the Israeli government's agenda. I hereby announce that we will retaliate against all terrorists, and any terror organization wherever it may be (. . .) the time for painful, comprehensive action is drawing near. We do not intend to wait endlessly. We will not succumb to the extortion of the Hamas terrorists." Some parties interpreted this statement as a threat to take action against Hamas leaders outside of the West Bank and Gaza, such as Khaled Mash'al, who is perceived by Israel as the mastermind behind the abduction. "We do not act rashly. That is why we have weighed our actions carefully," claimed Olmert. "But we are running out of time, and a painful operation is imminent. We will act with all the force at our disposal to put a stop to terrorism, to ensure the kidnapped soldier's well-being, and bring him home safely and quickly."

Despite these assertive warnings, proxy contacts between Hamas and Israel continued behind the scenes in an attempt to negotiate the soldier's release. The Egyptian representative in Gaza served as a main contact. The French Foreign Office also became involved after it turned out that Shalit holds French citizenship.[18]

The reaction of the IDF forces

Once it became clear that a soldier had actually been abducted, the IDF crossed the Palestinian border with armor and infantry forces. The forces fanned out and scanned an area of one square kilometer west of the fence. The kidnappers' tracks, which disappeared into Palestinian territory, were found at this time. Tanks and helicopters shot warning fire during the activity on the Palestinian side. Only in the afternoon did the IDF find the hatch on the Palestinian side, about half a kilometer west of the border. The hatch was discovered under a house east of Rafah and the IDF prepared to detonate the tunnel. At the same time, special units were summoned to the border. However, these units were not activated due to the lack of accurate intelligence and the Israeli desire to avoid arousing international censure.

On June 26, 2006, Prime Minister Olmert and Minister of Defense Peretz met to approve operational programs submitted by the IDF for extensive action in the Gaza Strip. The Prime Minister instructed the security forces to hunt down all those involved in the planning, including entities outside of Israel. Meanwhile, the IDF continued preparations for a large-scale ground operation in the Gaza Strip, in the event that political efforts to release Shalit failed.

That night, large forces were concentrated along the Gaza Strip. The intention was to operate two brigade-size infantry forces, Givati and Golani, combined with armor.

Nonetheless, military sources admitted that these forces would not be sent in for the purpose of rescuing the soldier. Circumstances permitting, any rescue mission was to be carried out by special units. The concentration of forces, alongside direct threats on the life of the Palestinian prime minister, were meant to signal Israel's intentions in the event that its demands were not met in the ensuing days. The IDF came up with a plan for prolonged action and began implementing it on June 26, when a marine and land closure was enforced upon the Gaza Strip. Traffic ceased at the border crossing, with the exception of humanitarian supplies. June 28 marked the initiation of the first stage of the Summer Rain Campaign – a "rolling" operation in the Gaza Strip.

The goal of the operation was to exert pressure on the central Palestinian Authority to bring back the captured soldier and end the shooting of Qasam rockets at Israel. The approved operation included air strikes against infrastructure and an invasion of Qasam rockets launching sites by ground forces. Parallel to this operation, security forces arrested 60 Hamas officials, including government ministers and members of parliament. This act was meant to increase the pressure on the Hamas government, in order to bring about the release of the kidnapped soldier, Gilad Shalit.

The kidnapping and murder of Eliyahu Asheri [19]

On June 25, 2006, an 18-year-old student from Itamar named Eliyahu Asheri was kidnapped. Asheri was enrolled at a premilitary preparatory school in Neve-Zuf. When his father realized that he had neither returned to school nor come home, he reported his son's disappearance at the police station in Ariel.

On June 26, a spokesperson of the "Popular Resistance Committees" in Gaza announced that his organization's activists had managed to kidnap an Israeli citizen in the West Bank. No details were provided regarding the abducted citizen's identity, and therefore the Israeli reaction to the announcement was cautious. On June 28, a press conference was held in Gaza, in which a spokesperson of the "Popular Resistance Committees" displayed Eliyahu Asheri's identity card. The spokesperson also mentioned his middle name, Pinhas. The spokesperson declared that Asheri would be murdered if Israel continued its activities in the Gaza Strip.[20] That day Asheri's body was found shot in the head near Bitunya by an IDF force. He was buried on June 30.

On July 4, 2006, Asheri's three kidnappers and murderers were arrested. Their interrogation revealed that Asheri had been kidnapped on June 25 at the Ofra junction. Asheri had been brought to Ramallah where he was murdered a short while later.

Abductions by Hizballah in the Zar'it Sector

In 2005, a prisoner exchange deal was carried out between Israel and Hizballah with Germany serving as intermediary. The Hizballah returned Elhanan Tenenbaum and the bodies of three Israeli soldiers kidnapped at Mt. Dov in October 2000, in exchange for the release of Palestinian prisoners and the return of the bodies of Hizballah fighters. During 2005 and 2006, following the second stage of negotiations between Israel and the Hizballah, Nasrallah threatened to kidnap Israeli soldiers for bargaining purposes. On November 21, the Hizballah tried to realize its threat.

The Rajar abduction attempt

On November 21, 2005, an abduction attempt was thwarted at an IDF position in the village of Rajar. An infantry attack against the Gladiyola outpost was thwarted at the same time. During the skirmish, Hizballah used widespread artillery, anti-tank missiles, sniping and light arms against all of the outposts in the Mt. Dov sector and other posts along the Lebanese border. During the exchange of fire, houses in Metullah were hit, and mortar shells fell near other settlements – Galilee residents were forced to sit in bomb shelters for several hours.

The fighting took place in inclement weather conditions including heavy fog, low cloud, local rain and intense cold. Under the diversion of the shooting in all sectors, a Hizballah cell attempted to infiltrate Rajar and penetrate an IDF post with the aim of abducting a soldier. An IDF force stationed in the village recognized the enemy squad, opened fire, and hit a number of terrorists, thereby thwarting the abduction attempt.

The Zar'it abduction incident

On July 12, 2006, eight IDF soldiers were killed and two abducted in a planned attack by Hizballah near Zar'it in northern Israel. Five civilians were hurt, in addition to five soldiers. The incident began in the morning, when two armored vehicles were on a routine patrol alongside the border. The patrol was ambushed and attacked between Zar'it and Shtula. A group of terrorists had cut the border fence and penetrated Israel. The terrorists took advantage of a blind spot in the IDF lookout coverage which they had duly noticed in advance, and were able to pass through the fence undetected.

They stalked the IDF force 200 meters inside Israeli territory, and surprised the patrol with a lethal spray of gunfire. Three soldiers were killed in the initial attack, one was severely hurt and another was lightly injured. The terrorists abducted two soldiers, Eldad Regev and Ehud Goldwasser, and took them into Lebanese territory.

As soon as the IDF became aware of the abduction, it began to pursue the terrorists inside Lebanon. In the course of the chase, a Merkava tank was hit by an explosive device and four of its crew members were killed. In attempts to extricate the crew, a soldier from the Nahal Brigade was killed and two others were lightly injured.

Hizballah's demands and Nasrallah's speech [21]

Shortly after the abduction, the Hizballah claimed responsibility, and demanded indirect negotiations for a prisoner exchange deal, indicating that it might include Gilad Shalit, who was kidnapped in Gaza. Hizballah's general-secretary Nasrallah demanded the release of Samir Quntar, Nassim Nasser and Yehye Sahhaf, and promised that he would demand the release of still more prisoners. Israeli Prime Minister Ehud Olmert summarily rejected the organization's demands.

On July 12 Hassan Nasrallah held a press conference in Beirut, declaring, "the kidnapped soldiers are far, far away." He addressed Israeli Prime Minister Ehud Olmert as follows: "I strongly recommend that you act responsibly. Any military action to release the abducted soldiers on the Israeli side, and any military escalation will be met by Hizballah surprises . . . we will respond with force to any action. The two soldiers will only be released through negotiations." Nasrallah mocked the lack of experience of the Israeli Prime Minsiter, its Defense Minister and the Chief of Staff, and advised them to consult with the people they had replaced.

Israel's response to the attack   At the end of an emergency session held near midnight, the Israeli government decided to open all-out war against the Hizballah until the thousands of missiles that the organization had aligned along Israel's border were completely annihilated.[22] The government unanimously approved Operation "Change of Direction" – a series of military actions against the Hizballah and the Lebanese government. Amongst other issues, they discussed massive bombardment of Lebanese infrastructures, as well as the elimination of Hizballah officials. No time limit was to be placed on the military operation – which was to include air raids, massive use of artillery, seaside bombings and ground operations. The overall goal was to renew Israel's deterrence capabilities in Lebanon, set new ground rules and push Hizballah back from the border.

"We will not allow ourselves to be held hostage to the threat of rockets," declared Prime Minister Ehud Olmert in response to security agencies' assessments that Hizballah might launch dozens or hundreds of rockets towards Israel. "We will act because the current reality forces us to respond to this threat once and for all." Olmert told cabinet members that the incidents on the northern border could not be perceived merely as a single event in a series of incidents *vis-à-vis* the Hizballah, but rather as a crossing of a red line that no other country would tolerate. Sources close to the Prime Minister defined the emergency meeting and its resolutions, as "a declaration of war."[23]

Defense Minister Amir Peretz met late that night with the Home Front Commander, and briefed him about impending events. Peretz noted that the Hizballah had built up a massive arsenal in recent years, and now the time had come for the inevitable confrontation. Peretz informed the cabinet: "we intend to act with all the force at our disposal so that when the conflict ends, the Lebanese government and the Hizballah will rue the moment they initiated the conflict." At the end of the meeting, cabinet members agreed that operative decisions would be approved by a special team that would include the Prime Minister, Foreign Minister Tzipi Livney, Deputy Prime Minister Shimon Peres, Defense Minister Amir Peretz, and the ministers Shaul Mofaz and Avi Dikhter.[24] In the aftermath of the cabinet's green light, on the night between July 12 and July 13, the IDF launched Operation Fair Pay – whose declared goal was to "exact a fitting price and restore Israel's deterrence effect" (later the operation's name was changed to "Change Direction").

The abduction and murder of an Israeli citizen near Qalkilya [25]

On July 28, 2006, Dr. Danny Yaakobi from the settlement of Yakir in

Samaria was abducted and murdered. His body was found in the trunk of his Subaru car, which had been torched in the fields of Funduk, a village near Qalkilya. Security forces investigating the murder suspected that he had been abducted and murdered when he went to Funduk for car repairs. Another theory was that a terrorist masquerading as a Jewish hitchhiker had abducted and murdered him. The Al Aqsa Martyr Brigades claimed responsibility for the incident.

Conclusions: Different Patterns of Terror Events and Changes in Israel's Response

At the time that these conclusions are being presented (October 2006), there exists a tenuous ceasefire in the Gaza Strip and Lebanon. Following the terror attacks perpetrated in June and July 2006, it is possible to discern different types of patterns adopted by the terror organizations, as well as changes in Israel's response.

The main points are set out below:

- The abduction perpetrated in June 2006, at Kerem Shalom, constitutes a new pattern adopted by Palestinian organizations, and particularly by the Hamas, as the leading organization to initiate this event. This is the first time that an abduction was carried out in the form of a complex military operation – a border crossing – that combined the attack of numerous military targets, and the abduction of a soldier in the heat of battle. As noted, all previous Hamas abductions were of a lone soldier or civilian hitchhiking in Judea and Samaria. The current pattern is similar to the modus operandi used by the Hizballah on the Lebanese front. Thus, there is reason to believe that the Kerem Shalom incident marks the adoption of the Lebanese pattern.
- From the point of view of modus operandi, the Hizballah abduction on July 12, 2006 does not constitute a new development. It bears great similarity to the abduction perpetrated in October 2000. Nevertheless, the skilled planning and high performance abilities are worthy of notice.
- As far as methods of operation are concerned, abductions in Judea and Samaria have not changed. They generally involve the abduction of civilians hitchhiking on the roads of Judea and Samaria. While the acts at the Lebanese front and the Gaza Strip necessitated prolonged and complex preparations as well as sophisticated performance, the abductions in the West Bank remain relatively "simple", although many of them ended tragically, with the murder of the abductees.

- The reaction of the Israeli government to the attacks in Kerem Shalom and at the Lebanese border are to be distinguished from those that preceded them. The Israeli response can be characterized in three main categories:
  - An ultimatum was issued to the organizations that perpetrated the abductions to return the kidnapped soldiers. In addition, the governments in whose territories the abducted soldiers are being concealed are to be held responsible – namely, the Hamas government in the Palestinian Authority and Fuad Saniora's government in Lebanon.
  - An Israeli declaration that no negotiations will be conducted for the release of prisoners in exchange for the kidnapped soldiers.
  - The initiation of wide-scale military operations in Gaza and Lebanon, whose declared goal was to change the security reality in these sectors and ensure the release of the abductees.

These military actions are far more extensive than the responses that characterized IDF steps in previous abduction incidents in Lebanon and certainly against the Palestinian Authority. Since these military actions are still in process (October 2006, at the time of writing), it is not yet possible to assess their success, and we will need to wait and see how the abduction incidents will end.

Appendices

Appendix A

Interview with the Chief of Staff Ehud Barak following the IDF operation to rescue Nachshon Wachsman [1]

HAIM YAVIN: We are about to speak to the Chief of Staff at his bureau in Tel Aviv.

Hello, Mr. Chief of Staff.

CHIEF OF STAFF EHUD BARAK: Good evening.

HAIM YAVIN: You will probably want to start with a few words in memory of Nachshon Wachsman and Nir Poraz.

CHIEF OF STAFF EHUD BARAK: We offer our condolences to the families, the Wachsman and Poraz families, on the loss of the two soldiers, our fighters. Nachshon was murdered when he was bound hand and foot and could not put up a fight. Nir Poraz, one of our most promising commanders in an elite unit, was killed while realizing a principle that has accompanied the IDF throughout its history, the principle that there is no limit to the risk that we are willing to take in order to save a comrade in distress.

HAIM YAVIN: After a day of debriefing, twenty-four hours after the operation, how would you summarise it? How was this operation different from other operations in the past?

CHIEF OF STAFF EHUD BARAK: Maybe the fact that it was prepared in a very short time. Within a matter of hours we had to plan it and carry it out against the background of the ultimatum that was about to expire in a few short hours, knowing that this terror cell had aready murdered Simani and Frankental, and it was the same type of cell that had killed Sasportas and Sa'adon, and Toledano subsequently. There were no negotiations and we had to act. The conditions were not the occupation of a bus or a building followed by a subsequent demand for negotiations. The reality was that the abductors themselves were in hiding and demanding that the Israeli government capitulate completely to their demands. This is unacceptable. As far as we knew at that time, there was no entity that truly represented this cell or even had a connection to it. Under these conditions, when it is an area under our control, despite the complexity, the right thing is to take action. That was my recommendation and that is what we did.

HAIM YAVIN: Major General Barak, when considering this mission, it seems impossible. Impossible to succeed, to save Nachshon's life. Do you believe that all other options were exhausted?

CHIEF OF STAFF EHUD BARAK: First of all, there was no other choice. Our assumption was that at nine o'clock, or even before nine o'clock, the cell would exterminate Nachshon, and disappear. It was unaware that it was surrounded and could probably negotiate for the return of the body. We have already experienced similar things. Thus we had no choice, even when we faced an extremely complex and intricate operation, and the special unit accomplished it with great determination under very difficult conditions, facing serious resistance. I believe that it was the right thing to do, and it always carries certain risks. You cannot promise perfect results. We have perhaps the best units in the world to carry out this kind of mission, but even they cannot ensure the desired results with complete certainty.

HAIM YAVIN: Do you observe greater sophistication in the Hamas, in its military branch, from the aspect of sophistication that did not exist in the past? The preparation of the house, the arms, the organization, the entrenchment, renting the house.

CHIEF OF STAFF EHUD BARAK: The Hamas' organization throughout the years has always been very sophisiticated, from the aspect of compartmentalization, planning, and determination and willingness to be killed along the way. Also, the wilingness to pluck at our heartstrings. I do not exclude the possibility that the ultimate intention of the extortion is to make us torment ourselves with the question – could we have saved Nachshon Wachsman with some kind of deal? The setting of impossible conditions, the inability to negotiate even under these conditions, and the creation of a situation whereby whether he was killed by them because we could not obtain information, or if, like the way it actually happened, he fell during a military rescue operation; either way we will carry this torment, that perhaps by capitulating to extortion, we would have moved forward. And in this regard I say, we are a people that has learned from experience.

We have already observed cases where an attempt to diminish the risks or the cost at a given moment, led to consequences that today, looking back, we know cost us dearly and took a higher toll on human life. Due to the nature of this prolonged struggle in which we are involved, it is important to know how to confront reality head on, to understand the jungle in which we live, and be able to call up all of the stamina and fortitude that are necessary for our society. Capitulation to extortion is a sure recipe for the next extortionist to show up and raise the ante.

CHIEF OF STAFF EHUD BARAK: Ultimately, in this case, a very important terror cell that had killed several Israelis was exterminated. The accomplice who was apprehended and the collaborator will lead us to additional information. Mainly to the operators in Gaza, and to other cases that these operators supervised. The Palestinian Authority will have to take action against them. If it does not, we will need to consider how to act against them, even if it is inside Gaza. I am pleased to note that for the first time since its inception, the Palestinian Authority has begun to take practical action. This is a matter that they must handle and determine. We should not do so in their stead. I think that ultimately the cell failed in its extortion. The State of Israel did not submit. Sorrowfully, the price is painful and heavy, and even so we must accept that we will have to face similar tests in the future and we will again be forced to confront this type of dilemma. All of the stamina and unity that surface during these difficult times must be preserved for future tests. This unity is ultimately our main force and in the end it is this element that will break the Hamas and the Islamic Jihad.

Appendix B
Interview with senior Hamas leader Mahmoud a Zahar

An interview with MAHMOUD A ZAHAR, one of the senior Hamas leaders in Gaza, conducted by ODED GRANOT during the abduction of Nachshon Wachsman by the Hamas.

MAHMOUD A ZAHAR was deported to Lebanon following the abduction and murder of Border Guard policeman Nissim Toledano, and returned to Gaza in 1993.

The interview shed light on several issues connected to the organization's policy regarding terror attacks, the relationship between the "internal and external" leadership, and his approach to negotiations for the release of a hostage in exchange for the release of Palestinian prisoners.

There have been publications (newspaper and radio reports) that you met with Arafat regarding the hostage.

No, I haven't. I have not spoken to him at all about this matter.

Where is Nachshon Wachsman being held?

I don't know. Whoever abducted him knows. There are Iz a-Din Al-Qasam Brigades everywhere. In northern Palestine and the south.

What does the Hamas say about this act?

The abduction is not a goal but a means to release all of the prisoners. All of the means used in the past failed. All of the attempts to conduct negotiations failed. All of the Palestinian Authority's meetings with the Israeli government failed. Appeals to human rights organizations failed. Demonstrations and protests and the pleading of women and children did not help. We had no other choice but to choose the path that we followed several times in the past. I think that the Israeli government is mainly responsible for this. If it had released the prisoners there would be no need for the abduction.

There were rumors that the Israeli government planned to release Sheikh Yassin.

Israel released this rumor only after the abduction. Just to make you and other journalists think that the abduction hindered Sheikh Yassin's release. In 1992, when Nissim Toledano was abducted, instead of releasing Sheikh Yassin, Israel's response was to arrest 2500 men and deport 400 of them to Lebanon. Then it had excuses, but now, after signing the agreement with the PLO, how can it justify detaining people? What does Israel want from a prisoner like Sheikh Yassin? It claims that if he is released in the West Bank, he will incite acts of terror, but what damage can occur if he is released to Gaza, which is surrounded by an electronic fence? There is no reason not to release him, except for revenge and a desire to kill the man.

What is your stance regarding Sheikh Yassin's call not to hurt Nachshon Wachsman?

Islam commands us to preserve the life of a captive, but Israel does not protect the lives of captives and prisoners. How long can this unbalanced situation continue? Israel should be the one to answer this question.

Do you mean that the Hamas disregards Sheikh Yassin's call?

Should we hold the hostage for eternity?!

He clearly called for the Hamas to spare him.

Sheikh Yassin's call was directed at the Iz a-Din Al-Qasam Brigades that carried out the abduction and they will take it into consideration. This matter is not connected to the political leadership but to the cells of the Iz a-Din Al-Qasam Brigades.

But the cells receive their instructions from the political level.

No. They receive their instructons from the military leadership.

Do you think Sheikh Yassin's call will have an effect?

I think this also depends on Israel's approach. If Israel continues along its current path and the Palestinian Authority continues to attack us – this will have a negative influence on the military leadership when making a decision regarding the abducted soldier.

Does the Hamas intend to enter a military confrontation with the Palestinian Authority?

I think the Palestinian Authority is headed for a confrontation with the Hamas. They have begun crackdowns and violent acts. In my house, on the night between Wednesday and Thursday, they shattered the windows and doors. Maybe the pictures will be aired on Israeli television.

Could this confrontation end in bloodshed?

The Palestinian Authority should answer that question. Islam dictates the Hamas' actions and it permits self-defense.

The Hamas issued an ultimatum to the State of Israel. Who is responsible for negotiations in the Hamas?

Those who perpetrated the abduction clearly defined their demands and demanded that Israel announce Sheikh Yassin's release. We have had bad experiences with this. We know that Israel behaves arrogantly in these cases.

Do you believe that Israel will not respond this time either?

It is clear that Israel will not release him.

You did not even leave an address with whom negotiations can be conducted.

What for? So you can abduct the man? Just like you kidnapped Abd al-Karim Obeid or Dirani?

For example, so that we can conduct negotiations and see evidence that the soldier is alive . . .

If Israel is serious, it should call the Red Cross.

The Red Cross was not mentioned in the Hamas' manifest.

Because we do not trust Israel.

Arafat is trying to help Rabin rescue the soldier.

The political echelon deals with politics, and the military entities deal with the abduction. Everything depends on them.

What do you think of Israel's decision to stop the talks with the PLO in Cairo?

This is an attempt to get the PLO to make political concessions which are not connected in any way to the abduction. Israel wants to exploit the soldier's abduction for the elections in order to prevent the IDF's redeployment. Israel is acting cunningly and the PLO does not realize it. We issued a warning that Israel does not want peace, but rather to shut the door on the PLO. That is what happened. We told them: You will get Gaza and Jericho in the beginning and Gaza and Jericho in the end. The process does not have the impetus to continue. They received Gaza and Jericho and you received the gate to the Arab world. Rabin was in Jordan and Peres visited Tunisia. The Gulf opened up to economic ties. What is left to propel the negotiations with the Palestinians forward? Nothing.

Appendix C
Al Qaida claims responsibility for the murder of the Egyptian Ambassador in Iraq [1]

Al Qaida executes the ambassador of the tyrants, Ihab a-Sharif.

In the name of Allah the merciful.

Oh, Allah! Allow our bullets to reach their target and tighten the grasp of our feet on this earth.

Praise to Allah, He who protects the worlds. The final triumph is in the hands of the faithful, and there will be no violence, except against those who cross all boundaries. Peace and prayers were just on the Imam of the Mujahidin, our Prophet, Muhammad, his family and retinue.

Our stand regarding those who fight a war against the Muslims is clear: They are infidels, missionaries, and outside of the Islamic family. Here are some reasons:

1   They rule with manmade rules, something which excludes them from Islam.
2   They have become allies of Allah's foes and enemies of the just.
3   The first to operate a war against Islam were the Egyptian authorities, several decades ago. Allow us to ask: Who killed Sayyid Qutb? May Allah take pity on him. Who killed Khaled al-Islamabuli and his group after they killed Anwar al-Sadat?
4   The Egyptian prison is full of Mujahidin. Egyptian courts, that are not subject to Allah's Sharia, sentenced our brothers in the Tawahid to death, including our beloved Sheikh Aiman A-Zawahiri, may Allah guard and protect him.
5   The betrayal of Jerusalem began through the Egyptian administration.
6   IThe Egyptian authorities were the first to obey the cross worshippers and disobey Allah's authority by sending the first ambassador to the missionary government in Iraq. They clearly obeyed instructions issued by the cross worshippers.
7   The Egyptian authorities were the first to agree to train those serving in the Iraqi army and the missionary police.

Your brothers in the Al Qaida organization will continue to kill every person who cooperates with the Jews and Christians in their war against Islam and the members of the Tawahid, with Allah's grace.

One of the reasons for delaying the announcement about the abduction of the Egyptian tyrant was to enable us the opportunity to apprehend as many ambassadors as possible.

Yesterday, we saw and heard how the world was helpless when the Sharia court sentenced this missionary to death. How is it that we did not hear a word when thousands of women, children and the elderly were killed in Faluja, Qum and Qarbala? And how is it possible that we never heard a word when hundreds of houses were bombed and collapsed on their inhabitants? What about the intentional murder of Sunnis in Iraq?

The entire world has heard about the rape and torture of Sunni women in Iraqi jails by the Americans and the Shiites. Have we heard anything about this?

The way to handle these tyrants is described by Allah:
"Behold you see that those in whose heart the afflication has spread are to be approached and told, we fear that you will return to inflict us. But God will bring triumph to his people and make his word true, and they will then regret that which they schemed in their heart." (Sura 5, Aya 52).

Allah, supreme God, gave us a precious religion, the religion of Abraham, and we would never have been led along the true path, if not for Allah, who guided us.

During his interrogation, the infidels' ambassador confessed to an alliance between the infidel's government with the Jews and the Christians. His confession was taped.

Let us let everyone, near and far, know that our Sheikh Abu Musab al Zarqawi (may Allah guard his soul), and the Sharia committee of Al Qaida in the Land of Two Rivers are determined to stand and fight the men of al-Alkami (ascribed to the Shia), and those who serve the cross, and any person who cooperates with them in any way.

We warn all tyrants that the Land of Two Rivers is no longer safe for the infidels because Allah gave strength to a small group of chosen warriors who fight for His goals. The joint goal of the cross worshippers and the missionaries in Iraq is to fight the "Umma" of Muhammad, may he rest in peace.

We, the organization of Al Qaida in the Land of Two Rivers, hereby announce that Allah's verdict has already been executed on the infidels' ambassador.

Oh, enemy of Allah, Ihab, this is your shame in your life, and terrible torture awaits you on Judgment Day.

Oh, Allah, you commanded the clouds to reach predetermined places, you sent us the Book (the Koran), you vanquished the allies. We urge you to vanquish the Jews and the Christians and anyone who helps them in their battle against the Muslims. Oh, Allah! Give us our victory over them.

Oh, Allah! Guard and protect the Mujahidin leaders and make their aim true so they can achieve the targets set for them.

Oh, Allah! Liberate Muslim prisoners wherever they are and grant us victory over our enemies and yours.

Communications Department
Al Qaida in the Land of Two Rivers
7.7.2005

Notes

I   Terror and Abductions – Western Vulnerability and Dilemma

1   Martha Crenshaw, *Terrorism, Legitimacy and Power* (Middletown Connecticut: Wesleyan University 1983), pp. 1–4.
2   Ibid., p. 3.
3   Ibid., p. 1.
4   Ibid., p. 2.
5   Alex P. Schmidt and Albert J. Youngman, *Political Terrorism* (New Brunswick: Transaction Books, 1982).
6   Ibid., p. 10.
7   Schmidt and Youngman, *Political Terrorism*, p. 11.
8   Boaz Ganor, *The Labyrinth of Countering Terror: Tools for Decision Making* (Herzliya: Mifalot Publishing, IDC, 2005), p. 32.
9   Ibid., pp. 32–33.
10 Ibid., p. 35.
11 Ibid., p. 35.
12 RAND Corporation Chronology of International Terrorism.
13 Paul Wilkinson, *Terrorism and the Liberal State* (Macmillam Education Ltd., 1997), p. 182.
14 Ibid.
15 Ray. S. Cline and Yona Alexander, *Terrorism as a State-sponsored Covert Warfare* (Virginia: Fairfax, 1986).
16 Edward Luttvack, *Strategy: The Logic of War and Peace* (Tel Aviv: Ma'archot Publishing, 2002), pp. 11–13.
17 This is a relatively simple model that addresses a scenario in which a single hostage is abducted for negotiation purposes within the boundaries of a state; negotiations are conducted with the government of that state.
18 Shaul Shay, *The Axis of Evil: Iran, the Hizballah and Palestinian Terror* (New Brunswick: Transaction Publishers, 2005).

2   Abductions in the Palestinian Arena and the Nachshon Wachsman Affair

1   The Hamas Movement, *Asharq al Awsat*, London, November 30, 1992. The article is based on interviews with senior members of the Hamas.
2   Ibid.
3   Ibid.
4   Anat Kurtz, Maskit Burgin, and David Tal, *Islamic Terror and Israel* (Tel Aviv University: Papyrus Publishing, 1993), pp. 157–158.

5 Ibid., p. 160.
6 Reuven Paz, *The Islamic Covenant and its Implications* (Dayan Centre, September 1998), p. 47.
7 Ibid., p. 47.
8 *Palestin al-Maslama*, April 1990, Hatzav translation, 5.6.90/843/001.
9 *Asharq al Awsat*, London, November 30, 1992.
10 Anat Kurtz, Maskit Burgin, David Tal, *Islamic Terror and Israel*, Papyrus Publishing (Tel Aviv University, 1993), p. 173.
11 Ibid., p. 173.
12 *Ha'aretz*, September 22, 1989.
13 Kurtz, Burgin, and Tal, *Islamic Terror and Israel*, p. 173.
14 *Ha'aretz*, December 19, 1990.
15 *Ha'aretz*, January 12, 1993.
16 The deportation injunctions signed by the commanding officers of the Southern and Central Commands on the basis of regulation 112 (1) of the Emergency Defense Regulations.
17 *Asharq al Awsat*, London, November 30, 1992.
18 Ibid.
19 Benjamin Netanyahu, *Terror – How Can the West Win?* (Tel Aviv: Sifriat Ma'ariv, 1987).
20 *Yediot Aharonot*, December 16, 1993.
21 Ronnie Shaked, The Murderers' Hill, *Yediot Aharonot*, August 14, 1994.
22 Ibid.
23 These details were divulged by Jihad Yamur during his trial at an Israeli military court.
24 Ibid.
25 Ibid.
26 *Ma'ariv*, October 16, 1994.
27 Ibid.
28 Testimonies by Salah a-Din Drawza and Jihad Yamur.
29 See wording in Arabic and Hebrew.
30 Perpetrators of the attack in the Nahalat Shiva Quarter of Jerusalem.
31 Alquds Radio – Ahmad Jibril's radio station broadcasting from Damascus.
32 Examples from the Arab press include: *A-Nahd* (the Hizballah newspaper), *Al-Quds, A Sapir, Biladi* and others.
33 *Ma'ariv*, October 16, 1994.
34 *Ma'ariv*, October 12, 1994.
35 *Ma'ariv*, October 16, 1994.
36 Ibid.
37 Ibid.
38 Ibid.
39 Ibid.
40 *Call-bi*, October 20, 1994.
41 *Ma'ariv*, October 12, 1994.
42 *Davar*, October 13, 1994.
43 This section is based on the testimonies of the rescue force's commanders and soldiers given at Jihad Yamur's trial as well as items published in the Israeli press.

44   *Yediot Aharonot*, October 17, 1994.

3   The Hizballah and Abductions in the Lebanese Arena

1   This chapter is based on Shaul Shay, *The Axis of Evil: Iran, Hizballah and Palestinian Terror* (New Brunswick: Transaction Publishers, 2005).
2   US Department of State, Patterns of Global Terrorism, 1993–2004.
3   The most prominent instances were the "Mikonos Affair" in Germany and testimony given by Iranian defectors.
4   This section is based on Shay, *The Axis of Evil*.
5   Alan Taylor, *The Islamic Question in the Middle East Politics* (Boulder: Westview Press, 1988).
6   David Menshari, *Iran in a Revolution* (Tel Aviv: Hakibbutz Hameuhad, 1988), p. 217. An interview with the Ayatollah Ali Mantzari, Jamhuri Islami, December 8, 1984.
7   Shaul Bakash, *The Reign of the Ayatollahs in Iran and the Islamic Revolution* (London: Unwin Paperbacks, 1986), p. 21.
8   Menshari, *Iran in a Revolution*, p. 217.
9   Magnus Ranstorp, *Hizballah in Lebanon – The Politics of the Western Hostage Crisis* (New York: St. Martin's Press, 1997), pp. 25–30.
10   Amir Taheri, *The Holy Terror – The Inside Story of Islamic Terrorism* (London: Sphere Books, 1987), p. 287. Examples of these types of publications include: *Alliue Altsadar*, bulletin of the "Islamic Revolution of Iraq"; and *Alhakima* – a Shiite quarterly edited by Muhammad Hussein Fadallah, published in Beirut.
11   Menshari, *Iran in a Revolution*, p. 217.
12   *Kihan*, December 14, 1982.
13   *Atala'at*, November 2, 1981.
14   *Jamhuri Islami*, January 26, 1984.
15   *Atala'at*, August 23, 1981.
16   Ayatollah Khomeini, *Al-Khakoma al-Islamiya*, pp. 18–22, pp. 133–139.
17   Menashri, *Iran in a Revolution*, p. 57.
18   Ibid., pp. 51–57.
19   Graham E. Fuller, *The Center of the Universe* (Boulder: Westview Press, 1991), pp. 12–14.
20   Hizballah, Special Collection of Information, the Center for Intelligence Heritage, the Information Center for Intelligence and Terror, March 2003, p. 45.
21   Fuller, *The Center of the Universe*, pp. 271–273.
22   Ibid., pp. 119–122.
23   Edgar O'Balance, *Islamic Fundamentalist Terrorism, 1979–1995* (New York: New York University Press, 1997), pp. 137–139.
24   This section is based on Shaul Shay, *The Axis of Evil: Iran Hizballah and the Palestinian Terror* (New Brunswick: Transaction Publishers, 2005).
25   Ibid., pp. 40–48.
26   Ibid.
27   Ibid.
28   Iran – *A Country Study*, Library of Congress Federal Research Division, USA, 1996.

29 Ibid.
30 *Ma'ariv*, Tel Aviv, June 28, 1996; Iran – *A Country Study*, Library of Congress Federal Research Division, USA, 1996; Amir Taheri, *The Spirit of Allah* (London: Hutchinson Press, 1985).
31 *Ma'ariv*, Tel Aviv, June 28, 1996.
32 *Ma'ariv*, Tel Aviv, June 28, 1996.
33 *U.S. News and World Report*, March 6, 1989.
34 *Independent*, July 1, 1987.
35 *Ma'ariv*, Tel Aviv, June 28, 1996.
36 Valiat Fakia refers to the supreme spiritual and political leader, who all Shiite believers are obliged to obey.
37 *Der Spiegel*, April 9, 1997.
38 *Ma'ariv*, Tel Aviv, June 28, 1996.
39 Marvin Zonis, Daniel Brumberg, "Khomeini, The Islamic Republic of Iran and the Arab World," *Harvard Middle East Papers*, 5, 1987, p. 34.
40 A. Fishman, *Hadashot*, February 18, 1992.
41 *Ma'ariv*, Tel Aviv, February 2, 1987.
42 Small numbers of members of the Revolutionary Guards began arriving in Lebanon already in 1979 and 1980.
43 Shimon Shapira, "The Origins of Hizballah," *The Jerusalem Quarterly*, Spring 1988.
44 Based upon "An Open Letter to the Oppressed," which was read out at a general meeting held by the Hizballah on March 16, 1985. The main points of the document serve as the organization's "political manifesto". These principles are reinforced by repeated statements made by the organization's leaders.
45 Martin Kramer (ed.) *Shi'ism, Resistance and Revolution* (Boulder: Westview Press, 1987), pp. 47–50.
46 Martin Kramer, *The Moral Logic of Hizballah*, Occasional Papers, No. 101, The Dayan Center for Middle Eastern Studies, Tel Aviv University, August 1987, pp. 63–66.
47 *Al-Nahar*, May 19, 1985.
48 *Al-Itihad*, September 13, 1988.
49 Anat Kurtz *et al.*, *Inter-International Terrorism*, JCSS, Tel Aviv University, 1989, pp. 55–58.
50 Interview with Fadallah for the periodical *Journal of Palestinian Studies*, Vol. Winter 1987.
51 Friday sermon by Fadallah as quoted by the French News Agency. See *Le Figaro*, August 5, 1989.
52 *Al-Muharar*, Lebanon, July 28, 1989.
53 Anat Kurtz, Maskit Burgin, and David Tal, *Islamic Terror and Israel* (Tel Aviv: Papyrus Publication, Tel Aviv University, 1993), pp. 52–55.
54 This section is based on Shaul Shay, *The Axis of Evil: Iran, Hizballah and Palestinian Terror* (New Brunswick: Transaction Publishers, 2005), pp. 127–132.
55 *Ma'ariv*, February 18, 2003.
56 "Al-Manar," Lebanon, April 9 2002.
57 "Al-Manar," Lebanon, September 28, 2001.

58 "Al-Manar," Lebanon, May 7, 1998.
59 "Al-Manar," Lebanon, February 7, 2003.
60 Shlomo Brom, *Israel and South Lebanon Prior to a Peace Agreement with Syria* (Tel Aviv: Jaffee Center, Tel Aviv University), 1999, pp. 18–19.
61 Hizballah, A Special Collection of Information, the Center for Intelligence Heritage, The Information Center for Intelligence and Terror, March 2003, p. 44.
62 Ibid., p. 46.
63 Ibid., p. 47.
64 Ibid., p. 48.
65 *Al Liwa'a*, October 9, 2002.
66 Iran – the state that supports and operates terror, A Special Collection of Information, the Center for Intelligence and Terror, March 2003, pp. 25–26.
67 Shaul Mishal and Avraham Sela, *Hamas Time* (Tel Aviv: Yediot Aharonot, Sifrei Hemed, 2003), p. 139.
68 *Asharq al Awsat*, London, November 30, 1992.
69 Efraim Kam, *From Terror to Nuclear Power, the implication of the Iranian threat* (Ministry of Defense publication, 2004), p. 278.
70 Ibid.
71 Ibid.
72 Ibid., p. 279.
73 Ibid.
74 *Ha'aretz*, April 16, 1996.
75 Iran – the state that supports and operates terror, a special collection of information, the Center for Intelligence Heritage, The Information Center for Intelligence and Terror, April 2003, pp. 38–39.
76 Ibid., pp. 28–36.
77 This section is based on documents from the court hearings in the matter of the petitions of Sheikh Obeid and Mustafa Dirani, as well as Ran Edelist and Ilan Kfir's book *Ron Arad, the Riddle* (Tel Aviv: Yediot Aharonot, 2000).
78 *Yediot Aharonot*, Tel Aviv, August 1, 1989.
79 The French weekly, *Paris Match*, as quoted in *Yediot Aharonot*, August 13, 1989.
80 *Yediot Aharonot*, August 1, 1989.
81 *Yediot Aharonot*, August 1, 1989.
82 *Al Hamishmar*, July 30, 1989.
83 Its translation was published in *Yediot Aharonot*, August 1, 1989.
84 *Yediot Aharonot*, August 4, 1989.
85 Quoted in *Yediot Aharonot*, August 13, 1989.
86 The information in this section is based on material from the legal discussions regarding Mustafa Dirani's incarceration in an Israeli prison. For example, Sheikh Obeid and Mustafa Dirani against the Minister of Defense, the High Court, December 26, 2000.
87 Protocols from Hassan Salameh's trial in an Israeli military court.
88 Protocols from Drawza's trial in an Israeli military court.
89 *Ma'ariv*, October 16, 1994.
90 Ibid.

91   *Alrai Alam*, November 16, 2001.
92   *Yediot Aharonot*, August 1, 1989.
93   Aluf Ben, Rabin, "Accepting the terrorists' demands would have been interpreted as Israeli surrender", *Ha'aretz*, October 16, 1994.
94   Shimon Schiffer, "Rabin promised the ministers: From now on the cabinet will decide about every military action", October 17, 1994.
95   Aluf Ben, Rabin, Accepting the terrorists' demands would have been interpreted as Israeli capitulation, *Ha'aretz*, October 16, 1994.
96   Ibid.
97   Benjamin Netanyahu, *Terrorism: How can the West Win* (Farrar, Strauss and Giroux, 1986).

4   The Abduction of Foreign Hostages in Lebanon

1   This section is based on: Ronen Bergman, "The Terrorist with Nine Lives", *Yediot Aharonot*, October 27, 2000; and Hizballah, a special collection of information, the Center for Intelligence Heritage, The Information Center for Intelligence and Terror, March 2003, pp. 36–39.
2   This section is based on *The Axis of Evil, Iran, Hizballah and Palestinian Terror* (New Brunswick: Transaction Publishers, 2005).
3   Maskit Burgin, Ariel Merari, Anat Kurtz, "Foreign Hostages in Lebanon," (Memorandum No. 25), JCSS, Tel Aviv University, August 1988.
4   Magnus Ranstorp, *Hizballah in Lebanon – The Politics of the Western Hostage Crisis* (New York: St. Martin's Press), pp. 86–88.
5   Martin Kramer, *The Moral Logic of Hizballah*, Occasional Papers No. 101, The Dayan Center for Middle Eastern Studies, Tel Aviv University, August 1987, p. 13.
6   Magnus Ranstorp – *Hizballah in Lebanon – The Politics of the Western Hostage Crisis* (New York: St. Martin's Press, 1997), pp. 41–49.
7   *International Herald Tribune*, March 12, 1987 (quoting *AFP*).
8   *Le Monde*, May 6, 1988. In one of its declarations, the Hizballah condemned the Socialist Party for its ties with Zionism. In March 1986 the organization's periodical *al-Ahad* wrote that the safety of French citizens worldwide depends upon the defeat of the Socialist Party in the upcoming elections.
9   The declaration made by Sheikh Yizbakh of the Hizballah, as it appeared in *al-Anwar*, July 12, 1990.
10   R. K. Ramazani, "Iran's Foreign Policy Contending Orientations," *The Middle East Journal*, Vol. 43, No. 2 (Spring 1989), pp. 204–206.
11   This section is based on *Terror at the Imam's Bidding* (Herzliya: Mifalot Publishing, the Interdisciplinary Center, 2001), pp. 41–43. The example of holding hostages at the US Embassy in Teheran is presented here despite the fact that it does not meet the definition of abductions under discussion in this study because it was a definitive incident that subsequently affected Iranian terror policy and drove home the potential inherent to the capture of Western hostages to the Iranian regime. Conclusions and lessons drawn by the Iranians in this context were implemented several years later in the Lebanese arena via the Hizballah.

12 This section is based on documents included in the claim which William Buckley's partner made against Iran.

13 Ilan Kfir (ed.), The "Irangate" Affair, the Tower Committee Report, Modan Publishing, p. 8.

14 Maskit Burgin, Ariel Merari, Anat Kurtz, "Foreign Hostages in Lebanon" (Memorandum No. 25), JCSS, Tel Aviv University, August 1988.

15 Ilan Kfir, (ed.), The "Irangate" Affair, the Tower Committee Report, Modan Publishing, p. 17.

16 The hijacking of aircraft is not a topic of this study, but I considered it appropriate to include the hijacking of TWA flight 847 for two main reasons: First, it sheds light on the complexity of the situation when there is state involvement in an abduction, and second, from the moment that the hostages on the aircraft were spread out in different hideaways in Beirut, the incident took on the character of a terror abduction.

17 This section is based on documents from a trial in the United States in which Higgins' family sued Iran as the party responsible for his abduction and murder. *Robin L. Higgins vs. The Islamic Republic of Iran, United States District Court for the District of Columbia*, September 21, 2000.

18 *Le Monde*, May 6, 1988.

19 *Jerusalem Post*, March 27, 1986 (quoting *Reuters*).

20 *Newsweek*, June 23, 1986.

21 *International Herald Tribune*, December 26, 1986 (quoting *Reuters*).

22 *Ma'ariv*, November 12, 1986.

23 *Al Nahar*, March 24, 1986.

24 *Times*, June 23, 1990, quoting an interview with British Prime Minister Margaret Thatcher.

25 *Yediot Aharonot*, June 20, 1986, quoting *The Daily Express*.

26 *Ha'aretz*, September 11, 1987, quoting *The Times*.

27 *Ma'ariv*, September 20, 1987, quoting *The Times*.

28 *The Times*, May 30, 1989, quoting the *DPI* German News Agency.

29 Sharam Chubin, "Iran and Its Neighbors: The Impact of the Gulf War," *Conflict Studies*, Vol. 204, 1981, pp. 12–14.

30 Anat Kurtz, Maskit Burgin, David Tal, *Islamic Terror and Israel* (Tel Aviv: Papyrus Press, Tel Aviv University, 1993).

31 Benjamin Netanyahu, *Terror, How Can the West Win?* (Tel Aviv: Sifriat Ma'ariv, 1987), p. 237.

32 Kurtz, Burgin, and Tal, *Islamic Terror and Israel*, pp. 94–97.

33 Ibid.

34 Ibid.

35 Ibid.

5 Abductions in the Iraqi Arena

1 CBC News Online, News Indepth: Iraq, May 15, 2005.

2 GRC – Gulf Research Center

3 Ibid.

4 Ibid.

5 *Ha'aretz*, March 10, 2005.
6 Robert Worth, *New York Times*, quoted in *Ha'aretz*, November 23, 2004.
7 *Ha'aretz*, March 19, 2005.
8 *Ha'aretz*, July 4, 2005
9 *Asharq Alawsat*, July 19, 2005.
10 Shahar Samuha, "Death News," *Ha'aretz*, June 29, 2004.
11 Amit Cohen, *Ma'ariv*, July 2, 2004.
12 Islamic Fundamentalists' Global Network Modus Operandi: Bosnia Documentation Center of the Republic of SRPSKA, Banja Luka, September 2002, pp. 59–60.
13 Based on an article in MEMRI: "The international federation of the Muslim Ulama led by Sheikh al-Qardawi: The resistance in Iraq is an obligation that applies to every Muslim", *Al Quds al Arabi*, London, August 23, 2004.

6 Abductions in Yemen

1 This sections is based on: Shaul Shay, *The Red Sea Terror Triangle – Sudan, Somalia and Yemen – and Islamic Terror* (New Brunswick: Transaction Publishers, 2005).
2 Yossef Bodansky, *Bin Laden, the Man Who Declared War on America* (New York: Forum, 1999), p. 314.
3 International Institute for Counter Terror Policy (ICT), Herzliya, International Terror Attacks <http://www.ict.org.il>.
4 Bodansky, *Bin Laden*, p. 246.
5 *Christian Science Monitor*, "Yemen Fights Own Terror War", February 5, 2002.
6 *Christian Science Monitor*, "Yemen Quakes in Cole's Shadow", September 5, 2002.
7 *Yemen Times*, Issue 7, February 17, 2002.
8 Interview with Yemen's President (CNN).
9 *Christian Science Monitor*, "Yemen Fights Own Terror War", February 5, 2002.
10 <ABC.NES.com>, Yemen New Terrorist Capital, October 8, 2001.
11 Peter L. Bergen, *Holy War Inc., Inside the Secret World of Osama Bin Laden* (London: Weidenfield and Nicolson, 2001), p. 193.
12 ICT – Yemen, Terror attacks.
13 <Arabic News.com>, December 6, 2001.
14 Ibid.
15 Ibid., pp. 190–191.
16 Ibid., pp. 190–191.

Epilogue: Abduction of Israeli Soldiers and Civilians (June and July 2006)

1 Roni Shaked, Guy Meytal Yossi Yehoshua and Shani Mizrahi, "The Fear: a wave of abductions," *Yediot Aharonot*, July 13, 2006.
2 Ibid.
3 Amos Harel, "The terrorists penetrated through a tunnel", *Ha'aretz*, June 26, 2006.

4   Avi Yisasharof, "Three organizations claimed responsibility, Abu Mazen's party: Khaled Mash'al gave the order", *Ha'aretz*, June 26, 2006.
5   *Yediot Aharonot*, July 4, 2006.
6   Avi Yisasharof, "Conflict between the organizations: who will hold the soldier", *Ha'aretz*, June 27, 2006.
7   Zvi Barel, "Hamas Source, the plan was not to abduct a soldier", *Ha'aretz*, June 27, 2006.
8   Avi Yisasharof, "Conflict between the organizations: who will hold the soldier", *Ha'aretz*, June 27, 2006.
9   Ibid.
10 Ibid.
11 Aluf Ben and Amos Harel, "Olmert to the IDF, prepare a large-scale operation in Gaza", *Ha'aretz*, June 26, 2006.
12 Ibid.
13 Ibid.
14 Ibid.
15 Ibid.
16 Ibid.
17 Amos Harel and Aluf Ben, "Olmert: there will not negotiations on prisoner release", *Ha'aretz*, June 27, 2006.
18 Ibid.
19 *Yediot Aharonot*, June 26, 2006.
20 *Yediot Aharonot*, June 29, 2006.
21 *Yediot Aharonot, Ma'ariv, Ha'aretz*, July 13, 2006.
22 Shimon Shiffer, Itamar Eichner and Eitan Gleikman, "The rules have changed", *Yediot Aharonot*, July 13, 2006.
23 Ibid.
24 Ibid.
25 Ronnie Shaked, *Yediot Aharonot*, July 30, 2006.

Appendix A

1   Interview with chief of staff of the IDF, Ehud Barak, broadcast on TV Channel One, October 15, 1994. Stenography by the Yifat Company.

Appendix B

1   Interview with Mahmoud Zahar, senior Hamas member, Oded Granot, *Ma'ariv*, October 11, 1994.

Appendix C

1   Interview with Mahmoud Zahar, senior Hamas member, Oded Granot, *Ma'ariv*, October 11, 1994.

Bibliography

Official Published Materials

Documents of the court hearings in the petitions of Sheikh Obeid and Mustafa Dirani in Israel's High court.

Hizballah, Special Collection of Information, the Center for Intelligence Heritage, the Information Center for Intelligence and Terror, Herzliya Israel.

Protocols of the trial of Hassan Salameh in Israeli court.

Protocols of the trial of Jihad Yamur in Israeli court.

Protocols of the trial of Salah Darawza in Israeli court.

U.S. Departament of State, Patterns of Global Terrorism, 1993–2004.

U.S. Library of Congress, Federal Research Division country studies Iran, Syria, Lebanon.

Newspapers, Journals and Monitoring Services

Israel: *Al Hamishmar, Callbi, Davar, Ha'aretz, Hadashot, Jerusalem Post, Ma'ariv, TV chanel 1, Yediot Aharonot.*

Arab: Lebanon – *A Nahd, Al Nahar, Al Manar, Al Muharar,* Syria – Al Quds radio, *P.A. – Palestin al Maslama, Al Quds, Biladi, Al Ahad,* Iran – IRNA, *Kihan,* Egypt – *Al Ahram, Al Jumhuriya Islami,* Saudi Arabia – *Al Itihad,* Yemen – *Yemen Times,* U.K. – *Asharq Al Awsat.*

Other languages U.S. – *Newsweek, Time, News* and *World Report, New York Times, Christian Science Monitor, Wall Street Jurnal, USA Today,* U.K. – *Independent, Herald Tribune,* France – *Le Figaro, Paris Match, French News Agancy,* Germany – *Der Spiegel, A.P, Reuters,* ABC news on line, CNN news on line, CBN news on line, NBC news on line.

Primary and Secondary Published Sources

Books

Bakash, Shaul, *The Reign of Ayatollahs in Iran and the Islamic Revolution* (London: Unwin Paperbacks, 1986).

Bodansky, Yossef, *Bin Laden, the Man Who Declared War on America* (New York: Forum, 1999).

Cline, Ray S. and Alexander, Yona, *Terrorism as a State-sponsored Covert Warfare,* (Virginia: Fairfax, 1986).

Crenshaw, Martha, *Terrorism, Legitimacy and Power* (Middletown, Connecticut: Wesleyan University 1983).

Edelist, Ran and Kfir's, Ilan "Ron Arad, the Riddle" (Tel Aviv: Yediot Aharonot, Publishers, 2000).

Ganor, Boaz, *The Labyrinth of Countering Terror: Tools for Decision Making* (Herzliya: Mifalot Publishing, IDC, 2005).

Fuller, Graham E., *The Center of the Universe* (Boulder: Westview Press, 1991).

Kam, Efraim, From terror to nuclear power, the implication of the Iranian threat (Tel Aviv, Ministry of Defense publication, 2004).

Kurtz, Anat, Burgin, Maskit, and David, Tal, *Islamic Terror and Israel* (Tel Aviv University: Papyrus Publishing, 1993).

Luttvack, Edward, *Strategy: The Logic of War and Peace* (Tel Aviv: Ma'archot Publishing, 2002).

Magnus, Ranstorp, *Hizballah in Lebanon – The Politics of the Western Hostage Crisis* (New York: St. Martin's Press, 1997).

Menshari, David, *Iran in a Revolution* (Tel Aviv: Hakibbutz Hameuhad, 1988).

Mishal, Shaul and Sela, Avraham, *Hamas Time* (Tel Aviv: *Yediot Aharonot*, Sifrei Hemed, 2003).

Netanyahu, Benjamin, *Terror, How Can the West Win?* (Tel Aviv: Sifriat *Ma'ariv*, 1987).

O'Balance, Edgar, *Islamic Fundamentalist Terrorism, 1979–1995* (New York University Press, 1997).

Paz, Reuven, *The Islamic Covenant and its Implications* (Tel Aviv Dayan Center, 1998).

Schmidt, Alex P. and Youngman, Albert J., *Political Terrorism* (New Brunswick: Transaction Books, 1982).

Taheri, Amir, *The Holy Terror – The Inside Story of Islamic Terrorism* (London: Sphere Books, 1987).

——, *The Spirit of Allah* (London: Hutchinson Press, 1985).

Shay, Shaul, *The Axis of Evil, Iran, the Hizballah and Palestinian Terror* (New Brunswick, Transaction Books, 2005).

——, *Terror at the Imam's Bidding* (Herzliya: Mifalot Publishing, the Interdiscliplinary Center, 2001).

——, *The Red Sea Terror Triangle – Sudan, Somalia and Yemen – and Islamic Terror* (New Brunswick, Transaction Books, 2005).

Articles

Brom, Shlomo, *Israel and South Lebanon Prior to a Peace Agreement with Syria,* Jaffee Center, Tel Aviv University, 1999, pp. 18–19.

Burgin, Maskit, Merari, Ariel, and Kurz, Anat, "Foreign Hostages in Lebanon", (Memorandum No. 25), JCSS, Tel Aviv University, August 1988.

Islamic Fundamentalists' Global Network Modus Operandi: Bosnia Documentation Center of the Republic of SRPSKA, Banja Luka, September 2002, pp. 59–60.

Kfir, Ilan (ed.), The "Irangate" Affair, the Tower Committee Report, Tel Aviv Modan Publishing 2000, p. 8.

Kramer, Martin, *The Logic of Hizballah,* Occasional Papers No. 101, The Dayan Center for Middle Eastern Studies, Tel Aviv University, August 1987, pp. 63–66.

Kurz, Anat, *et al.*, *Inter-International Terrorism,* JCSS, Tel Aviv University, 1989, pp. 55–58.

Shapira, Shimon, "The Origins of Hizballah", *The Jerusalem Quarterly,* Spring 1988.

Zonis, Marvin and Brumberg, Daniel, "Khomeini, The Islamic Republic of Iran and the Arab World", *Harvard Middle East Papers,* 5, 1987, p. 34.

Index